The New Face of Evangelicalism

The New Face of Evangelicalism

An International Symposium on the Lausanne Covenant

edited by

C. René Padilla

HODDER AND STOUGHTON
LONDON SYDNEY AUCKLAND TORONTO

Foreword

John R. W. Stott

MANY A CONFERENCE has resembled a firework. It has made a loud noise and illumined the night sky for a few brief brilliant seconds, only to fall to the ground in smoke, silence and darkness. What is exciting about Lausanne, however, is that its fire continues to spark off other fires. The debate refuses to die down.

In this symposium, the Lausanne Covenant is not so much a text for exposition as a basis for further theological construction, a springboard for fresh innovative thought. Some of the big issues of the Congress – culture, church, mission, social responsibility, dialogue and presence, moratorium, leadership, worldliness — are taken up here and developed. The fact that ten of the fifteen contributors are Third World citizens or residents introduces a freshness of perspective and a pungency of comment to which the rest of us (especially from Europe and North America) need to pay close and humble attention.

In saying this, I speak for myself as much as for anybody else. Although I do not find myself in full agreement with every opinion expressed by this team of authors, I welcome the freedom with which they have expressed themselves. One of Lausanne's most important achievements was the discussion in candour and mutual respect of evangelical differences. We shall never attain maturity in Christ if we find some nettles too painful to grasp or, if we grasp them, pretend they don't sting when they do. More evangelical dialogue is badly needed, in which we listen open-heartedly to each other's constructive criticism. This volume should prove a valuable stimulus in this direction.

No doubt some will jib at the title *The New Face of Evangelicalism* and will insist that in their view the old face was better. For myself I would want to argue that the face of evangelicalism presented at Lausanne and in this book is still the true evangelical face. For one detects here without difficulty the familiar birthmarks of biblical authority and the unique salvation of Christ. Perhaps a more accurate — though less felicitous — title would have been *Evangelicalism with a Face-Lift*. For if the face is the same, the expression has altered. The old face now wears a new seriousness, is lit with a new smile of joyful confidence in God, and is newly turned in the direction of the contemporary world's agony and need.

John Stott

Contents

Introduction

C. René Padilla

THE INTERNATIONAL CONGRESS ON WORLD EVANGELIZATION
held at Lausanne, Switzerland, July 16—25, 1974, has been
described by *Time* magazine as 'a formidable forum, possibly
the widest-ranging meeting of Christians ever held'. It
brought together 2,473 participants from 150 countries and
135 Protestant denominations. And it issued a very significant statement on evangelism which was personally signed
by a high percentage of the participants at the end of the
Congress and which is rapidly becoming a rallying point for
Christians around the world — the Lausanne Covenant.
The Introduction to the Covenant draws attention to the
participants and their intention in issuing this important
document:

> We, members of the Church of Jesus Christ, from more
> than 150 nations, participants in the International Con-
> gress on World Evangelization, praise God for his great
> salvation and rejoice in the fellowship he has given us with
> himself and with each other. We are deeply stirred by what
> God is doing in our day, moved to penitence by our
> failures and challenged by the unfinished task of evan-
> gelisation. We believe the gospel is God's good news for
> the whole world, and we are determined by his grace to
> obey Christ's commission to proclaim it to all mankind
> and to make disciples of every nation. We desire, there-
> fore, to affirm our faith and our resolve, and to make
> public our covenant.

The Covenant took shape through a series of draftings that began several months before the Congress. The first draft, prepared by Dr James D. Douglas on the basis of the main papers to be discussed at the Congress, was submitted by mail to a panel of consultants. Revised in the light of the comments received from the advisers, the document was then submitted to a drafting committee made up of five members: Rev. John Stott, Dr James D. Douglas, Mr Samuel Escobar, Mr Leighton Ford and Dr Hudson Armerding. The drafting committee made a further revision at Lausanne, and this third draft was submitted to all the participants in the middle of the Congress, with the invitation to send their comments, either as individuals or as groups. Hundreds of amendments were suggested and a number of them were then incorporated into the final draft. The result was a document that undoubtedly reflects the general mind and mood of the Lausanne Congress.

The Covenant is divided into fifteen sections which are placed in the following order:

1. The Purpose of God
2. The Authority and Power of the Bible
3. The Uniqueness and Universality of Christ
4. The Nature of Evangelism
5. Christian Social Responsibility
6. The Church and Evangelism
7. Co-operation in Evangelism
8. Churches in Evangelistic Partnership
9. The Urgency of the Evangelistic Task
10. Evangelism and Culture
11. Education and Leadership
12. Spiritual Conflict
13. Freedom and Persecution
14. The Power of the Holy Spirit
15. The Return of Christ

That a 2,700-word statement on evangelism should deal with such a wide range of subjects is in itself a proof that Evangelicalism on the whole is no longer willing to be identified as a movement characterised by a tendency to isolate evangelism, in both theory and practice, from the wider context represented by the nature of the Gospel and the life and mission of the Church. To be sure, the whole Covenant is permeated with a real concern for the unevangelised and a deep personal commitment to the task implied by the Congress motto, 'Let the Earth Hear His Voice'. Furthermore, a number of the topics included in it could be expected in practically any traditional statement on the same subject — the inspiration, truthfulness and authority of Scripture; the uniqueness and universality of Christ and the subsequent rejection of universalism and syncretism; the need of personal commitment to Christ for salvation; the primacy of evangelism and the need for Christian nurture. But the Covenant goes far beyond that to show that biblical evangelism is inseparable from social responsibility, Christian discipleship and church renewal.

In quite a remarkable way, the Covenant, in the first place, eliminates the dichotomy between evangelism and social involvement. No one would claim that socio-political concern was a new discovery for evangelicals at Lausanne. The fact remains, however, that Christian social responsibility (as grounded in the doctrine of God, the doctrine of man, the doctrine of salvation and the doctrine of the Kingdom and therefore inextricably connected with evangelism) is given in the Covenant a place of prominence that can hardly be regarded as characteristic of evangelical statements. In fact, a cursory look at the differences between the third draft and the final version of the Lausanne document shows that the statement on social responsibility was considerably strengthened by (a) the replacement of the expression 'social action' with 'socio-political involvement', (b) the addition of direct references to alienation, oppression and discrimination and to the denunciation of evil and injustice, and (c) the promotion of the whole section from No. 7 to No. 5. Of course, enough is said on this subject to make it clear that the position upheld is quite distinct from that in which salvation is reduced to socio-politico-economic liberation. But the recognition that Christians should share God's concern 'for justice and reconciliation throughout human society and for the liberation of men from every kind of oppression' and that 'evangelism and socio-political involvement are

both parts of our Christian duty' (section 5) leaves no room
for a lopsided view of the mission of the Church. The Covenant does, however, fail to answer many an important
question regarding the connection between evangelism and
social concern. As Carl F. H. Henry has pointed out,

> Instead of the emphasis that social action is not (in
> any way? exhaustively?) evangelism, we must ask whether
> the overcoming of social alienation is not rather a neces-
> sary aspect of the evangel. Instead of the emphasis that
> political liberation is not (in any way? exhaustively?)
> evangelism, we must ask whether it is not rather a legiti-
> mate and even intrinsic aspect of the evangel. (*Christianity
> Today*, Vol. XVIII, No. 24, September 13, 1974, p. 67)

Despite this shortcoming that the Radical Discipleship
Group sought to overcome by issuing 'A Response to Lausanne' at the end of the Congress, the Covenant is a death
blow to the superficial equation of the Christian mission
with the multiplication of Christians and churches. Evangelicalism is definitely getting over the 'Church Growth' syn-
drome and over the unbiblical divorce between the *kerygma*
and the *diakonia*.

In the second place, the Covenant eliminates the
dichotomy between evangelism and Christian discipleship.
Quite obviously, Christian nurture does not automatically
promote evangelism. The question, however, is whether
genuine evangelism is ever possible without a call to discipleship and without a concern for the whole counsel of God. The
Lausanne statement leaves no doubt on the matter. In defining the nature of evangelism it asserts that 'in issuing the
gospel invitation we have no liberty to conceal the cost of
discipleship' (Section 4). Further on, it decries the pursuit
of church growth at the expense of church depth and the
divorce of evangelism from Christian nurture (Section 11).
Thus it is quite clear in the Covenant that conversion is
inseparable from discipleship and that discipleship involves
a radical change in life-style. Those who signed the Covenant
sided against any attempt to separate evangelism from
Christian nurture, the *kerygma* from the *didache*.

Finally, the Covenant eliminates the dichotomy between evangelism and church renewal. This is done, for instance, in the way it deals with the question of Christian unity. Over against those who would concentrate their efforts on unity to the neglect of evangelism, it rightly affirms that 'organisational unity may take many forms and does not necessarily forward evangelism' (Section 7). Nevertheless, in the same vein it asserts that, 'Evangelism also summons us to unity because our oneness strengthens our witness, just as our disunity undermines our gospel of reconciliation.' In the light of such a statement, it can hardly be claimed that the cause of Christian unity as viewed in the Covenant is no more than 'a good thing' that may or may not be a legitimate concern, since co-operation does not necessarily foster evangelism. The Covenant goes far beyond a mere concession to the importance of Christian unity; it throws into relief the impossibility of separating evangelism from church unity. Those who signed the Covenant pledged themselves 'to seek a deeper unity in truth, worship, holiness, and mission'. Again, when it comes to the question of life-style, the Covenant presupposes the need for Christians to make it their concern to illustrate the validity of their message with their own lives. From 'A Response to Lausanne', it quotes the striking words, '. . . a church which preaches the cross must itself be marked by the cross', and it warns that the church 'becomes a stumbling block to evangelism when it betrays the gospel or lacks a living faith in God, a genuine love for people, or scrupulous honesty in all things including promotion and finances' (Section 6). It leaves no foothold for that evangelism according to which the end justifies the means. And it goes beyond that to the expression of a firm commitment on the part of those who live in affluent circumstances to the duty 'to develop a simple life-style in order to contribute more generously to both relief and evangelism' (Section 9). The assumption is clearly made, that evangelism is of one piece with church renewal, that the *kerygma* is inseparable from the *koinonia*.

A note of repentance permeates the whole Lausanne Covenant. Beginning with a reference to 'penitence' for past failures it goes on to acknowledge that 'we have often denied our calling and failed in our mission, by becoming conformed to the world or by withdrawing from it' (Section 1), that we have 'sometimes regarded evangelism and social concern as mutually exclusive' (Section 5), that 'our testimony has sometimes been marred by sinful individualism and needless duplication' (Section 7) and that the fact that more than 2,700 million people are still unevangelised is 'a standing rebuke to us and to the whole church' (Section 9). Such statements express an important aspect of the 'spirit of Lausanne', namely, the recognition of the Church's failure to live up to her vocation — a breath of fresh air coming from people who have oftentimes been too prone to parade their feats in the evangelisation of the world. After Lausanne, every sign of triumphalism among evangelicals may be legitimately interpreted as an attempt to cling to the past.

In the final analysis, the greatest accomplishment of the Congress was to clarify the meaning and nature of the Christian mission. Over against an unbiblical isolation of the proclamation of the Gospel from the total mission of the Church, there emerged a concept of evangelism in which the proclamation was seen as inextricably connected with social responsibilty, discipleship and church renewal. However disappointing to those who expected the Congress to be a big display of the numerical power of evangelicals or a great world gathering aimed exclusively at the multiplication of Christians and churches, the Lausanne meeting turned out to be an updating of the evangelical agenda, made possible by a renunciation of fierce pragmatism and a return to biblical theology. Evangelism remained intact, but was no longer understood as ecclesiocentric activism, but rather as God's means of placing the totality of life under the lordship of Jesus Christ. The need to proclaim Jesus Christ 'with a view to persuading people to come to him personally and so be reconciled to God' (Section 4) was confirmed, but not without a recognition that 'our Christian presence in the world is indispensable to evangelism, and so is the kind of dialogue whose purpose is to listen sensitively in order to understand' (*ibid.*). The Church was seen not only as 'the appointed means of spreading the Gospel' (Section 6), but also as a new community that stands 'at the very centre of God's cosmic purpose' (*ibid.*). The importance of missionary work was ratified, but due weight was given to the fact that 'the dominant role of western missions is fast disappearing' (Section 8) and it was admitted that 'a reduction of foreign missionaries and money in an evangelised country may sometimes be necessary to facilitate the national church's growth in self-reliance and to release resources for un-evangelised areas' that (Section 9) and 'missions have all too frequently exported with the gospel an alien culture' (Section 10).

The Lausanne Covenant is little more than a detailed outline for an evangelical theology of mission. But it raises a number of issues that define the agenda for theological reflection in the coming years. And it clearly sets the direction in which such a reflection will have to move, for it concludes with the following words:

> Therefore, in the light of this our faith and our resolve, we enter into a solemn covenant with God and with each other, to pray, to plan and to work together for the evangelisation of the whole world. We call upon others to join us. May God help us by his grace and for his glory to be faithful to this our covenant! Amen. Alleluia!

Those who signed the covenant pledged themselves 'to pray, to plan and to work together for the evangelisation of the whole world', and to do so in line with the understanding of evangelism that emerged at Lausanne. The function of theological reflection will be to deepen this understanding with a view to obedience. With the Lausanne Covenant, Evangelicalism has taken a stand against the mutilated Gospel and the narrow view of the Church's mission that were defacing it, and has definitely claimed for itself a number of biblical features that it had tended to minimise or even destroy. Thus it has not only enhanced its appearance but has also given evidence of its intention to be a faithful reflection of its Saviour and Lord, Jesus Christ.

In keeping with the desire that the Lausanne Congress should be regarded as a process more than as an event, the

authors of the present symposium have undertaken the task
of discussing the fifteen sections contained in the Covenant.
Having participated in the Congress, they were asked to
expand on the topics that are raised in the Covenant and to
carry on the debate that took place at Lausanne. Each
author was given the freedom to express his own views, but
the hope was nourished that the final product would be a
fairly accurate portrayal of 'the new face of Evangelicalism'
— the face that emerged at Lausanne — as well as a demonstration of the value of theological cross-fertilisation among
Christians from different areas of the world. The reader will
have to judge the measure to which that hope has been
fulfilled.

It remains for me to express my appreciation for the assis-
tance received from Mr Samuel Escobar in the planning
of this symposium and from Miss Linda Sellevaag in the
editing of the manuscripts.

C. RENÉ PADILLA
Buenos Aires, Argentina

CHAPTER I

The Purpose of God

Carl F. H. Henry

'WE AFFIRM OUR belief in the one eternal God, Creator and Lord of the world, Father, Son and Holy Spirit, who governs all things according to the purpose of his will. He has been calling out from the world a people for himself, and sending his people back into the world to be his servants and his witnesses, for the extension of his kingdom, the building up of Christ's body, and the glory of his name. We confess with shame that we have often denied our calling and failed in our mission, by becoming conformed to the world or by withdrawing from it. Yet we rejoice that even when borne by earthen vessels the gospel is still a precious treasure. To the task of making that treasure known in the power of the Holy Spirit we desire to dedicate ourselves anew.'

(Isa. 40: 28; Matt. 28: 19; Eph. 1: 11; Acts 15: 14; John 17: 6, 18; Eph. 4: 12; I Cor. 5: 10; Rom. 12: 2; II Cor. 4: 7)

(LAUSANNE COVENANT, CLAUSE 1)

THE GOD OF the Bible is the purposeful sovereign Lord, not some aimless divinity or monarch with obscure and revisable objectives. All God's mighty deeds fall within the eternal hinterland of his decree and decision. Overarching our moment in time stands the vast realm of eternity with its divine decrees and imperial election. No doctrine of God can be biblical unless it limelights such scripturally-prominent themes as God's predetermination, election, initiative, promise and fulfilment. The living God is a deciding and disposing deity.

God's omnipotent will is eternally active, this purpose and volition being vigorously exercised even before the creation of the world.

First of all, God eternally wills himself in the inner triune life of the Godhead, not indeed by some internal necessity but in free and lively vigour.

Secondly, everything outside God is in the first instance referable to his will as the basis and criterion of all that is, and not to involuntary factors or some extraneous and foreign will. God's purpose in respect to the created universe is not conditioned by the universe but solely by his own 'good pleasure'.

Thirdly, the universe, existing first only as a divine possibility, is a real creation limited not by the nature of the cosmos itself but by God's purpose alone. Because it expresses God's sovereign will, moreover, the created universe is not an arbitrary and capricious phenomenon.

Fourthly, God's will is revealed in all his works and in his intelligible, verbal instruction of his creatures, specifically in the inspired Scriptures. God who created for specific objectives, by his sovereign divine decision and deed, alone knows and alone can disclose his purpose. Man has no covert ability to foretell God's inscrutable will, and sin frustrates his desire for divine illumination. Solely as a matter of free grace God has published to fallen man the origin, meaning and aim of all his works. In consequence mankind is confronted by and subjected to the revealed and unrelenting will of God in a binding way.

Exhibiting what is unqualifiedly true and unreservedly good, divine righteousness and love leave no doubt that man's 'autonomy' is affirmed wholly by the antecedent will of the Creator.

The International Congress on World Evangelization (Lausanne, 1974), like the World Congress on Evangelism (Berlin, 1966), was an evangelical response to God's decision, initiative and promise within the context of our own generation. The evangelisation of the earth clearly falls within the declared purpose of the holy Creator and Judge of all and gracious Redeemer of those whose sins are forgiven (Matt. 28: 19–20, Acts 1: 8). Only the world-wide proclamation of the biblical good news will enable the four billion human beings now inhabiting our planet to call upon the Lord's name for salvation (Rom. 10: 13–14) in line with the scripturally-declared purpose and promise of God.

God's Overall Plan for the World

God has a highly specific plan for mankind — for every man — in the context of his purpose for the created universe. In Scripture, God has published his divine intention for man and the universe for fallen man's benefit. The creation narrative emphasises the mandate given Adam in the garden. In view of his created likeness and relationship to God, man is made steward of the earth and assigned dominion over the lower creatures (Gen. 1: 26 ff.). God purposes that man promote those spiritual and moral priorities which the Creator had actualised in calling man and the world into being.

God's decree to create and govern includes such possibilities and eventualities as Satan, sin, and death — a dark realm that exists not independently of God's will (as dualism has it) but through that will itself. It is a rebellion that the Bible deplores and condemns as anti-God and anti-Christ, and whose conquest God pledges and achieves at a staggering price. It is a condition that does not demolish his divine lordship and governance of the created world; it finds its decisive counter-force in man's redemption. It is a turn of fortunes that will ultimately and profoundly exhibit the glory of God who seeks to bless all who obey and serve him.

All that God wills is good. Evil is what renegade creatures will contrary to divine purpose. God's omnipotent will does not preclude the origin of evil but rather accommodates it in a way that neither reflects on the unconditional righteousness of the Creator nor diminishes the fiendish nature of evil. Surely the sovereign Creator does not will what is contrary to his purposes; only his creatures have the dubious prerogative of willing for some purpose alien to God's (and hence for evil) what God himself wills for good. They — or rather we — not God, are the source of evil in this world.

The Creator works through this very evil to undo it. God is free to command his creatures and to withhold or to confer his grace upon rebellious spirits. From eternity God wills election in Christ; under stipulated conditions, flowing from his internal perfection and proposed relationship to the cosmos and man, he shapes a renewal in fellowship for a redeemed remnant who are to receive and trust the Redeemer. God's supreme good for his creation is not found in the manifestation of a creaturely obedience and blessedness invulnerable to sin and not coupled with redemption. It is rather found in the bestowal of divine salvation whereby man is reminded not only of his creation from the dust of the earth but also of his re-creation by the Holy Spirit and of moment-to-moment privileges shaped solely by the sovereign grace of God. Into his holy image he refashions a race of creatures that not only rejoice in the good, but also know, by experience, the terrible ravages of a past wickedness from which no escape is possible save by God's gift of the Saviour-Son. God is all the greater in that he forgives sin and rescues lost souls from damnation and hell.

Man's original commission, his primal charter, was authority over nature, and all that his Maker ever commanded him concerning interpersonal relationships could be summarised as wholehearted love for God and love for one's neighbour as oneself. Walking upright among the animals with superior powers of disposal and control, he was endowed with reason, conscience and language. His clear assignment was to tend and cultivate the garden God had planted, to implement God's purpose in this world as an intern serving the cosmic Craftsman. As God's representative he had a faint shadow of a bequeathed royalty but not absolute lordship, since God alone is creator of all life, his own included. He is at once last and first among many creatures, as the creation account makes plain. In many respects he shares a common dependence with the lower animals. Yet the fish and cattle feed him, and the sheep clothe him; he roams the land and soon sails the seas and then soars the skies. He mitigates climates and conquers diseases; he reclaims jungles and mountains and exhumes mineral and petrochemical resources. He promenades the planet and then turns it into a launching pad to the moon and outer space.

But what of spiritual and moral obedience? What did man's dominion imply? Surely not that man 'made in the image and likeness of God' (Gen. 1: 26) should 'become like one of us, knowing good and evil' (3: 22), that is, a surrogate sovereign and autonomous stipulator of right and wrong and, in effect, himself god. A hallmark of contemporary civilisation is this ancient notion that man's creative identification of the true and the good is a sign of his 'coming of age'; in short, the Fall is esteemed a virtue. Instead of obedience to his Maker and deference to revealed truth and unchanging commandments, contemporary man is encouraged to disown the deity and to accept only perpetually revised standards and theories.

God has set his witness against this distortion of the

divine plan of creation in the biblical narrative of the Fall of man. Someone has noted that human life begins in a garden (Gen. 2: 8) and ends in a city (Rev. 21). Many tragic things happen on the way from one to the other — Eden despoiled, Babel ensconced — as depicted in Augustine's *The City of God and the City of Man.* Adam blames his wife, Cain murders Abel, and sin escalates into a global conflagration. The cry of the hungry and destitute goes unheard, exploitation and oppression run riot, helpless minorities are victimised by social injustice — so the Old Testament prophets protest. Man fallen into sin ravages nature which, sharing in the curse, becomes a reluctant servant. He recombines nature's forces for destructive ends; sky and sea and land move his monstrous war machines and are laid destitute by conflict as predatory powers invade helpless neighbour states. The air is polluted and minefields stripped naked of cover. Management and labour inveigh against each other — and yet not infrequently produce and sell for profit consumer goods that are shoddy, substandard (if not harmful and dangerous) and covered by ineffective guarantees. Beasts are cruelly hunted or sentimentally coddled for pleasure while human foetuses are aborted and children starve for hunger. Hijackers commandeer passenger planes, human guerrillas take fellow humans captive and terrorise them for gain. Fallen man seeks to make nature serve only his welfare, but has no wisdom about where his welfare truly lies; he exploits the creation for greed and convenience and comfort. He has eclipsed the why of life through his preoccupation with the what and how; his pursuit of the quantitative dimensions of human existence smothers the qualitative (life that is truly life). The dominion he exerts through science readily becomes demonic through his loss of moral norms.

But the created universe exists and continues under conditions laid down by God alone in respect to its preservation, government, and all else. God intends a 'new heaven and a new earth' wherein righteousness dwells. In the final judgment of a fallen race he will institute the universal reign of righteousness and cancel his proffered opportunity for repentance and redemptive restoration. The vocational calling violated by the First Adam is exemplified anew by the

Second Adam, Jesus Christ, God's sinless Son. Man's creation mandate still confronts him, but the rule for which man was destined through his likeness to God has been transferred to the Messiah (cf. Pss. 2, 110) as the forerunner and representative of a perfect humanity. Jesus' obedience has ramifications for all human relationships. The creation mandate given at the outset of Genesis has been supplemented by the evangelistic mandate given at the climax of the Gospels. The news of man's redemption, of God's gracious promise and fulfilment in Jesus Christ, must be carried to a race snared in moral and spiritual revolt.

The fallen followers of evil, however violently they may rage, can never destroy the reality and conditions of creaturely existence. The Devil and his wicked host are doomed, whereas Christ's kingdom with its call for righteousness in all the relationships of life is invincible. It is the resurrection of Jesus Christ from the dead which exhibits the goal toward which both world history and church history are moving. His is the humanity of unblemished righteousness that God approves on earth and for the eternal order, that of the sinlessly obedient Son in whom the Father delights (Matt. 3:17). The apostle Paul sounds the trumpet-call anticipating God's coming judgment of philosophers and plebians alike on Mars Hill: 'He commands all men everywhere to repent, because he has fixed a day on which he will judge the world in righteousness by a man whom he has appointed, and of this he has given assurance to all men by raising him from the dead' (Acts 17: 30, 31).

What God seeks in the world is man's full devotion to love and justice. What the world in its disobedience merits is divine judgment. What God in mercy now offers is a prospect of redemption. The world is to be the kingdom where God rules and reigns in human affairs. It has, however, sunk out of spiritual orbit into the sludges of spiritual revolt in sin. But Christ came into this world as the gift of a holy God of love. From eternity God chose to proffer redemption provided by the righteous Saviour's obedience in life and death, and his victory over Satan and sin.

God's Overall Purpose for the Church

God's plan to vindicate righteousness encompasses the entire universe — the world of humanity gripped by sin's powers and the cosmos snared in its consequences. God pledges the absolute reign of righteousness — a messianic kingdom in which personal holiness, social justice, and universal peace prevail. In view of the grace he extends to the penitent he pledges the surety of eternal felicity for the redeemed and eternal punishment for the rebellious.

If God's plan for man concerned only his final destiny in the life to come, there would be no indispensable role on earth for the church. But the Christian hope is more than eschatological dimensions in the distant future. It does not forfeit to secular ideologies the definition of authentic personal existence and social life in the here and now. While indeed oriented to God's final goal of eschatological restoration in Jesus Christ, the New Testament Gospel nonetheless vigorously disputes the pretensions of every other hope for humanity in the present. It offers a persuasive alternative to both the revolutionary and the reformist secular challenges to human alienation and social injustice, whether an instant ideal society be proposed through a Marxist transformation of proletarian man or through the scientific, technocratic computerisation of human existence.

Jesus Christ is God's elect man to whose image redeemed humanity is to be fully conformed (I John 3: 2): so also the church is the new society, the distinctive body of twice-born men and women whose divine calling is to live by the standards and criteria of the coming King. The church is the new humanity living under God's revelation and authority as a new community. Enlivened to God's general revelation — revealed externally in nature and history, and internally in every man's conscience and reason — and obediently acknowledging his special prophetic-apostolic revelation in Scripture, she is integrated into God's redemption covenant to put all things under Christ's rule (Eph.

1: 10). The declaration that 'Jesus Christ is Lord' means among other things that he alone ultimately mediates the governance of the world and the fortunes of mankind. His purpose in the conquest of sin is not a mere cleansing of rebellious creatures from guilt, but their full liberation from the power of Satan and sin, and their transfer from the realm of spiritual and moral darkness to the messianic kingdom which has already been manifested in Christ.

Christians are called 'out of the world' yet stand in a divinely mandated relationship to it. They live through transcendent spiritual resources in a fallen realm. Within that realm they are entrusted with a 'light' and 'salt' mission (a role of illumination and preservation) and an evangelistic mission (a role of grace and salvation). They have a duty in relation to civil government and the socio-political order generally, and in relation to the church as a beachhead for the kingdom of God.

Yet who can delude himself into thinking that the church in the world today actually fulfils this role in a conspicuous and apparent way? The world that shapes human experience, the culture that conditions human commitments, even the Devil that Christians insist Christ holds at bay, all leave their mark upon believers in some measure. This is clearly seen in the divisions among Christians, the controversies over doctrine and life even among evangelicals, and the withdrawal from society and indifference to social injustice as if this were a requirement of evangelistic fidelity. Happily, the modern hesitancies have not always been characteristic of evangelical Christianity in this degree, and even today a new climate of concern over evangelical disunity and social disengagement is emerging. This carries its own sometimes equally pernicious dangers, endorsing principles, policies and programmes of others simply because they have been energetically involved in the social and political areas.

Let us be clear about three things.

First, in the person of Jesus Christ alone the kingdom of God had already entered human history in an unqualified way. 'The kingdom of God is in your midst' (Mark 1: 15), announced Jesus. His personal resistance to Satan and sin and his unblemished victory over them, his self-denial and unreserved obedience to the Father, the fullness of the Holy Spirit in his daily life, his rescue of fallen individuals from their ensnarement in sin, the 'signs' of healing and raising the dead, and his progressive contraction of Satan's power and sealing of Satan's doom through his own death and resurrection — all these are hallmarks of the kingdom decisively manifested in the midst of mankind.

Second, the final and universal triumph of the kingdom is assured. The good news or Gospel proclaimed by Jesus is that Israel's central hope, God's messianic rule, had now moved beyond the stage of promise to the era of fulfilment — although that fulfilment has several stages. The joyous proclamation of 'the kingdom of God' or 'the kingdom of heaven' forms as Peter Beyerhaus puts it, 'the heart of the evangelistic ministry of Jesus' (cf. Matt. 4: 17, Luke 4: 43). The kingdom anticipated by the Hebrew prophets had not come in Old Testament times because of Israel's violation of God's covenant: God pledges that Gentiles as well as Jews will share in spiritual regeneration vouchsafed through his obedient Son, the promised Messiah. In and through the Messiah the kingdom will break liberatingly into human history. Jesus applies the Isaian promise of eschatological salvation to his own mission and, in fact, prefaces his public ministry by it (Isa. 61: 1–2, Luke 4: 18 ff.) with the significant deletion of the phrase 'the day of vengeance of our Lord'. Still future, beyond the present age of grace, stands the day of final judgment of men and nations, when the Messiah coming in power and glory forcibly consummates the rule and reign of God throughout creation, subdues all rebellion, binds Satan and his hosts, and dooms the wicked. In Jesus Christ the promised kingdom has come and will be consummated.

But many Christians have been sadly confused about the role of the church in the interval between the coming and the consummation, that is, in this present age of grace. This confusion has in some ways inspired and in other ways encouraged modern secular utopian aberrations. One costly misunderstanding was the Constantinian mistake. The church-state was viewed as a religious unity in which the institutional church now seeks to rule the earth through strategic control of all historical powers. Today, some Moslem as well as Roman Catholic nations come near to this view. Another was the Anabaptist notion of Christian withdrawal from society in order to establish the kingdom in a pure church. Many fundamentalists early in this century approached this viewpoint in some respects. Still another was the modernist misunderstanding which viewed the church as the conscience of the world and regarded its task as the 'christianisation' of society. This view is still influential among some neo-Protestants. A fourth misunderstanding is the 'theology of revolution' — sometimes modified into a 'theology of liberation' – which considers violence in some if not all circumstances an acceptable method to implement socio-economic ideals. It appeals to the eschatological elements of the Bible to justify such reliance on force.

As a result, we must, thirdly, be clear about the church's role in the age of grace, the modern world. The church is, as we have already said, the new redeemed society, distinct from the unregenerate fallen world whose only final destiny, outside of the orbit of evangelisation and regeneration, is doom. As the new society of the twice-born, the church is the community most nearly approximating to the kingdom of God on earth. Her motivation and conduct ought in principle and practice to exemplify what personal and social obedience to the coming King involves. She has, however, a further mission and duty in relation to the larger world. In the age of grace the body of Christ is still a distinctive segment of the body of humanity: for all the church's regeneracy, sanctification is not yet glorification; for all the world's unregeneracy, moral obstinacy is no mere animality, that is, an existence without obligation to truth and right. In a fallen world wherein both non-Christians and Christians live, God wills civil government for the preservation of justice and restraint of disorder. Christians no less than non-Christians are obliged in conscience to support, mould, advance and defend it, insofar as government is an instrument achieving God's objectives, and to criticise and resist it insofar as it requires what contradicts God's commands.

The church is to be light of the world and salt of the earth. It illuminates earth's bleak problems, and extols Christ as light of the world, and in a degenerating cultural climate preserves whatever is meritorious. Christ is extending his kingdom in the world in and through the church's victories over sin and Satan. These victories are both personal and social. They include the regeneration of doomed sinners and the rescue of man and society from every conceivable form of interpersonal and social as well as theological alienation: oppression, exploitation, racial and sexual discrimination, and anything that runs counter to God's New Covenant. Social justice is not, to be sure, a task for Christians only, but Christians have most reason to formulate and champion it.

The Place of Evangelisation

The social implications of the Gospel are integral to evangelistic fulfilment, and social concern is an indispensable ingredient of the evangelistic message. That Christ died and rose for our sins has for its divine context a creation restored to the purposes for which God intends man and the cosmos.

Social concern cannot therefore be isolated and compartmentalised as a marginal or secondary consideration which the evangelist leaves to others because he has a special calling to evangelise. The question arises, assuredly, as to how much social ethics one addresses to the sinners in proclaiming the Gospel, and this — along with the precise content — will vary from place to place, time to time and audience to audience. But there must assuredly be some minimum, some point at which evangelism comes to grips with social evil if it authentically proclaims the lordship of Christ, some situation in which the evangelist must prefer imprisonment and even martyrdom if necessary to any and every alternative, even if his calling is 'to preach the Gospel'.

The church is in the world for three reasons. One of these,

that of glorifying God's name, continues throughout time and eternity, but it has special implications nonetheless for a world that defames or blasphemes the name. To glorify the name of God in word and deed means nothing less than a total identification with and dedication to the purposes of the Creator who calls us above all else to love him with our whole being and our neighbours as ourself.

A second duty is to edify the body of Christ. The endowments and gifts peculiar to each person are to be used for the enrichment of all. In heaven believers will all be sinlessly conformed to Christ's image and unbelievers will be inaccessible; here and now we have opportunity for mutual 'edification' (Rom. 14: 19, I Thess. 5: 11). This term, *oikodomeoo*, has messianic import. The church is first and foremost an edifice of Christ's building. But our calling as believers includes the upbuilding of the community of which Christ Jesus is the foundation, a foundation laid by apostolic missionary preaching. We are to contribute to the evangelical growth of fellow believers and thus to be builders of a heavenly fellowship, bringing to this task whatever spiritual, intellectual, moral and charismatic possibilities are available to the biblically disciplined believer.

Extension of the kingdom is the third prong, and this is most effectively fulfilled by those whose lives are God-glorifying and church-edifying. The gathered church aims in the age of grace to equip all believers to function effectively as the church dispersed. Lord's Day morning ought therefore to radiate the realities of Resurrection morning: the Risen Christ gathers with his followers and, renewing them by the Spirit, invigorates them for witness and service in the world. Not until the church is gathered on high will this dispersion of believers for evangelism become less important than congregational assembly in praise of the Lamb that was slain. The church can hardly glorify God's name in the age of grace or be truly edifying if she neglects her ambassadorial role of beseeching the lost to be reconciled to God. 'As the Father has sent me, even so I send you' (John 20: 21), said Jesus.

The church's sense of the urgency of global evangelism is governed by inspired Scripture, which affirms the impossibility of salvation through alien ideologies and religions. Not only in the world, but even in the professing church some thinkers today affirm that God is savingly active in all perspectives. But the Bible is clear: no name but Jesus Christ's is given whereby sinners must and can be saved (Acts 4: 12).

Evangelisation of the lost is not a matter of mere radio accessibility to a Gospel broadcast, a Gospel-portion slipped under the front door, a tract passed out on a street corner, or even a brief word of witness on an elevator, although all these may be significant contributory elements. No person is evangelised until becoming a Christian seems to him or her a genuine option, and when rejection of this option means setting one's self against powerful evidence. Ideally it includes the presence in one's neighbourhood of an obedient believing congregation, so that the unbeliever knows his choice is not only between Christ and false gods but also between distinguishable societies with which he may identify.

Key 73 shared the diverse methods of evangelism used by co-operating participants throughout America; Lausanne shared the many strategies for evangelism now being successfully employed in various parts of the world. Yet the fact remains that a one-to-one approach initiated by every believer still holds the best promise of evangelising the earth in our century. This is not to devalue the importance of literature, radio and television which often leap otherwise impenetrable barriers and are significant contributory and supportive media in reaching vast masses. But were every Christian to win another in a single calendar year, the multiplication of believers would far surpass any harvest of souls yet reported in the modern missionary era. Evangelising the lost in one's own neighbourhood is at once the most natural and most strategic place to begin. Some Christians are called and despatched to distant lands as missionaries, though they are comparatively few; all are called and despatched to their neighbours near or far.

A Christian who cannot walk across the street to converse with a neighbour about the Lord of glory ought to hasten to the altar rail, confess to fellow believers that he is part of the modern church's problem, and seek prayer and power to desist from frustrating God's evangelistic purpose for the church and to become an obedient disciple. I am ready to join that procession.

God's purpose for world and church is rooted in eternity past. It comprehends decision in the here and now, in our time, on our street, and in our own lives in relation to our many neglected neighbours. That is what the parable of the Good Samaritan, and behind that the reality of the Incarnation, is all about. It has in view a new man and a new society; indeed, its ultimate issue is a new heaven, and earth, the home of justice.

CHAPTER II

The Authority and Power
of the Bible

John R. W. Stott

'WE AFFIRM THE divine inspiration, truthfulness and authority of both Old and New Testament Scriptures in their entirety as the only written word of God, without error in all
that it affirms, and the only infallible rule of faith and practice. We also affirm the power of God's word to accomplish
his purpose of salvation. The message of the Bible is addressed to all mankind. For God's revelation in Christ and
in Scripture is unchangeable. Through it the Holy Spirit
still speaks today. He illumines the minds of God's people in
every culture to perceive its truth freshly through their own
eyes and thus discloses to the whole church ever more of the
many-coloured wisdom of God.'
(*II Tim. 3: 16; II Pet. 1: 21; John 10: 35; Isa. 55: 11; I Cor.
1: 21; Rom. 1: 16; Matt. 5: 17, 18; Jude 3; Eph. 1: 17, 18;
3: 10, 18*)

(LAUSANNE COVENANT, CLAUSE 2)

SOME READERS OF the Lausanne Covenant will doubtless think it very odd that a statement on evangelism should not only include a paragraph on the Bible but also place it in such a prominent position, second only to God himself and his purpose. 'Those evangelicals are incorrigible,' our critics may say; 'they always insist on dragging the Bible in somewhere. It's a positive obsession with them.'

But our critics do not always understand us. Far from being irrelevant to a declaration on evangelism, biblical authority and power are fundamental. At least three reasons may be given. First, if evangelism means precisely 'spreading the evangel', it is impossible to discuss evangelism as an activity apart from the message which is being communicated. Any definition of evangelism is nonsensical which does not include a definition of the evangel. And we have no authoritative statement of the Gospel except in Scripture.

Secondly, if evangelism leads to conversion, the evangelist should be concerned for the nurture of the converts. What teaching shall they be given? Jesus himself anticipated this question by commissioning the church to teach disciples everything he had commanded (Matt. 28: 20). Christians cannot grow in worship, faith or obedience unless they know whom to worship and what to believe and obey. Thus the biblical revelation is indispensable to Christian maturity.

Thirdly, there is more than content in God's Word, in God's revealed truth, which instructs us for salvation; there is power. Evangelism is not a merely human enterprise. Men cannot win souls by their own ingenuity or effort. Only God can give life to the dead. And his power is exercised through his Word and Spirit. The Gospel itself is the power of God for salvation (Rom. 1: 16).

So the Covenant's second paragraph alludes to the authority and power of the Bible, and adds a third reference, namely to its interpretation.

The Authority of the Bible

Three familiar words are used to indicate our view of Scripture, namely 'inspiration', 'truthfulness' and 'authority'. They belong together, for each involves the others. 'Inspiration' describes the process by which the Bible came into existence, namely that God himself 'breathed' the words (II Tim. 3: 16). 'Truthfulness' is the inevitable result, for what God speaks is true, while the word 'authority' indicates the practical consequence. Truth from God has authority over men.

Nothing is said in the Covenant about the nature of the process called 'inspiration'. Evangelicals do not (or at least should not) hold the mechanical view which has led people to use typewriters, tape-recorders and dictaphones as illustrations. For Scripture itself shows that God treated the authors of Scripture as persons, not as machines. This is evident from the differences of theological emphasis and literary style which we perceive in their writings. God did not obliterate their personality. Nor did he make their own thinking and researching unnecessary (cf. Luke 1: 1–4). On the contrary, he spoke through them in such a way that all their background, convictions and gifts were fully and freely expressed in what they said and wrote. At the same time, if God's inspiration did not destroy their personality, neither did their personality destroy God's inspiration. We believe that the words of the Bible are equally the words of God and the words of men. On the one hand, men spoke from God (II Pet. 1: 21); on the other God spoke through men (Heb.

1: 1). This is what we mean when we affirm that all Scripture in its entirety is 'the only written word of God'.

'Truthfulness' is the result. For 'God is not man, that he should lie' (Num. 23: 19). On the contrary, God's word is truth (John 17: 17). To assert that all Scripture is true is not the same thing as asserting that it is all equally important. Jesus himself spoke of 'the weightier matters of the law', insisting that 'justice, mercy and faith' were more important than the tithing of garden herbs (Matt. 23: 23). Again, the Old Testament revelation though true was incomplete ('in many parts', Heb. 1: 1 literally), while most of us would agree that the Sermon on the Mount is a more profitable study than the genealogies! Nevertheless, all God's Word is true. And this positive affirmation inevitably involves the negative corollary that it is 'without error in all that it affirms'.

The addition of the phrase 'in all that it affirms' is important. Not everything included in Scripture is true, because not everything recorded in Scripture is affirmed by Scripture. It would be extremely naïve (to say the least) to declare one's belief that 'every word in the Bible is true'. It plainly is not. A good example is the Book of Job. Its first thirty-one chapters contain speeches by Job's so called 'comforters', Eliphaz, Bildad and Zophar. We have no liberty to pick out any random sentence they uttered and say 'this is the word of God'. For their speeches are a strange mixture of truth and error. We know this because in the book's last chapter God specifically says to the three comforters: 'you have not spoken of me what is right' (42: 7). So then, in declaring that Scripture is 'without error in all that it affirms' we commit ourselves to its study, to the responsible work of biblical interpretation, so that we may discern the intention of each author and grasp what is being affirmed.

The third word is 'authority'. God's inspired and truthful Word has authority over us, both as individuals and as churches. It is 'the only infallible rule of faith and practice'. Most churches accept additional rules, a creed or confession or catechism which defines the church's position on disputed points. But these are themselves subordinate to Scripture, and being the composition of men, are fallible documents.

There is only one supreme and infallible rule which determines the beliefs and practices of the church, and that is Scripture itself. To this we may always appeal, even from the confessions, traditions and conventions of a church.

Jesus himself clearly distinguished between Scripture and tradition. He regarded Scripture as God's Word and tradition as man's, and insisted on the subordination of the latter to the former. One of his major quarrels with the Pharisees was that they gave more respect to tradition than to Scripture, and in so doing often annulled the authority of Scripture. 'You leave the commandment of God, and hold fast the tradition of men,' he said. Again, 'you have a fine way of rejecting the commandment of God, in order to keep your tradition! ... thus making void the Word of God through your tradition which you hand on' (Mark 7: 8, 9, 13).

There is an urgent need for the contemporary church to recover our Lord's own perspective. All churches have their own traditions, and Jesus did not forbid these. What he prohibited was on the one hand the holding of traditions which are contrary to Scripture and on the other the teaching of any human tradition — even if not contrary to Scripture — as a doctrine which must of necessity be believed (Mark 7: 7). The Church of Rome appeared to take a significant step forward at Vatican II when it declined to endorse the Council of Trent's position that Scripture and tradition were two equally authoritative *sources* of revelation. Instead it spoke of them as two *streams*. Although this is still an unsatisfactory formulation, it at least indicates that tradition must run parallel to Scripture and cannot stand on its own as an independent source of truth. This gives us liberty in Protestant-Catholic debate to press Roman Catholics to prove their traditions from Scripture and, if they cannot, to have the courage to abandon them.

In ecumenical circles the problem is an exaggerated deference not so much to church tradition as to human reason. A study of recent ecumenical assemblies discloses astonishing attitudes to Scripture, and in particular a token respect which is little more than a mask. For example, the application at Uppsala of the eschatological text 'Behold I make all things new to the revolutionary movements of the day was such a glaring misuse of Scripture as scarcely to need refutation. Similarly, no biblical scholar could claim that there was any serious attempt at Bangkok to define salvation biblically. What was offered instead was a series of bright ideas, with a half-hearted attempt to find biblical warrant for them. At the root of the evangelical-ecumenical debate is the question of biblical hermeneutics. What are the true principles of biblical interpretation? If the leaders of the World Council of Churches hope for the respect of evangelicals, let alone their active collaboration, they must give more solid evidence of a desire to take Scripture seriously and live under its authority than they have done in recent years.

It is an easy game, however, for evangelicals to criticise Roman Catholic and ecumenical Christians. What about ourselves? 'We affirm the divine inspiration, truthfulness and authority' of Scripture, we say. Yet far too often we fail to practise what we preach. We are not always aware how much we also can be in bondage to tradition. In many churches the 'traditions of the evangelical elders' appear to be more sacrosanct than Scripture itself. Of course such evangelicals will defend themselves by saying that their traditions are all *biblical* traditions. And I do not doubt their sincerity. But what they are really doing is to exalt their own interpretation of Scripture as a 'doctrine' which must be believed, and this is exactly what Jesus accused the Pharisees of doing. I readily agree that in the central Christian doctrines and duties Scripture speaks in a plain, perspicuous way. But there are other areas in which devout Bible-believing students reach different conclusions. Some are doctrinal issues, concerning (for example) the order and ministry of the church, the nature and effect of the sacraments, and the interpretation of prophecy. Others are ethical, concerning (for example) alcohol, tobacco and cosmetics. Evangelicals must be mature enough to give each other liberty in such matters.

Every church should be engaged in a process of continuous self-evaluation and reformation. It is a painful, threatening situation to be in. We would all find it easier to make up our minds about controversial issues once and for all, and then let our minds set in a hard, inflexible mould. We make the same mistake with our culture. Because it is congenial to us, and an important part of our personal security we invest our cultural background with the sanctity and permanence which belong to Scripture alone. We need instead to develop a certain detachment to all tradition, convention and culture, so that we subject them to constant, rigorous, biblical scrutiny. Only so can we display that realistic submission to Scripture which we affirm.

The Power of the Bible

Talk about submission to biblical authority suggests to many people's minds a concept of Scripture as a dead letter. But this is not our view. Although the Bible is the 'written Word of God', or (to use a scriptural formula) 'what stands written', nevertheless we do not forget that 'The Word of God is living and active, sharper than any two-edged sword' (Heb. 4: 12).

The biblical understanding of God's Word is not just that he speaks it, but that he acts through it. His words are not merely speech; they are deeds as well. This is clear of creation, which was effected by God's words of command. 'God said ... and it was so'; 'He spoke, and it came to be; he commanded, and it stood forth' (Gen 1: 6, 7 etc., Ps. 33: 9). The same is true of salvation, which indeed is a new creation. For the same God who said 'Let light shine out of darkness' has shone in our hearts, revealing Christ to us (II Cor. 4: 6). His Word was creative; it brought to us both light and life.

Perhaps the best known biblical statement of the power of God's Word is that which this paragraph of the Covenant echoes, namely Isaiah 55: 11. God likens his Word to the rain and snow which fall from heaven, water the earth and make it fruitful. 'So shall my word be,' he says, 'that goes forth from my mouth; it shall not return to me empty, but it shall accomplish that which I purpose, and prosper in the thing for which I sent it.' God never speaks his words aimlessly. He has a purpose in speaking, and his Word accomplishes his purpose.

The Covenant refers to 'his purpose of salvation', and this echoes another verse (II Tim. 3: 15) which asserts that the Scriptures 'are able to instruct you for salvation through faith in Christ Jesus'. Scripture is God's own testimony to Jesus Christ. Its overriding purpose is to bear witness to Christ. He himself said so: 'it is they that bear witness to me' (John 5: 39). And God uses Scripture to elicit faith in Christ and thus to bring salvation. Testimony to Christ — faith — salvation: the order is the same according to both John and Paul (John 20: 30, II Tim. 3: 15). Further the 'salvation' Scripture brings is to be understood broadly as including our growth into maturity. For Paul goes on to write: 'all Scripture is inspired by God and profitable for teaching, for reproof, for correction, and for training in righteousness, that the man of God may be complete, equipped for every good work' (II Tim. 3: 16, 17).

Once more this is easy to say. But in the spirit of Lausanne, which was a spirit of humble self-criticism, we evangelicals have to admit that we do not live up to our profession. We declare our confidence about Scripture that 'through it the Holy Spirit still speaks today'. If we mean this, it will have at least two practical results.

First, we shall listen to the voice of the Spirit through Scripture. We shall neither look for visions and revelations apart from Scripture, nor shall we read Scripture as a lifeless ancient document. Instead, we shall read Scripture regularly and expectantly, with the strong confidence that the living God can and will speak to us through his Word today. With what a dull and unbelieving spirit we customarily open the pages of the Bible! We expect nothing, and we receive nothing. Our spirit is stale, our appetite jaded, our heart dull and our ear deaf. Yet God says to us as we read: 'he who has an ear, let him hear what the Spirit says to the churches' (Rev. 2: 7 etc.). It is a striking statement. The reference is to a letter of John's, yet through it the word of the Spirit could be heard. The letter was written, yet through it a voice was speaking. The letter had been written weeks, perhaps months, previously, yet through that dated written message a contemporary voice, the living voice of the Spirit of truth, was still speaking. He who has ears to hear, let him hear!

The second logical consequence of a sincere belief in the authority and power of the Bible would be a recovery of expository preaching. By 'expository preaching' I am not referring to a particular homiletical method, one option among many, but to all our preaching. For all true Christian preaching is expository preaching, that is to say preaching which faithfully draws out the message of the biblical text and applies it relevently to the present day. Do we really believe that it is God's good pleasure 'through the folly of what we preach [i.e. the *kerygma*, the biblical Gospel] to save those who believe' (I Cor. 1: 21), and that through the same message Christians become 'mature in Christ' (Col. 1: 28, 29)? Then we shall spare no pains to study Scripture in order to expound it accurately and meaningfully. This calls for a greater measure of integrity than we often display. If the Bible is God's Word written, we must pray over it and pore over it until it yields its message. We have no liberty to falsify the Word of God, twisting it to suit our prejudice or to conceal our laziness. We evangelicals have a higher view of Scripture than anybody else in the church; then our study and exposition of it should be correspondingly more conscientious. The current dichotomy between how we regard Scripture and how we treat Scripture is one of the greatest scandals of contemporary Christendom. It is also a major cause of the weakness of the church, of the spread of error and of the prevailing Christian superficiality and immaturity.

The Interpretation of the Bible

The last four sentences of the Covenant's second paragraph broach the important subject of biblical interpretation. They do not outline the principles which should guide us in interpreting Scripture, but they lay a vital foundation by contrasting with the unchangeability of Scripture as God's revelation the fresh and growing understanding of it which the Holy Spirit continues to give his people.

Notice the statements that 'the message of the Bible is addressed to all mankind' and 'God's revelation in Christ and in Scripture is unchangeable'. Neither the passage of time nor the variations of culture can alter it. God has revealed himself fully and finally in Christ and in the whole biblical witness to Christ. His Word cannot be broken (John 10: 35). Not an iota or dot will pass from it (Matt. 5:18). It is intended for all men in all places and at all times. Indeed we are sure of its universality precisely because we are sure of its finality.

Yet this assertion of the unchangeability of Scripture does not mean that our view of it is static and wooden. On the contrary, as has already been emphasised, 'the Holy Spirit still speaks today' with a living voice through the very message which he spoke centuries ago and caused to be written for our learning. The Bible is not a museum of ancient words, but the medium of a contemporary voice.

This present work of the Spirit is expressed by the word 'illumination'. Indeed, the Covenant deliberately sets 'revelation' and 'illumination' together as complementary terms. 'God's revelation', it says, took place 'in Christ and in Scripture'. For revelation is an objective unveiling of truth, progressive throughout Scripture and culminating in Jesus Christ, the Word made flesh. Illumination, however, is a subjective process, taking place 'in the minds of God's people'. The two processes are necessarily related, not only because the Holy Spirit is the author of both but also because the Scriptures are involved in both. Scripture is the result of revelation, and it is what has been revealed in Scripture that the Spirit illumines our minds to perceive.

This gracious teaching ministry the Holy Spirit exercises among God's people 'in every culture'. Culture was a major topic of debate at Lausanne, and clearly evangelical Christians still have to grapple further with the relation between Christianity and culture. On the one hand, culture can distort the Gospel. We tend far too readily to identify our cultural way of life with the Christian way of life. Once this identification has been made we find ourselves in bondage to some form of what Dr René Padilla rightly styled 'culture-Christianity'. There are many brands of it — in North America and Latin America, in Europe, Africa and Asia. On the other hand, although our culture can be a barrier to our understanding, it can also be the medium of it. Indeed, the understanding of the Gospel which each of us has is bound to have been to some extent determined by our cultural background. Our culture is part of us. We cannot escape from it. Inevitably we see things through our own eyes, from our particular cultural perspective.

Nor is this fact always to be deplored. On the contrary, it is often enriching. For we see those facets of the Gospel which are relevant to us, and the Holy Spirit uses our existential situation to illumine and emphasise to us some appropriate biblical truth. For example, it was natural for the American Negroes in the terrible days of their slavery to identify themselves with Israel under Egyptian oppression, to listen with eager ears to the message of Moses and to derive comfort from the prospect of the promised land. Similarly, Christians suffering under communist, Muslim or Hindu persecution are fortified by the Book of Revelation, with its assurances that Jesus Christ is already on the throne and is soon coming back in power and triumph. Again, our vision of the family of God will be affected by whether our personal experience has been of a 'nuclear' family (as in the West) or an 'extended' family (as in Africa). The way in which any biblical concept strikes us, whether it be the concept of love or justice or freedom, is sure to be influenced by our cultural milieu.

We should not, therefore, react with immediate hostility to the notion of 'black theology' or 'African theology', insisting that we believe only in biblical theology, and biblical theology is everywhere exactly the same, whatever our skin pigmentation or cultural situation. It is true that the substance of God's revelation is the same. But once we have asserted its unchangeability we should be ready to add that, nevertheless, different facets of it shine with particular brilliance for particular people. As with the authors of Scripture so with its readers, the Holy Spirit does not bypass our personality and teach us in a vacuum. He used the cultural background of the biblical writers in order to convey through each a message appropriate to them as real people in real situations. In the same way he uses the cultural inheritance of Bible readers to convey to them out of the Scriptures living and appropriate truth.

Three expressions in the final sentence of the Covenant's second paragraph deserve special mention. First the phrase 'perceive its truth freshly through their own eyes'. Our evangelical presentation of the Gospel has often become stale and stereotyped because we have neglected this. There is a great need for *faithfulness* in our proclamation, it is true, but there is an equal need for *freshness*. Just as no child can receive a faith from his parents like a package, or inherit it like a legacy, but must appropriate it for himself personally, so no convert can receive the Gospel from an evangelist as if it were a mere formula of words. Each new Christian must make the Gospel his own, as the Holy Spirit authenticates it to him in his own mind, heart and life. Yet some of our evangelistic missions resemble Gospel factories. We give the impression that we want to mass produce converts, with each an exact replica of the rest.

The same is true of the tension between mission and church in Third World countries. Some missionaries have tried to force their converts into an alien cultural mould. The converts' rebellion against this form of oppression was as healthy as it was inevitable. Indeed, the enormous multiplication of African Independent Churches (six thousand listed in Dr David Barrett's *Schism and Renewal in Africa*) is to be understood at least partly as the quest for an authentic *African* expression of Christianity shorn of western cultural clothing. To allow and even encourage other Christians to perceive the truth of the Gospel 'freshly through their own eyes' is a mark both of respect for human beings and of confidence in the Holy Spirit.

The second expression is that the Holy Spirit discloses his truth 'to the whole church'. This concept reflects the apostle Paul's prayer that we 'may have power to comprehend *with all the saints*' the full dimensions of the love of Christ. It will take 'all the saints', the whole church, to grasp the fullness of God's revelation. We evangelicals need to be reminded of this, because without doubt our doctrine of the Holy Spirit has usually been too individualistic. We think of him as a gracious indwelling guest, who illumines *my* mind and teaches *me* and increases *my* knowledge of the things of God. Quite right too. But does he teach nobody else?

Our individualism is in part a consequence of our history. We continue to thank God for our Reformation heritage, and not least for the Reformers' insistence on 'the right of private judgment', that is, on the individual Christian's liberty to appeal to Scripture over against the whole hierarchy. But this undoubted right sometimes degenerates into a claim to personal infallibility, as if we believed not in the priesthood but in the papacy of all believers! In some evangelical circles there is such an unbalanced emphasis on the personal ministry of the Holy Spirit to each Bible reader that the authorised teachers of the church are despised and rejected. But God has set teachers in his church. Pastors and teachers are permanent gifts which the exalted Christ bestows on his church (Eph. 4: 7–12). And it is the Holy Spirit's purpose to teach his people through human teachers as well as directly and immediately.

Moreover, we can often gain fresh insights into the revealed truth of God from teachers of a different culture who see and express things differently from us. We talk much of the need for cross-cultural evangelism, but not enough about cross-cultural teaching. Those of us who come from the West assume too readily that the best teachers in the church are westerners. But the bubble of our arrogant assumption is quickly pricked when we are exposed to the openness and integrity of a brother from the East African revival area, or the mystical mind of a Chinese expositor or the imagination and enthusiasm of a Latin American Christian.

The third expression is the last one, that the Holy Spirit discloses 'ever more of the many-coloured wisdom of God'. 'Ever more.' The enlightening, teaching ministry of the Holy Spirit has been gradual and cumulative throughout the history of the Christian church. Some of us evangelicals speak as if we thought the Holy Spirit virtually ceased to exist, certainly ceased to teach, when the last apostle died and the canon of New Testament Scripture was complete! What we should rather affirm is that the character of his teaching ministry changed. 'Revelation', conceived as the objective disclosure of new truth, did cease with the apostles. God's self-revelation came to its climax in Christ and in the apostolic witness to Christ. It is inconceivable that there should be any higher revelation than that. But the Holy Spirit's work of illumination has continued. Indeed he has been progressively clarifying the church's mind on the great doctrines of Scripture. This is the field of historical theology or the development of doctrine, and it is fascinating to watch the story unfold as the great councils, confessions and teachers of the church define successive biblical doctrines. True, all these clarifications belong to the realm of 'tradition'. They are human and fallible formulations of Scripture and do not possess the infallibility of Scripture itself. Nevertheless, they bear witness to the continuing ministry of illumination which the Spirit has exercised, and we in the twentieth century are privileged to have entered into the rich heritage of the Christian centuries. We ought to prize it more than we customarily do.

The same work of illumination continues today. The Holy Spirit is still disclosing 'ever more of the many-coloured wisdom of God'. The expression is borrowed from the apostle Paul (Eph. 3: 10). He likens God's wisdom to an oriental carpet or tapestry, woven from many threads of many colours. God's revelation in Christ and in Scripture is indeed complete and unchangeable. But may God give us the humility to recognise that out of this unique, final and colourful revelation we still have much more to learn, and that in this learning process we have much to receive from one another.

CHAPTER III

The Uniqueness and Universality of Christ

Saphir Philip Athyal

'WE AFFIRM THAT there is only one Saviour and only one gospel, although there is a wide diversity of evangelistic approaches. We recognise that all men have some knowledge of God through his general revelation in nature. But we deny that this can save, for men suppress the truth by their unrighteousness. We also reject as derogatory to Christ and the gospel every kind of syncretism and dialogue which implies that Christ speaks equally through all religions and ideologies. Jesus Christ, being himself the only God-man, who gave himself as the only ransom for sinners, is the only mediator between God and man. There is no other name by which we must be saved. All men are perishing because of sin, but God loves all men, not wishing that any should perish but that all should repent. Yet those who reject Christ repudiate the joy of salvation and condemn themselves to eternal separation from God. To proclaim Jesus as "the Saviour of the world" is not to affirm that all men are either automatically or ultimately saved, still less to affirm that all religions offer salvation in Christ. Rather it is to proclaim God's love for a world of sinners and to invite all men to respond to him as Saviour and Lord in the wholehearted personal commitment of repentance and faith. Jesus Christ has been exalted above every other name; we long for the day when every knee shall bow to him and every tongue shall confess him Lord.'

(*Gal. 1: 6–9; Rom. 1: 18–32; I Tim. 2: 5, 6; Acts 4: 12; John 3: 16–19; II Pet. 3: 9; II Thess. 1: 7–9; John 4: 42; Matt. 11: 28; Eph. 1: 20, 21; Phil. 2: 9–11*)

(LAUSANNE COVENANT, CLAUSE 3)

THE THIRD SECTION of the Lausanne Covenant strongly reaffirms the extraordinary claim that the Christian church has always made: namely, that Christ is the Saviour of the world, the only mediator between God and man, and that there is 'no other name in heaven and on earth' whereby the totally lost world may be saved. Men have through their sin and rebellion alienated themselves from God, but God has not abandoned them to the full consequences of their separation from him. In diverse ways he gives them some knowledge of himself and of truth, and tries to lead them to a saving knowledge through his unique self-revelation in Christ.

We must ask ourselves, what is the nature of God's unique revelation through Jesus Christ in the context of his diverse means of self-disclosure to mankind and his general dealings with them? What should be a Christian's attitude to other religions and ideologies which in their own right claim to offer man his salvation and knowledge of goodness, light and truth?

General and Special Divine Revelation

In Christian theology a distinction is often made between general revelation and special revelation. The former refers to God's dealing with all men through which they have some knowledge of him, and the latter refers specifically to the absolute and unique revelation of God in Christ which is expressed in his Word. The problem of the relationship between the two has become a very relevant and urgent question particularly in recent years.

What is General Revelation?

Those who have not come to the knowledge of Christ are not ignorant of God altogether, for God has revealed something of himself in 'many and various ways' outside of his self-revelation through his Son (Heb. 1: 1–2). While only a believing Christian can understand the beauty and wonders of God's creation to any great depth, the so-called 'nature Psalms' (Pss. 8, 19, 65, 104) speak of how God's handiwork communicates his power and glory. Paul, speaking of the ungodly and the wicked, says, 'ever since the creation of the world his invisible nature, namely, his eternal power and diety, has been clearly perceived in the things that have been made' (Rom. 1: 20).

All men also have some understanding of God's moral demands on them as they show that 'what the law requires is written on their hearts' (Rom. 2:15; cf. 1: 32). The very fact that man lives and that there is some orderliness and concept of justice underlying the continuance of human society, gives evidence that God's grace and presence envelop all his creation. Paul's speeches to the men of Lystra and of Athens describe God as the one who guides man and governs the history of nations, who is not far from anyone and has not left himself without witness, having the ultimate purpose that all men should leave their ignorance and come to the true knowledge of him (Acts 14:15–17; 17: 22–31).

With the recent widespread interest in non-Christian religions, general revelation is often understood to mean that truth is so vast and broad that no religion can claim any absolute or unique character, that God speaks to man equally through all religions and ideologies. Instead of the absolute denials of this position which characterised the last few centuries, today it is affirmed from every quarter that truth is so marvellous that none can define it: thus everyone may be right and every idea is a part of truth.[1] But this 'relativism of truth' and universalism is not what we mean by general revelation.

The Limits of General Revelation

The teaching on general revelation should in no way jeopardise the doctrine of special revelation. It is not a second or an alternative source of the knowledge of God to special revelation. First, general revelation in itself cannot give man a true knowledge of God and lead him to salvation without special revelation. These two kinds of revelation do not have separate identities, but are one unity. Special revelation is God's self-disclosure in Christ and his ministry; likewise, general revelation is also given through Christ. Natural revelation comes to man through the works of creation which are all made through Christ, since without him nothing was made (John 1: 3; Col. 1: 16). If God deals with men through their consciences and they have his laws written upon their hearts, this is because Christ is 'the true light that enlightens every man' (John 1: 9). Outside of Christ, the special revelation of God, there is no ground for general revelation.

Second, Paul's discussion in Romans 1 demonstrates that the concept of general revelation carries with it a note of awesomeness and warning. The knowledge of God available to all men deals with his deity, power, and holiness, not his saving love and forgiveness (cf. Rom. 1: 20, 32). Because men generally are incapable of responding worthily to what they know of God in obedience and submission, 'by their wickedness [they] suppress the truth', become futile in their thinking and darkened in their minds so that they are led to idolatry and immorality (Rom. 1: 18–23). General revelation brings condemnation and restlessness to those estranged from God and makes them aware of their need for Christ. 'General revelation remains a reminder of the guilt of the "closed eyes". Precisely this doctrine, therefore, uncovers for us the absoluteness of the revelation of God in Jesus Christ.'[2] Their partial knowledge of God through general revelation leads them to God's judgment and wrath. Thus general revelation is linked with guilt and the anger of God (Rom. 1: 18, 21).

Third, we should not presume that general revelation can invariably convince men of God's existence and work in the world. We cannot concur with the Roman Catholic theology of the 'natural knowledge of God' according to which the natural law of reason in man leads him to a true, though incomplete, knowledge of God even apart from the revelation through Christ. Reason does not lead man to a knowledge of God, much less can it prove his existence. Proofs for the existence of God have value in strengthening the faith of those who already believe, but reason cannot create faith. On the other hand, there is very much in the world, nature and human history today which can be more readily used to disprove the existence of a sovereign and just God rather than to prove his existence.

Special Divine Revelation

The fundamental characteristic of Christian faith which constitutes its uniqueness in the face of other religions and ideologies is its emphasis on the knowledge of God through his self-revelation in Christ within the context of human history at a given time and place.[3] Divine revelation is primarily personal. Christ 'was manifested in the flesh' (I Tim. 3: 16). Apart from this central event, God often intervened in human history through his mighty acts in fulfilment of his plan of salvation. The Old Testament is primarily a record of the events which God initiated.

The redemptive acts of God and his gracious interpretation of them in human terms as recorded in the Bible are inseparably related to each other, and together they constitute revelation. The Bible without the historicity of the revelatory events and saving acts of God is a compilation of mere religious ideas and myths like any other religious scripture; at the same time the redemptive history signifies nothing if it stands without divine interpretation.

Providing God's people with the written Word should be considered a part of God's great redemptive acts in history. God's historical and personal self-disclosure came to have a scriptural or written embodiment, lacking which we would have been for ever blind to his revelation.

If one isolates the Bible from the historical acts of God, the life and ministry of Christ, and the work of the Holy Spirit in the world today, one gives it an absolute and divine character similar to what is claimed for the Koran, which is believed to have been eternally coexistent with Allah. This kind of attitude forces us to formulate different foolproof theories of inspiration which fence us in and tend to lead us to some form of bibliolatry.

But a graver danger with Christian theology today is an over-emphasis and insistence on history as the primary and sole means of God's revelation. If 'redemptive' events *per se* constitute divine revelation, how much would the biblical history of an insignificant, subjugated nation of Israel, and an unfortunate carpenter-preacher from Nazareth, speak for itself? Viewed objectively in the perspective of the history of great ancient nations, biblical events only prove the opposite of what the Bible claims regarding the power and greatness of Yahweh and of Christ the King of kings. The audacity of the biblical claims makes no sense if biblical events are viewed in terms of pure history.

Events in themselves can say very little. For example, the event of a good man from Galilee hanging on the cross cannot give one any knowledge as to who the man is. It is also true that the historical biblical narratives themselves represent verbal communications rather than the events as the actual revelation of God. If revelation comes only through history, several parts of the Bible which are outside the framework of history will have to be rejected as invalid — for example, the Wisdom literature, Proverbs and many Psalms. Again, the prophets' understanding of God's Word went far beyond their own understanding of their contemporary events and state of affairs.

The coming of Christ was the great salvation event that Israel expected throughout the Old Testament times. All the other saving acts of God are related to this one and foreshadowed it. The 'event of Christ' was interpreted by God through the apostles who themselves participated in this event and through those teachings and writings the supreme significance of the Christ-event is made known. Apostolic tradition carries with it the authority of the life and teachings of Christ as God spoke through them. Their words as written down in the New Testament are thus God's unique revelation in Christ.

There is, in addition to the redemptive acts of God and their spoken divine interpretation, a third distinguishable aspect of special revelation: the work of the Holy Spirit in the hearts of men. Just as the act of God and the Word of God are inseparable, so are the Word of God and the Spirit of God. The special divine revelation is accepted and understood as such only by the witness of the Holy Spirit and his appropriation of the revelation in the experience of a believer. The Spirit of God which interpreted the saving acts of God in terms of the Scripture, today interprets the Scripture to us as God's unchanging word for us. The objectivity and the ultimate authority of God's special revelation in Christ and the Word are made real to us and authenticated by the work and testimony of the Holy Spirit in us.

Christian Faith and Other Faiths

Our belief in God's unique revelation in Christ poses the question of what should be our attitude to other living religions of today with all their various values and profound teachings. Major religions such as Hinduism and Buddhism have been undergoing significant renewal during recent years in response to the growth of the nationalistic spirit and the revival of old values and traditions. The basic teachings of these religions are reinterpreted in terms of contemporary philosophies and sciences. Their relevance to social and political problems is underlined. Allegorical interpretations, similar to those which the Christian church used for over a thousand years, are applied to stories and myths in their scriptures to make them relevant to present-day situations and needs.

The Problem Stated

The attitudes of Christians to other faiths generally fall under the following categories:

1. Man should develop one global religion and one culture, pooling together the relevant values in all religions and philosophies, as the world's space and communication barriers are fast disappearing and the world is shrinking into one community. A synthesis of all major religions should be man's goal.

2. The present status quo of the religions should be maintained as each of them represents a valid and true way to the absolute truth.

3. Christianity should be open to borrow heavily from other religions and expand itself to make it richer and more universally acceptable.

4. The Christian faith offers something unique and distinctive, revelation in Christ is the only truth while other religions only tend to lead man astray from the true and only way. One should work towards the goal of all men submitting themselves to Christ.

Certain Christian circles and influential Christian theologies consider Christianity 'as a species of genus religion, as a sub-division of the general preoccupation with the divine'.[4] Thus, not only is a broad and universal approach to religion encouraged, but also Christianity is reduced to one of the many different paths to God.

Christians in Asia and Africa are a minority living amongst non-Christian majorities, and in their life and witness they are always in 'dialogue' with people who are of other faiths. To state the fundamentals of the Christian faith using native categories of thought and indigenous expressions, they always confront the religious overtones and implications of words and thought patterns they have to use, just the same as St John must have experienced in his use of the Greek word *logos*. To them Christianity's relation to other religions is not just an academic question, but rather their grass-roots-level daily situation.

In our discussion on this question, we should make a distinction between Christianity as a religious system and the core of the Christian faith as found in the Bible. A man who claims to be an adherent of the Christian religion can be just as far from God as any pagan. If in our comparative study of religions, we make a distinction between popular, empirical Christianity and the fundamentals of the Christian faith — that is to say, between what Christian religion is and what it should be — then this type of distinction should be applied to other religions also. Thus it may be more correct to say 'Christian faith and other faiths' rather than 'Christianity and other religions'.

Certain people hold that non-Christian religions point to Christ just as the Old Testament religion does. Just as we find unfulfilled longings for a more complete knowledge and experience of God in the Old Testament, the same is found also in other religions and religious scriptures. They all, like the Old Testament, represent 'the promises', and revelation in Christ or the New Testament becomes the 'fulfilment' of all. But the Old Testament itself represents a position very different from this. Perhaps the most striking description of Yahweh in the Old Testament is that he is a 'jealous God' who would not tolerate the worship of other gods. Following other gods and the religions of other nations was considered the greatest of offences and was punishable by death. Yahweh is declared to be the only living God; other gods are merely 'nonentities', 'worthlessness' and forms made of stone or wood (Jer. 10: 15; Isa. 40: 18–20). Israel's syncretic openness to the religion of its neighbours was vehemently opposed by the prophets.

Dangers of Syncretism

Those who have a syncretic approach to religions hold that all different faiths speak in their own ways of the ultimate Truth. At a certain level they all lose their particularities and are elevated to spiritual freedom and ultimate meaning.[5] They would say that Christians should abandon their claim to the uniqueness of their faith, and with openness and humility join hands with men of other faiths in their search for the ultimate truth. The differences between the religions are only superficial — the modes of worship and detailed beliefs — all of which we should overlook while we work towards developing one common faith. According to them any pretence of the superiority of Christianity is caused by lack of humility and love for our fellow men of other religions.

Most non-Christian religions of the past and the present show a syncretic nature, this being particularly true with Hinduism. Thus Hinduism has become a melting pot of religions, having within itself all forms of faith. Mahatma Gandhi, an ardent proponent of Hinduism and the one who is credited as the father-founder of the nation of India, speaks for many Hindu leaders and syncretic Christians when he says, 'The soul of religions is one, but it is encased in a multitude of forms . . . Truth is the exclusive property of no single scripture . . . I cannot ascribe exclusive divinity to Jesus. He is as divine as Krishna or Rama or Mohammed or Zoroaster.'[6]

The basic assumption in the syncretic approach is that God is too great, ineffable and unknowable to adequately reveal his true nature in any single experience or single revelation in history. No one scripture can claim to be a unique and final revelation of God. Even an infinite number of experiences of God by an infinite number of his saints would not actually reveal his true nature. In syncretism a great deal of emphasis is given directly or indirectly to man's mystical experience of God. It is held that persons who belong to different religions share with one another a 'common spirituality' through their direct and mystical experience of God which transcends their theological differences.[7]

The pitfalls and implications of this approach to truth and the revelation of God are quite apparent. First, when no single revelation of God is final and there are an infinite number of ways and times that God reveals himself, man has no certainty as to his knowledge of the truth. If there is anything like an ultimate truth, no one can ever come to know it. Man must always rely on his periodical experiences of God and his personal insights, although these may vary considerably from time to time and from those of his fellow believers. No revelation of God is normative, and there never can be a certainty in our understanding of God.

Second, the incarnation of Christ and God's self-disclosure in history become of no particular significance. Nevertheless, the whole basis of Christianity is neither the sublime thoughts of the greatest sages nor the profoundest mystical experiences of man, but rather a decisive event in history, namely the Christ-event. The Gospel is in its entirety the news about this event. Once the belief that God reveals himself in a unique way once for all in the person and ministry of Christ is given up, Christianity has no basis whatsoever on which it may stand.

Third, the syncretic view has a strong tendency to devalue the personal character of God and to consider religions as systems of the pious ideas of men. God is a Person with a purpose and a design for the world which he works out on his initiative. History is not a series of cyclical events, but a purposeful movement towards a goal guided by a God who is a person. Syncretism or any compromise with other religious systems, therefore, is a repudiation of the Christian faith which is not founded on the Bible.

Opportunities for and Limitations of Religious Dialogues

For a Christian who is personally and genuinely committed to Christ, 'dialogue' with people of other religions can be an enriching experience. For one thing, he cannot truly love a Hindu or a Buddhist or witness to him without taking seriously both the person and the religious convictions and traditions which have made him what he is. Dialogue is based on true reverence for the other person and his values. Both partners give themselves to each other, and in the case of a Christian this giving primarily involves his witness to Christ. As a Christian he shares his faith, a gift of grace from God to an unworthy sinner, with all humility.

The main basis of religious dialogue should be the equality of persons rather than the equality of religions. Dialogue can prove to be very valuable in such areas as common spiritual values, human rights and freedom, the development of nations, the dignity of labour, basic morals, etc. Also, dialogue will be extremely helpful in clarifying mutual misunderstandings and prejudices. However, those who engage in dialogue should realise that any resemblance the Christian faith may have to other religions is only superficial. Because of the manner in which religions — both empirical Christianity and empirical non-Christian religions — are generally practised, there may appear to be many more similarities between them than there actually are. But in some of the fundamentals of the Christian faith, one finds no common ground for dialogue. Consider, for example, the personal character of God as stressed in Christianity compared to the Hindu concept of an impersonal God, or the Buddhist concept of religion without a god; or, again, the biblical emphasis on history as opposed to the lack of any sense of history in most religions, except Judaism and Islam.

Any dialogue which devalues Christ's incarnation, death and resurrection at one time in history as recorded in the Bible, and which gives primary emphasis to 'a cosmic Christ' who works equally in all religious systems, smacks of syncretism and should be rejected. Thus one cannot agree with the stand that is generally taken in India today by those long engaged in the task of inter-religious dialogue. This view states, 'It seems that a more universal work of Christ in the history of mankind must be discerned, but that the model or key to such a discernment is the life, death and resurrection of Jesus, as recorded in the Gospel . . . The task of Christian mission, then, is to help the Hindu to recognise that his experience of God is an experience of the God who is fully made known in Jesus . . . The open approach of dialogue seems to be the only missionary method adequate to the intensely personal work of the Gospel.'[8] Speaking to this point the Lausanne Covenant affirms, 'We also reject as derogatory to Christ and the Gospel every kind of syncretism and dialogue which implies that Christ speaks equally through all religions and ideologies . . . To proclaim Jesus as "the Saviour of the world" is not to affirm that all men are either automatically or ultimately saved, still less to affirm that all religions offer salvation in Christ.'

Jesus Christ the only Saviour and Lord

The Uniqueness of Christ and His Authority

The main thrust of the third paragraph of the Lausanne Covenant is an affirmation of the uniqueness of Christ. Christ is wholly divine and fully human at the same time. He is the only God-man, the only ransom for sinners and the only mediator between God and man. This is the sum and substance of the whole Gospel and of the New Testament records. The person of Christ and the great mystery of his divine and human natures being perfectly combined in one person have been repeatedly discussed in the history of the church. There are numerous works written on the subject and the scope of this chapter does not permit us to deal with the issue adequately.[9]

I Timothy 2: 5–6 states, 'There is one God, and there is one mediator between God and men, the man Christ Jesus, who gave himself as a ransom for all.' This passage makes four clear claims for Christ: He is 'God', 'mediator between God and men', 'man', and 'ransom for all'.

The confession of the deity of Christ is based on the testimony of the Scripture and particularly Christ's own claims for himself. Those who deny this doctrine shut their eyes to the consistent scriptural evidence for Christ's deity. The single major charge brought against Jesus by his enemies was that he claimed Godhood for himself.

The word 'man' as applied to Christ speaks of the incarnation of Christ and his perfect humanity. His humanity was not an illusion, a phantom body, or a mere cloak he put on and put off at will, as is the case with the concept of the divine incarnations in Hinduism or in the teaching of Docetism. But the Word which was God 'became flesh and dwelt among us' (cf. John 1: 1, 14; Phil. 2: 6; Col. 2: 9).

The deity of Christ cannot be understood apart from his humanity, and neither his deity nor his humanity should be viewed apart from his being the only ransom for all, the only mediator between God and man. On the cross we do not see a glorified humanity but a condemned one; and the 'man' on the cross with a crown of thorns was at the same time 'the very God of very God'. In this mystery lies the hope of man's salvation. There is salvation in no one else (Acts 4: 12).

The whole structure of Christianity and all its claims stand or fall with the validity of its belief in the person of Christ. If the Gospel records about him are not entirely true, and if Christ is not really what he claimed to be, then there is nothing left of Christianity. Christ made supreme claims for himself, unless one falsely assumes that much of what the Gospels attribute to Christ are expressions of faith of the early church which were invented by them and unconsciously exaggerated. If we carefully examine the claims of Christ, we see that obviously no man can make such claims unless he is really God or has a mad delusion about himself.

Jesus said 'I am the way, and the truth, and the life; no one comes to the Father, but by me' (John 14: 6). He further stated that he is the 'bread of life' and those who come to him should never hunger or thirst (John 6: 35). He himself claimed to be 'the light of the world' and the source of eternal life (John 8: 12; 11: 25). He found in himself the fulfilment of the long-expected promises of the Messiah and Yahweh's kingdom, contained in the Old Testament (Matt. 13: 16–17; Mark 1: 15; Luke 4: 17–21, 24–27, 44). He accepted for himself the special title 'the son of man', used of a supernatural person in Daniel 7, and mentioned in the Gospels more than fifty times; so also the description given by Thomas, 'My Lord, and my God' (John 20: 28). He spoke of his eternal existence (John 8: 58; cf. Exod. 3: 14). To know him is to know God (John 8: 19) and to honour him is to honour God (John 5: 23). On two major occasions of Christ's ministry — at his baptism (Matt. 3: 17) and his transfiguration (Matt. 17: 5) — a voice came from heaven authenticating his deity.

When he taught he did not teach like the religious leaders of his time, but as one with extraordinary authority (Matt. 7: 28–29; Luke 4: 32). He claimed for himself power to forgive sins (Matt. 9: 1–8) and authority to judge the world (Matt. 25: 31–46; John 5: 22).

His character was perfect and blameless, far above even the best of the saints (I Pet. 2: 22; I John 3: 5). Even his enemies could not find any moral defect in him and had to bring in false witnesses at his trial. He was an innocent person (Matt. 27: 4, 19; Luke 23: 47). The miracles he performed — opening the eyes of the blind, stilling the storm, healing the sick, and raising the dead — were 'signs' pointing to the validity of his claims for himself.

It is useless to try to imagine that all the claims that Jesus made for himself were attributed to him by his early followers. As Stott[10] points out, 'We cannot any longer regard Jesus as simply a great Teacher, if he was so grievously mistaken in one of the chief subjects of his teaching, namely, himself,' and if Christ was not indeed God, there is a certain disturbing 'megalomania' about him. His life and character, particularly his resurrection and ascension, the life of his followers all through the centuries, and our own humble experience abundantly support his claims to uniqueness.

The Universality of Christ and His Work

Because truth as found in Christ is unique, the Christian faith claims for itself an absolute and universal character, considering that all other systems are either false or only partially true. This is naturally offensive to others, especially to a modern man who lives in an atmosphere of relativism. But 'we must not suppose that this claim to universal validity is something that can quietly be removed from the Gospel without changing it into something entirely different from what it is.'[11]

Again, because Christ is unique and there is no other Saviour for man, the scope of his work should cover all mankind for all time. The whole world is in sin and all men have sinned (Gen. 6: 5; Ps. 53: 3; Eccles. 7: 29; Rom. 3: 23; 5: 12). The sure result of sin is death and eternal separation from God (Rom. 6: 23). The Lausanne Covenant wording puts this truth in these words, 'All men are perishing because of sin . . . those who reject Christ repudiate the joy of salvation and condemn themselves to eternal separation from God.'

One may ask, how does this assertion relate to the doctrine of election as taught in the Scripture? Both the human responsibility and divine sovereignty are strongly and clearly taught in the Bible, and even found parallel in the same sentences (I Pet. 2: 7–8; Luke 22: 22; Acts 2: 23). There is no simple answer to this problem, with which the students of the Bible have struggled for centuries. One may say, though it sounds quite paradoxical, that 'those who are saved will ascribe all credit to God while those who are lost will accept all blame for themselves.'[12]

The salvation which we proclaim is not that through Christ's atoning death all people are automatically saved whether or not they acknowledge it, nor is it that, as the universalists claim, all mankind will be ultimately saved because God is too loving to condemn anyone to eternal hell. Further, the universal work of Christ does not mean that he is working out his plan and salvation *incognito* through all religious systems, redeeming those who faithfully follow their separate religious convictions.

Christ is to be preached to all the world without any racial and social distinctions (Rom. 1: 14–16; 10: 12). Our proclamation contains, as in the case of the apostolic teachings, the sum total of all that Christ has done and is as well as the claim of his total lordship over us. The core of the message is that Christ died in our place, for us and on our behalf (Isa. 53: 4–6; Rom. 3: 25; II Cor. 5: 21). He is 'the Lamb without blemish', destined before the foundation of the world to be our sacrifice (I Pet. 1: 19–20). In the Old Testament the victim that was sacrificed fulfilled a double role (Lev. 4, 5). It represented death, the punishment due to the one who brought the sacrifice. But it also represented the life of the worshipper offered afresh to God through the blood which was shed and offered to God. Through sacrifice, the broken relationship between man and God was restored. Christ became thus our sacrifice once for all. 'With this news we invite all men to respond to him as Saviour and Lord in the wholehearted personal commitment of repentance and faith' (Lausanne Covenant).

The name of Christ is exalted above every other name; he is Lord over all the world, and all authority in heaven and on earth is given to him (Matt. 28: 18; Phil. 2: 9–11). What does Christ's lordship and sovereignty over the world mean in relation to our ministry and the task of evangelism? It affirms that God is the one who initiates, guides and completes all our evangelistic tasks. The decisive factor in our evangelism is not our talents, valuable experiences, our use of the most modern methods or even the extent of our commitment to Christ, but rather his work carried out according to his plans (Zech. 4: 6). Christ's sovereignty means also that we are under his orders and his orders are based on the fact that he has absolute right over us in conducting our lives. Christ's universal lordship means that our field of ministry is not a limited area, but his vast domain, namely, the whole world and the total man. This includes not just the soul of man but also his mind and body, and not just individuals, but also societies, groups and nations. He has authority over the most obstinate person to whom we witness, the nations and bodies which give organised opposition to Christian work, and over our cities, our countries, and the whole world. The harvest which is plenteous, which we are to reap, is the harvest of Christ's own field and of no other.

CHAPTER IV

The Nature of Evangelism

Michael Cassidy

'TO EVANGELISE IS to spread the good news that Jesus
Christ died for our sins and was raised from the dead according to the Scriptures, and that as the reigning Lord he
now offers the forgiveness of sins and the liberating gift of
the Spirit to all who repent and believe. Our Christian presence in the world is indispensable to evangelism, and so is
that kind of dialogue whose purpose is to listen sensitively in
order to understand. But evangelism itself is the proclamation of the historical, biblical Christ as Saviour and Lord,
with a view to persuading people to come to him personally
and so be reconciled to God. In issuing the gospel invitation
we have no liberty to conceal the cost of discipleship. Jesus
still calls all who would follow him to deny themselves, take
up their cross, and identify themselves with his new community. The results of evangelism include obedience to
Christ, incorporation into his church and responsible service
in the world.'
*(I Cor. 15: 3, 4; Acts 2: 32–39; John 20: 21; I Cor. 1: 23; II
Cor. 4: 5; 5: 11, 20; Luke 14: 25–33; Mark 8: 34; Acts
2: 40, 47; Mark 10: 43–45)*

(LAUSANNE COVENANT, CLAUSE 4)

Introduction and Background

THUS SPAKE THE Lausanne Covenant on what is possibly the key issue in the church of Jesus Christ today — namely the nature of evangelism. That evangelism should have defied definition in universally acceptable terms, in spite of its central place in a spate of contemporary conciliar and evangelical conferences, reveals the extent to which the modern church has lost both its nerve and its way regarding that which is meant to be at the heart of its life. It was against the background of this uncertainty that the Lausanne International Congress on World Evangelization took place.

The Lausanne Covenant's statement on the nature of evangelism confronts this uncertainty head on with clear answers to basic questions:

(1) What is Evangelism?
(2) What is the Evangel?
(3) How is the Evangel communicated?
(4) Why communicate the Evangel?
(5) What are the results of Evangelism?

What is Evangelism?

'To evangelise,' says the Covenant, 'is to spread the Good News ...' Evangelism is thus an activity by which a particular body of truth, the Evangel (see following section), is 'spread'.

Of immediate and obvious significance is the fact that the matter of fruit or 'success' in spreading the News is omitted from the definition, and rightly so, in my judgment. This is not to deny the vital importance of aiming for fruit, but only to insist that evangelism's authenticity does not depend on whether it has been fruitful or not.

This understanding would seem to be in line with the exegetical data of Scripture. The verb *euangelizomai* seems clearly to refer to announcing the Good News or *euangelion*. The verb is very common in the New Testament and is applied to Scripture (Gal. 3: 8), to Christ (Luke 20: 1) and to ordinary church members (Acts 8: 4), as well as to the apostles on their missionary journeys. Thus Acts 14: 7 says of Paul and Barnabas in Lycaonia: 'There they evangelised.' No comment is made on the outcome.

Often the verb is used along with reference to the message preached. Thus Jesus felt constrained to 'evangelise' or proclaim 'the kingdom of God' (Luke 4: 43); persecuted Christians went everywhere 'evangelising' or announcing 'the word' (*ton logon*; Acts 8: 4); Philip told the Ethiopian eunuch the good news of 'Jesus' (Acts 8: 35); Paul preached the evangel (*euangelion*; Gal. 1: 11), and 'God's gospel' (II Cor. 11: 7). In all these instances the verb to 'evangelise' is used, while in only one of them (Acts 8: 35) are we positively assured of conversion as the consequence.

This holds true in other passages where the verb *euangelizomai* is used with mention of those who receive the message: e.g., 'the poor' (Luke 4: 18), 'you ... in Rome' (Rom. 1: 15), 'many villages of the Samaritans' (Acts 8: 25), 'all the towns' (Acts 8: 40), etc. All these recipients were 'evangelised' in terms of the biblical usage of the word, though little or nothing is said of the consequences. To evangelise is to sow the seed of the word, and not necessarily to reap. All four soils of the parable (Matt. 13: 1–23) were 'evangelised', though only one was really fruitful.

This, we repeat, is not to say that we are not to aim for converts, but simply to assert that one can evangelise without winning souls, though winning souls is the aim of evangelism. Likewise one can play football without necessarily scoring goals, though scoring goals is the aim of playing football.

The Lausanne Covenant also strongly resisted any confusion between evangelism and socio-political engagement. As this is fully dealt with in Chapter V (Christian Social Responsibility), I shall not deal with it at length here. It will suffice to note Canon Douglas Webster's helpful distinction between mission and evangelism, as made in the South African Congress on Mission and Evangelism (March 1973). He pointed out that 'mission' is a comprehensive word with a large meaning, while 'evangelism' is a more restricted word with a sharply defined meaning. Thus Jesus' own mission (see Matt. 11: 4–5 and Luke 4: 18–19) included many things (healing, cleansing, liberating, proclaiming), only one of which can properly be described as evangelism. Thus, 'all evangelism is mission. Not all mission is evangelism.' Likewise:

> He sends his church to do many things. Their totality is the Christian mission. Of these things evangelism has its unique importance. But healing, teaching, baptising, liberating, protesting, working for peace and justice, feeding the hungry, reconciling those at variance, are all essential parts of mission, as we see it in the New Testament ... Nevertheless, [affirms Webster] however closely we may associate these activities with evangelism, the New Testament does not identify them with it. Evangelism is the proclaiming of the Gospel, particularly to those who have not heard it, or who have not understood it, or who have not responded to it, or who have forgotten it.[1]

What is the Evangel?

If 'to evangelise is to spread the Good News', what is the Good News? What is the content of the Evangel? This question is all important, because the church's whole attitude to the world, and its whole approach to evangelism, depends on what it believes about the content of the Gospel.

The first matter about which Lausanne was quite firm and unequivocal was this: while our presentation of the Gospel may vary, its content may not. The Gospel, if true for any, must be true for all. As I have noted elsewhere: 'The fact that aspects of the message may be either unacceptable or offensive to modern, rationalistic man must not make us restructure the message to accommodate him, but explicate its meaning relevantly to touch him not simply in his cultural or social context, but in his existential need, perplexity and moral guilt.'[2] Modernity and our desire for relevance must never result in any reworking, restructuring or amputating of the basic *kerygmatic* content of the message. While our manner of presenting the message will take into account a man's contextual life and situational need, it will never avoid declaring the *kerygma* as that fixed deposit of truth which constitutes the Evangel. Francis Schaeffer put it this way at Lausanne: 'Christianity is a specific body of truth ... and we must hold that truth.'[3]

The Lausanne Covenant articulated the *kerygmatic* content as follows: 'That Jesus Christ died for our sins and was raised from the dead according to the Scriptures, and that as reigning Lord he now offers the forgiveness of sins and the liberating gift of the Spirit to all who repent and believe.'

This formulation, which follows, broadly speaking, C. H. Dodd's celebrated statement of the *kerygma*,[4] suggests that Dodd's outline is still broadly serviceable, even though recent scholarship has broken down his rigid distinction between *kerygma* and *didache*.

However, in a nutshell, the message we have for the world is *Jesus* (e.g. Acts 8: 35, Rom. 1: 1–4). The Rev. John Stott, in his superb address at Lausanne, observed that within the message of Jesus there are at least four elements — (1) Gospel events, (2) Gospel witnesses, (3) Gospel promises, (4) Gospel demands.

Gospel Events

These are primarily the *death* and *resurrection* of Jesus. Interestingly enough, I gather Francis Schaeffer believes the first item of proclamation should not be 'Jesus died for your sins', but 'God is'. In the theistic context of the first century, in contrast to the agnostic context of the twentieth, this was possibly self-evident. But perhaps twentieth-century man does need reminding of the 'God who is there' before he hears our elaboration of the Gospel events. One might also note that in moving directly into the cross of Christ as the first item within the Good News, the Lausanne Covenant does lay itself open to the charge of minimising the incarnation. Those ready to accuse Lausanne of being weak on the incarnational responsibilities of the church might well isolate the start of the problem at this point. Be that as it may, the Covenant is right to give pride of place to the atoning death of Jesus and to his resurrection from the dead. These are Gospel events — factual, actual, historical, literal. For the Christian, the *locus* of revelation is history and events of history.

Gospel Witnesses

Stott noted that:

> the apostles proclaimed the death and resurrection of Jesus both according to the Scriptures (Acts 2: 25ff., 3: 18, 24; cf. I Cor. 15: 3–4) and according to the evidence of their own eyes ... (e.g. Acts 2: 32, 5: 32). So we today have no liberty to preach Christ crucified and risen according to our own fancy or even according to our own experience. The only Christ there is to preach is the biblical Christ, the objective historical Christ attested by the joint witness of the prophets of the Old Testament and the apostles of the New (cf. Acts 10: 39–43). Our witness is always secondary to theirs.[5]

Dr Stuart McWilliam of Glasgow affirms the same truth thus: 'Biblical preaching is preaching which allows the Bible to speak, to be heard.'[6]

Gospel Promises

(a) *The forgiveness of sins.* The Covenant, along with Dodd and his *kerygma*, speaks of the Gospel promises whereby 'the reigning Lord now offers the forgiveness of sins and the liberating gift of the Spirit' (see Acts 2: 38). Forgiveness deals with the past, while the experience of the indwelling Spirit gives power for the present and hope for the future. And indeed forgiveness and justification are desperately needed by man, for without them he remains under condemnation and wrath (John 3: 36). But the glory of the Gospel is that it promises a way out from *wrath* (John 3: 18; Eph. 2: 3–6). Evangelism's concern, as the Great Commission affirms (e.g., Luke 24: 47) is therefore to declare this Gospel promise of forgiveness.

(b) *The liberating gift of the Spirit.* It was also noteworthy, in a conference attended by many Pentecostals, that the Covenant affirms that 'the liberating gift of the Spirit' is given at the time of repentance and faith (Eph. 1: 13) rather than in a subsequent 'baptism' or 'infilling'. This would strike the present writer as exegetically sound. However, I also judge it healthy that world evangelicalism, as seen at Lausanne, moved forward to an acceptance of biblically based charismatic movements, and hopefully some of the evangelical fears of charismatic renewal will now begin to ease up a bit. Significantly, 'the Spirit' is referred to in the Covenant as 'the liberating gift'. While not minimising the importance of political liberation (see Chapters V and XIII), Lausanne clearly and rightly saw the Spirit as the ultimate liberator of man from those forces that render life dark, empty and meaningless. It is he who illumines (I Cor. 12: 3), convicts of sin (John 16: 9), regenerates (John 3: 5–6), assures (Rom. 8: 16) and seals our salvation (Eph. 1: 13–14). It is he who produces spiritual fruit (Gal. 5: 22), comforts (Acts 9: 31), fills (Acts 2: 4, 4: 31), liberates (II Cor. 3: 17–18; Gal. 5: 1; Rom. 8: 2), guides (Acts 16: 6–7), and equips for service (Acts 1: 8), ministry (I Cor. 12: 4–11) and life (Gal. 5: 25).

Gospel Demands

The Gospel promises of forgiveness and the gift of the Holy Spirit are not automatically conferred upon all, but are conditional upon our meeting the Gospel demands of repentance and faith. 'Forgiveness of sins and the liberating gift of the Spirit,' says the Covenant, 'are offered to all who repent and believe.' In this the Gospel demands a radical decision, yes or no, for or against. Jesus presents men with an either-or. In this sense the preaching of the Gospel always brings the hearers under judgment.

We consider these two demands in turn:

(a) *Repentance*. Speaking at Lausanne, René Padilla indicated that he saw preaching the Gospel as equivalent to preaching 'repentance and forgiveness of sins' (Luke 24: 47), or to testifying 'of repentance to God and of faith in our Lord Jesus Christ' (Acts 20: 21). 'Without this call to repentance,' says Padilla, 'there is no Gospel.' Nor is repentance simply a bad conscience, 'but a change of attitude, a restructuring of one's scale of values, a re-orientation of the whole personality. It is not simply giving up habits condemned by a moralistic ethic, but rather laying down the weapons of rebellion against God, to return to Him.'[7]

Padilla also noted that while repentance has an eschatological significance, in that it marks the boundary between the old age and the new, between judgment and promise, nevertheless we must affirm that its significance is not purely eschatological, so that the present life has meaning only as a preparation for the 'hereafter'. In fact it is the escapist mechanisms operating in this understanding of repentance, he observed, which produced the Marxist criticism of Christian eschatology as 'the opiate of the people'.[8] In like vein Professor Brian Johanson noted at the South African Congress that 'an *eschatos* at hand is as important as, and indeed inseparable from, any in the future'.[9] He who repents must therefore recognise that the promise of eternal blessings is accompanied by serious temporal responsibilities.

(b) *Faith*. If repentance is a change of mind leading to a change of direction, (e.g., the Prodigal, Luke 15: 17, 20) and if it is conceived primarily in negative terms as turning *from* sin, then faith is the positive turning *to* Christ and receiving (John 1: 12) him as Saviour and Lord (Col. 2: 6).

However it is worth noting that the capacity for the response of faith, and indeed of repentance, is God-given and by his grace. It is 'through grace' (Acts 18: 27) that men believe. The Gentiles, St Peter said, were '*granted* repentance unto life' (Acts 11: 18). Likewise St Paul stressed to the Philippians that it had been '*granted*' them to believe in Christ (Phil. 1: 29), and to the Ephesians that their salvation 'by *grace* . . . through faith' was a '*gift* of God' (Eph. 2: 8).

The work of the Holy Spirit is thus essential, both in the forsaking which repentance demands and in the embracing which faith requires. Indeed, 'no one can say, "Jesus is Lord" except by the Holy Spirit' (I Cor. 12: 3). Reconciling repentance and faith as both the obligation of man (e.g. Acts 2: 38; Mark 1: 15) and the gift of God (Eph. 2: 8; Phil. 1: 29) need not exercise us unduly, provided we realise that the two truths are both in Scripture, and are therefore 'friends'. And, as Spurgeon once remarked, 'it is not necessary to reconcile friends!'

A man is thus called to repent and believe. He who does so with true sincerity becomes a Christian and is converted. He knows what the Evangel is and has embraced it.

How is the Evangel Communicated?

We come to our third question: 'How is the Evangel communicated?' The Lausanne Covenant gave the question a threefold answer. The Gospel is communicated by:

(1) Presence.
(2) Dialogue.
(3) Proclamation.

Our presence gives credibility to the Gospel and reflects its personal dimensions. Our dialogue creates relevance and reflects its situational dimensions. Our proclamation requires faithfulness and reflects its universal dimensions.

Presence

Says the Covenant: 'Our Christian presence in the world is indispensable to evangelism.' This was a refreshing stipulation to hear from world evangelicalism. The Word had to become flesh before there could be a Gospel to preach. In-

carnation preceded atonement. And did our Lord not say:
'As the Father has sent me, even so I send you' (John
20: 21)? In other words his pattern is ours. Thus every word
of witness has to become flesh, or credibility is lost. We are
'a letter from Christ', 'known and read by all men' (II Cor.
3: 2–3). If the letter is blurred it is because the tablet, rather
than the handwriting of God, is defective. The consequence
is a message which is both illegible and inaudible.

At Lausanne a group of brethren, mainly Latin Americans, issued a document of affirmation, confession, doxo-
logy and resolution. Basically a call for radical discipleship,
it addressed itself in more visceral terms than the Covenant
to a number of issues. On this matter of *presence*, they
affirmed that:

> the communication of the Evangel in its fullness to
> every person world-wide is a mandate of the Lord Jesus
> Christ to his community. There is no biblical dichotomy
> between the Word spoken and the Word made visible in
> the lives of God's people. Men will look as they listen and
> what they see must be one with what they hear. The Chris-
> tian community must chatter, discuss and proclaim the
> Gospel; it must express the Gospel in its life as the new
> society, in its sacrificial service to others as a genuine ex-
> pression of God's love, in its prophetic exposing and op-
> posing of all demonic forces that deny the lordship of
> Christ and keep men less than fully human, in its pursuit
> of justice for all men, in its responsible and caring trust-
> eeship of God's creation and its resources. There are
> times when our communication may be by attitude and
> action only, and times when the spoken word will stand
> alone: but we must repudiate as demonic the attempt to
> drive a wedge between evangelism and social action.[10]

In Holland there is a church with a lovely stained-glass
window symbolically portraying the message of I Corinthians 13. For those inside the building the sequence is the
Pauline one of faith, hope and love. But for someone looking from outside the church, the sequence is the opposite:
love, hope, faith. If the outsider does not look at us and see

love, he will not move on to hope and faith. The towel and washbasin must often precede the microphone. Compassionate, humble service (*diakonia*), and true community (*koinonia*) are integral to faithful witness (*martyria*).

Dialogue

However vital presence is as a method of evangelism, it is inadequate by itself to convey the full content of the Gospel. Verbalisation is essential, for evangelism is essentially an announcement of a message. One of the methods of verbalisation is dialogue. The Covenant, acknowledging that our Christian presence in the world is indispensable to evangelism, adds: 'So is that kind of *dialogue* whose purpose is to listen sensitively in order to understand.'

While the theology of dialogue has been given considerable attention in the last chapter, we must reiterate here that the Covenant is not sanctioning an uncommitted and open-ended type of dialogue in which the Christian is ready to embrace the other man's religious position. Rather he talks, discusses and listens, 'in order to *understand*'. On the basis of this sympathetic understanding the Christian hopes to convey the Gospel more relevantly 'with a view to persuading people to come to Christ personally and so be reconciled to God' (Lausanne Covenant, see also following section). Christian dialogue aims ultimately at conversion, even when it takes place with men of other faiths.

The committed nature of such dialogue, we must affirm, is not based on religious triumphalism, intolerance, or narrow-mindedness, but on an orthodox Christology which sees Jesus as Lord of all, the only *logos* of God (John 1), the Cosmic King of the Universe, through whom and for whom 'all things were created' (Col. 1: 16) that 'in everything he might be pre-eminent' (Col. 1: 18). The issue really is one of truth. This is not to say that the Christian has nothing to learn in dialogue, or to assert that there is no truth in other living faiths. Indeed, in meeting them in humility at their highest, the modern Christian apologist, like Justin and Tertullian in the second century, will find he can maximise those common elements of truth which originate in general revelation and in the spermatic word (John 1; Col. 1; Heb. 1) and which are present in the great world religions by virtue of that 'light that enlightens every man' (John 1: 9). Yet none of this absolves him from dialogue's ultimate aim of persuasion beyond the intermediate aim of sympathetic understanding. The point is that dialogue which drifts down from religious discussion to community problems and then to the plight of man in society is moving the wrong way. It must move upwards to focus ultimately on the unique thing, far beyond all other religions, which God has done in Christ.

Proclamation

The Covenant, having made its affirmation of the 'indispensable' importance of dialogue for evangelism, adds: 'But evangelism itself is the proclamation of the historical biblical Christ as Saviour and Lord.'

Clearly proclamation is here distinguished from dialogue as the *sine qua non* in evangelistic methodology. Yet in fact the two are related and complementary. Thus those who begin with dialogue will at some point be required to proclaim, while those who begin with proclamation will often need to supplement their proclamation with dialogue. The ministry style of the apostle Paul well illustrates this (cf. Acts 17).

It seems to me, however, that proclamation must retain its primacy. Speaking in Durban, Canon Webster noted: 'In the great majority of the seventy-six instances of the word "Gospel" in the New Testament, the verb that goes with it is "to preach" . . . Just as a game is something you normally play, so the Gospel is something you normally preach.'[11] In fact Helmut Thielicke affirms that the critical criterion of every theology is that 'it must be preachable, because its very origin is in preaching.'[12] But, as Thielicke also notes, 'the Gospel must be preached afresh and told in new ways to every generation, since every generation has its own unique questions. This is why the Gospel must constantly be forwarded to a new address, because the recipient is repeatedly changing his place of residence.'[13]

It is also noteworthy that the recipients of New Testament preaching were those who had *not* heard the Gospel before. The verbs used are all used primarily in that context. 'In the New Testament,' says Alan Richardson with perhaps a trace of hyperbole, 'preaching has nothing to do with the delivering of sermons to the converted, which is what it normally means today, but always concerns the proclamation of the "good tidings of God" to the non-Christian world.'[14] With this C. H. Dodd concurs. In the New Testament, preaching is 'the public proclamation of Christianity to the non-Christian world'.[15]

This focus of primitive New Testament preaching also reinforces our previous conclusions on the committed nature of Christian dialogue, and on the unashamed purpose of all Christian evangelism — namely conversion. To this we now turn.

Why Communicate the Evangel?

The Covenant states: 'Evangelism itself is the proclamation of the historical, biblical Christ as Saviour and Lord, *with a view to persuading people to come* to him personally, *and so be reconciled to God*. In issuing the Gospel invitation, we have no liberty to conceal the cost of discipleship. Jesus still calls all who would follow him to deny themselves, take up their cross, and identify themselves with his new community.' Why communicate the Gospel? Because we want to persuade alienated men and women to be reconciled to God and to become disciples in accordance with his expressed will in the Great Commission.

Thus in this clause of the Covenant we see:

(1) Persuasion as the aim of evangelism.
(2) Reconciliation as the consequence of persuasion.
(3) Discipleship as the goal of the Great Commission.

Persuasion as the aim of evangelism

When Stanley Jones went as a young missionary to India, an

Indian intellectual challenged him at a meeting with this question: 'Have you come here to try and convert us?' 'But, of course,' said Dr Jones. 'What do you think?' It was a good answer. Christian evangelism aims to convert. This does not mean that it does so by compulsion or pressure, but by persuasion. In this, personal sensitivities and freedom may not be violated. If they are, we cease to be true Christian evangelists, for the Gospel is not only a message, but a standard. The Gospel is not something we simply preach. It is something we 'obey' (cf. I Pet. 4: 17).

Take Paul's example. The apostle, compelled by love to proclaim the Gospel, says 'we persuade men ... God making his appeal through us. We beseech you on behalf of Christ, be reconciled to God' (II Cor. 5: 11, 20). The New English Bible speaks of Paul 'trying to convince Jews and Greeks' (Acts 18: 4). At Ephesus for three months 'he attended the synagogue and, using argument and *persuasion*, spoke boldly and freely about the Kingdom of God' (Acts 19: 8 NEB). Indeed the entire missionary enterprise in the book of Acts had conversion, response and spiritual fruit as its consuming aim. Clearly then, the Gospel is not offered on a take-it-or-leave-it basis. Without compelling men, we must aim to persuade them.

It is in magnifying this dimension of evangelism that Dr Donald McGavran, Peter Wagner, and others at the Fuller Seminary School of World Mission have brought such a fine and vital contribution to world mission. Their magnificent obsession is that the church should not betray the two billion who have not yet heard the Gospel. We must seek clearly, definitely, and aggressively to try and win them. This is why we communicate the evangel.

Reconciliation as the consequence of persuasion

The Lausanne Covenant asserts that evangelism is done 'with a view to persuading people to come to [Christ] personally *and so be reconciled to God*'. This understanding involves a tacit rejection of the universalist position that people will be reconciled to God, regardless of whether they come to Christ or not. Although the emotional and philo-

sophical appeal of the universalist position is undoubted.
Lausanne repudiated such a view as exegetically unsound
(Chapter III). As far as our evangelistic mandate is concerned, it can only be the course of wisdom to operate on the
assumption that men are only reconciled to God as they
come personally to Christ. We thus declare the Gospel so
that people who were 'enemies of the cross of Christ' (Phil.
3: 18) should become 'reconciled to God by the death of his
Son' (Rom. 5: 10) and be transferred from 'the dominion of
darkness ... to the kingdom of his beloved Son' (Col.
1: 13).

Discipleship as the goal of the Great Commission

The Covenant affirms that 'in issuing the Gospel invitation,
we have no right to conceal the cost of discipleship. Jesus
still calls all who would follow him to deny themselves, take
up their cross and identify themselves with his new community.'

Our goal in evangelism is not decisions, but disciples, men
and women who are obediently following Jesus, from within
the context of his church, regardless of the cost. This is also
the clear goal of the mandate given by Jesus in his Great
Commission.

For a long time, obedience to the Great Commission was
seen simply in terms of evangelism and proclamation (cf.
Mark 16: 15, 'Go into all the world and preach the Gospel
to the whole creation'). But increasingly, missionary-
minded people are focusing on discipling. In fact, within all
four Gospel accounts of the Commission, aiming for 'disciples' is evident as the goal of mission, a disciple being one
who *follows* (Matt. 4: 19) and *obeys* (Acts 5: 29) Christ, and
who in so doing is willing to take up his own cross (Matt.
10: 38).

Writing of Matthew's version of the Commission, Peter
Wagner notes helpfully:

> ... the passage contains four action verbs: go, make dis-
> ciples, baptise and teach. In the original Greek only one of
> them is imperative, and three are participles. The impera-
> tive 'make disciples' is the heart of the command. The par-

ticiples 'going', 'baptising' and 'teaching' are helping verbs ... Making disciples then, is the end. It is the right goal of mission strategy. Going, baptising and teaching are means to be used towards accomplishing the end. They are also necessary components of missionary strategy, but they are not ends in themselves.

The other four appearances of the Great Commission do not expand on the right goal. They do add to the list the means available to reach it. Mark 16: 15, 16 repeats baptising, but adds preaching. Luke 24: 47, 48 repeats preaching but adds witnessing. John 20: 21 mentions sending. Acts 1: 8 repeats witnessing and adds the geographical aspect of 'Jerusalem, Judea, Samaria and the uttermost part of the earth'.[16]

All this implies that we must not confuse means and ends. Preaching is not an end in itself, but a means to the end of bringing men to Christ and making them 'disciples'. To ignore this is to settle simply for decisions, pew-warmers or for nothing. That won't do. Evangelism's call requires that the cost of out-and-out discipleship be squarely faced and honestly presented. If it is, certain results will flow from the lives of those turning to Christ. To these we turn.

The Results of Evangelism

The Covenant states that 'the results of evangelism include obedience to Christ, incorporation into his church, and responsible service in the world'.

Interestingly enough, this outline follows Bishop Stephen Neill's celebrated specification of the three conversions subsumed in a true Christian conversion: conversion to Christ, conversion to the church, and conversion to the world.

Obedience to Christ

Assuming genuine repentance and faith in our hearers, we must now stress the priority of moral and spiritual obedience to Christ. Said Jesus: 'Not everyone who says to me "Lord, Lord," shall enter the kingdom of heaven, but he who does the will of my Father who is in heaven' (Matt. 7: 21). We dare not separate taking Christ as Saviour from following and obeying him as Lord. His lordship and saviourhood belong together. Indeed for the apostle John the only proof that we love God is 'that we keep his commandments' (I John 5: 3). Likewise Jesus had said: 'He who has my commandments and keeps them, he it is who loves me' (John 14: 21). To follow Jesus in this way is to be involved in what the apostle Paul called 'obedience to the faith' (Rom. 1: 5, 16: 26). The authenticity of our response can thus only be tested by the sincerity of our obedience. We who were once 'slaves of sin' are now to become 'obedient from the heart' (Rom. 6: 17).

Incorporation into his church

For the New Testament preachers, evangelism which did not involve incorporation into the church was unthinkable. An isolated Christian was seen as a contradiction in terms. To come to Christ was to come to his community, and be incorporated by regeneration into the invisible church or kingdom of God (John 3: 3, 5) and by baptism into the visible (Acts 2: 38). Comments John Stott: 'Baptism, which admits people into the visible church (the company of the baptised), does not admit to the invisible (the blessed company of all faithful people), that is, of believers. It is the sacrament of regeneration, visibly signifying and pledging it, but not the means of regeneration, invariably conveying it.'[17] Baptism thus points back to the redemptive work of God and forward to the obedient life of faith.

That into which we are incorporated by regeneration and baptism is the body of Christ (Matt. 28: 19; Acts 8: 16; I Cor. 12: 13), the messianic community, the church. And the marks of the messianic community, as Francis Schaeffer stressed at Lausanne, are two-fold: faithfulness to the Scriptures and beauty of community. 'We need two orthodoxies,' he said, 'first, an orthodoxy of doctrine, and second, an orthodoxy of community. If we do not show beauty in the way we treat each other,' he added, 'then in the eyes of the world . . . we are destroying the truth we proclaim.'[18]

In being incorporated into the church the new believer is incorporated into a visible fellowship with those two commitments — faithfulness to the Scriptures and beauty of community. This is also what it means to be devoted to 'the apostles' teaching and fellowship, to the breaking of bread and the prayers' (Acts 2: 42).

Responsible service in the world

Paradoxically, the Christian turns both *from* the world and *to* the world. He turns from its life-style and to its life-need. He turns from irresponsible sin to responsible service.

Lausanne, unlike some evangelical gatherings, had strong horizontal as well as vertical concerns. The world was not simply there to be evangelised, but to be loved and served. People are not just pew-fodder, scalps or statistics for our success-oriented evangelistic reports, but *people* with a wide range of personal, social, political and other needs. The church is not simply to boom its message at them from air-conditioned pulpits, but to reach out in caring service and compassion. The incarnational responsibilities of our faith can be neither evaded nor avoided. Jesus' kenotic pattern (Phil. 2: 5–8) is ever to be ours. And we are to try and actualise in the world externally that peace or *shalom* of God which we know internally.

This is not to embrace a humanistic theology or to succumb to unbiblical visions of utopia in the here and now, but to obey the imperatives of compassion in the world's varied and various day-to-day needs. There is to be no divorce between soteriology and ethics. The saved man is a man who serves. Faith and works go together (Jas. 2: 14–17). The evangelist, on the way from Jerusalem to his city-wide crusade in Jericho, will not, in passing, toss a tract or decision card to the man who has fallen among thieves, but will stop to minister and care for him.

Conclusion

What is evangelism? Evangelism is an activity by which the biblical Good News of Jesus' earthly life, atoning death, glorious resurrection, and liberating Spirit is heralded to all the world through Christian presence, humble dialogue and clear proclamation. Along with the heralded word goes a call which aims to persuade all men everywhere, regardless of cost, to respond to the cosmic Lord of Life in repentance, faith, obedient discipleship and willing incorporation into the messianic community of a biblically faithful and socially beautiful church. Forgiven, reconciled to God and liberated by the Spirit, the Christian is to serve his Lord and the world by joyful worship, faithful witness and compassionate service.

CHAPTER V

Christian Social Responsibility

Athol Gill

'WE AFFIRM THAT God is both the Creator and the Judge of all men. We therefore should share his concern for justice and reconciliation throughout human society and for the liberation of men from every kind of oppression. Because mankind is made in the image of God, every person, regardless of race, religion, colour, culture, class, sex or age, has an intrinsic dignity because of which he should be respected and served, not exploited. Here too we express penitence both for our neglect and for having sometimes regarded evangelism and social concern as mutually exclusive. Although reconciliation with man is not reconciliation with God, nor is social action evangelism, nor is political liberation salvation, nevertheless we affirm that evangelism and socio-political involvement are both part of our Christian duty. For both are necessary expressions of our doctrines of God and man, our love for our neighbour and our obedience to Jesus Christ. The message of salvation implies also a message of judgment upon every form of alienation, oppression and discrimination, and we should not be afraid to denounce evil and injustice wherever they exist. When people receive Christ they are born again into his kingdom and must seek not only to exhibit but also to spread its righteousness in the midst of an unrighteous world. The salvation we claim should be transforming us in the totality of

our personal and social responsibilities. Faith without works
is dead.'
*(Acts 17: 26, 31; Gen. 18: 25; Isa. 1: 17; Ps. 45: 7; Gen.
1: 26, 27; Jas. 3: 9; Lev. 19: 18; Luke 6: 27, 35; Jas. 2: 14–26;
John 3: 3, 5; Matt. 5: 20; 6: 33; II Cor. 3: 18; Jas. 2: 20)*

(LAUSANNE COVENANT, CLAUSE 5)

THE INTERNATIONAL CONGRESS on World Evangelization was convened primarily 'to arouse all believers to a new obedience to Christ in world evangelism'.[1] This was certainly the dominant theme of the Congress, but the theological issue which captured the attention of most participants and provoked many intense discussions was undoubtedly that of the relationship between evangelism and social action.

In expressing penitence 'for having sometimes regarded evangelism and social concern as mutually exclusive' and in emphasising that 'evangelism and socio-political involvement are both part of our Christian duty', the Lausanne Covenant marked a turning point in evangelical thinking, a turning point which may well have significant consequences for all Christians. It has already been warmly received by ecumenical leaders and the Covenant was studied at the Fifth Assembly of the World Council of Churches held in Nairobi last year.[2]

The Changing Scene

New Emphases at Lausanne

The dramatic nature of the change in evangelical thinking on social responsibility may be seen most clearly by com-

paring the Lausanne statements with those of its predecessor, the World Congress on Evangelism held in Berlin
in 1966.

The issue of evangelism and social concern was raised in
group discussions during the Berlin Congress, but it was not
adequately debated. At that time many evangelicals still
considered social involvement an enemy of 'biblical evangelism' to be avoided at all costs.[3] To be sure, the Congress
statement did include a lengthy section condemning racism,
but it did so in purely personal terms, and in describing the
'one task' of the church it spoke only of evangelism.[4] Of the
scores of papers delivered at that Congress only one dealt
with evangelism and social concern, and it was devoted
almost entirely to racism as a barrier to evangelism.[5]

Lausanne was quite different. The question of social responsibility was raised at the very beginning and was a re-
curring theme throughout the entire Congress. In his
opening address, Dr Billy Graham expressed the hope that
the Congress would accomplish four things: (1) frame a biblical declaration of evangelism, (2) challenge the church to
complete the task of world evangelisation, (3) state the relationship between evangelism and social responsibility, and
(4) develop a world-wide fellowship among evangelicals of
all persuasions.[6] At his final press conference he emphasised: 'If one thing has come through loud and clear it is
that we evangelicals should have social concern. The discussion in smaller groups about the contemporary meaning
of radical discipleship has caught fire.'

John Stott, who has come to be regarded as something of
a theologian-at-large among evangelicals, prepared the way
in the opening plenary session when he placed evangelism
within the context of the church's total mission of service to
the world.[7] The leading American evangelical, Carl F.
Henry, and George Hoffman made significant contributions
in major seminars on social ethics. In his paper Henry
affirmed that 'the church, under Christ's lordship is sent into
the world to proclaim personal and social redemption' and
the report of the seminar sessions asserted: 'Christian social
involvement includes not only personal but institutional
action. Institutionalised evil requires institutional action

for change.'[8] Hoffman quoted, with approval, the re-
tiring speech of Dr W. A. Visser 't Hooft at the Uppsala
Assembly of the World Council of Churches: 'A Christianity which has lost its vertical dimensions has lost its salt,
and is not only insipid in itself, but useless to the world. But
a Christianity which would use the vertical dimension as a
means to escape from responsibility for and in the common
life of men is a denial of the incarnation of God's life for the
world manifested in Christ.' He left no doubt where he
stood on the issue of social responsibility.[9]

But it was the younger Third World theologians René
Padilla and Samuel Escobar who really set the Congress
alight. Padilla launched an all-out attack on 'culture-Christianity' of the variety manufactured by North American
evangelicals and exported south in large quantities. This is a
Gospel obsessed with technology and numbers but truncated and distorted in its lack of emphasis upon the radical
nature of discipleship and its lack of interest in the social
implications of the Gospel. Escobar warned the Congress
that 'a spirituality without discipleship in the daily social,
economic and political aspects of life is religiosity and not
Christianity'.[10]

Coming less than two weeks before the resignation of
Richard Nixon as President of the United States (on whom
so many evangelicals had pinned their hopes) the prophetic
words from Latin America could not go unheeded! The Covenant drafting committee was forced to strengthen its earlier presentation by replacing the words 'social action' with
'socio-political involvement' and by adding more explicit
references to the denunciation of injustice and oppression.[11]

Over five hundred people met on the Sunday evening of
the Congress to discuss 'the social and political implications
of radical discipleship today', and a brief document, 'A Response to Lausanne', was prepared by a small group who
felt that the Covenant did not go far enough.

The 'Response', a rough collation of sentences and
phrases taken from major papers delivered at the Congress,
affirmed the Gospel as 'good news of liberation, of restoration, of wholeness, and of salvation that is personal,

social, global and cosmic'. It repudiated as 'demonic' any attempt 'to drive a wedge between evangelism and social action' and confessed evangelical shortcomings on a wide range of socio-political issues. It asserted that the Christian community must 'chatter, discuss and proclaim the Gospel; it must express the Gospel in its life as the New Society, in its sacrificial service to others as a genuine expression of God's love, in its prophetic exposing and opposing of all demonic forces that deny the lordship of Christ and keep men less than fully human; in its pursuit of real justice for all men; in its responsible and caring trusteeship of God's creation and its resources.'[12]

The new face of evangelicalism emerging from Lausanne may be seen, in part at least, in this renewed emphasis upon socio-political involvement as a constitutive part of the church's mission of sacrificial service, upon social action as an integral component of the life of discipleship, upon political involvement as the necessary outgrowth of the proclamation of the good news of liberation through the death and resurrection of Jesus Christ.

Historical Background

The shift in evangelical thinking represented in the movement from the position adopted at Berlin to that which found its expression at Lausanne has to be interpreted against the background of the bitter struggle waged for half a century in North America between so-called 'evangelicals' and 'liberals', 'fundamentalists' and 'modernists', 'pietists' and 'activists'.[13]

During the 1920s evangelicals, reacting to the extremes of the 'social gospel' and reflecting the middle-class values of the society in which they flourished, reversed their earlier interest in social action and concentrated their efforts almost solely upon denouncing personal evils and proclaiming individual salvation. Conservative in their theology, evangelicals became increasingly conservative in their approach to politics, economics, culture and social issues generally (even though the major thrust of their theological position should have pressed them in quite a different direction). They aligned themselves with right-wing political parties which were seeking to maintain the status quo and so frequently became deaf to the cries of the underprivileged and disenfranchised. The 'American Way of Life' was regarded as the epitome of Christianity as evangelicalism became almost inextricably bound up with western culture. To support the system was to proclaim the Gospel, to challenge it was to challenge God. The prophetic voice was muted, if not silenced, and involvement in social and political movements which sought to change existing structures was identified as 'liberalism' and, even, 'communism'. These were the dark ages of evangelicalism![14]

A countering of this 'great reversal' began in the 1950s when a small group of evangelical writers began to call for 'a new reformation', for a renewed interest in social issues. During the 1960s this interest began to be reflected in the public pronouncements of evangelical conferences, and now in the 1970s it has broadened to include not only 'social concern' but also 'social and political involvement'.

The 'Wheaton Declaration', adopted at *The Congress on the Church's Worldwide Mission*, Wheaton, 1966, confessed, 'We have sinned grievously. We are guilty of unscriptural isolation from the world that too often keeps us from honestly facing and coping with its concerns.' It urged all evangelicals 'to stand openly and firmly for racial equality, human freedom, and all forms of social justice throughout the world.'[15] *The United States Congress on Evangelism*, Minneapolis, 1969, also made a strong plea for Christians to address themselves to contemporary social evils[16] and *The European Congress on Evangelism*, Amsterdam, 1971, included a recognition of 'the social implications of the Gospel' in its fivefold aim.[17] Each Congress called for an end to the artificial polarisation between evangelism and social action, but on each occasion, however, the primacy of proclamation was reaffirmed and social involvement was conceived primarily in personal terms.

At the Inter-Varsity *Urbana 70* Convention the relationship between evangelism and social concern became the main theological issue. Samuel Escobar, Tom Skinner, George Taylor and Myron Augsburger all emphasised the

absolute necessity for the church to face concrete social and
political issues.[18]

The Declaration of Evangelical Social Concern signed in
Chicago in 1973 acknowledged the evangelicals' failure to
proclaim God's justice 'to an unjust American society', 'to
defend the social and economic rights of the poor and oppressed', to condemn 'the exploitation of racism at home
and abroad', and called for evangelical Christians 'to demonstrate repentance in a Christian discipleship that confronts the social and political injustice of our nation'. Going
much further than earlier declarations it asserted: 'We must
attack the materialism of our culture and the mal-
distribution of the nation's wealth and services ... Before
God and a billion hungry neighbours, we must rethink our
values regarding our present standard of living and promote
more just acquisition and distribution of the world's resources ... We must challenge the misplaced trust of the
nation and its institutions in objects of mere religious loyalty.'[19]

The Growth of Opposition

The transition from traditional evangelism with its stress on
personal salvation and the new-style evangelism with its emphasis on both personal salvation and socio-political action
has not been without its antagonists. In almost all denominations and para-church agencies there are significant
groups which consider the new move a swing back to liberalism to be resisted at all costs.[20]

This resistance to a greater degree of socio-political
action by evangelicals has been encouraged by the frequently inflammatory publicity given in religious and secular
media to the World Council of Churches' grants to liberation movements in southern Africa.[21] It has also been re-
energised by the generally negative attitude of evangelicals
to the *Commission on World Mission and Evangelism*,
Bangkok, 1973, which was seen as interpreting 'salvation'
almost solely in terms of 'this worldly improvements', more
food, more justice and more freedom.[22]

It reached its zenith in *The Berlin Declaration on Ecu-*

menism, 'prepared by the European Conference of Confessing Fellowships in co-operation with Christian leaders throughout the world', a frontal attack on the World Council of Churches. It claims that as a result of the ecumenical movements's acceptance of 'an ungodly humanism that deifies man' there is developing 'a new polarisation' which will inevitably lead to an 'unavoidable division' in the churches. 'On a world-wide basis the antithesis emerges between fellowship in the biblical profession of Jesus Christ and a secularist Ecumenical Movement.' The Liberation Programme of the Council indicates that it is 'on the way to substituting Jesus Christ with his antichristian counterpart' and is perverting the Gospel 'to an antichristian ideology'.[23]

The Declaration was prepared just a few months before Lausanne and was signed by a number of Congress leaders and speakers. European churchmen feared that the movement would lead to a further polarisation at Lausanne, but by the time Peter Beyerhaus, the movement's spokesman, was able to plead openly for 'a world-wide association of evangelicals' to combat 'the Mission of Barabbas'[24] the die had already been cast. The polarisation did not materialise and, in fact, a great deal of ground was covered in the attempt to bring the polarisation of the 1960s to an end. It is now over to Nairobi!

The Emerging Basis

The shape of the Christian community results from the interaction of the Word and the world, the form of its proclamation from an exegesis of the Word and an analysis of the world.

The Berlin Congress was held during *the glorious '60s.* The awe-inspiring space programmes of the Soviet Union and the United States were at their height, the civil rights movement was winning and the 'Green Revolution' was well under way. It was the golden age of science and technology. Evangelical writers optimistically espoused John R. Mott's call for 'the evangelisation of the world in this generation'.[25]

The Lausanne Congress met during *the troubled '70s*. Horrors of war, threats of ecological suicide, manipulation of the media by the technocratic elite, the energy crisis and devastating famines formed the background to the discussions. The Pentagon Papers trial and the Watergate scandals dampened the confidence of American evangelicals and led to a more realistic understanding of the Christian's responsibility in the world.[26]

Lausanne came to recognise that the key to understanding the Christian's responsibility in the world, of his mission of sacrificial service, is to be found in the preaching of Jesus with his emphasis upon the fact that in his words and works the kingdom of God had drawn near (Mark 1: 14–15).[27] The kingly reign of God, the hour of salvation, which the Old Testament longed to see, had begun to break into human history through the ministry of Jesus (cf. Luke 4: 16–21).

Jesus directed his mission especially towards those whom the orthodox regarded as beyond the fringes of respectability, outside the realm of salvation. Lepers, who had to live outside the camp, who were regarded as 'unclean' and denied fellowship with others (Mark 1: 40–45; Luke 17: 11–19); Gentiles who had no share in the privileges of Israel (Matt. 8: 5–13; John 4: 46–54); women and children who had no status in the community (Matt. 8: 14–17; 9: 20–26; Luke 13: 11–13; Mark 10: 13–16); notorious sinners, despised tax-collectors, drunkards and prostitutes (Matt. 11: 19; 21: 32; Mark 2: 16–17; Luke 7: 37–50; 15: 1–2; 19: 1–10). His 'following consisted predominantly of the disreputable, the uneducated, the ignorant, whose *religious* ignorance and *moral* behaviour stood in the way of their access to salvation, according to the convictions of the time'.[28]

Jesus' concern for the 'little people' of society, her outcasts, was inextricably bound up with his preaching of the coming kingdom (Matt. 10: 7–8; 11: 5–6; Luke 4: 18–19)[29] and underlines the fact that it is an act of grace. The kingdom belongs to the poor (Luke 6: 20) and for this reason he came to call notorious sinners (Mark 2: 17).

In the light of this good news of the nearness of God's kingly reign, in preparation for its breaking into human history, and in response to this act of supreme grace, Jesus demanded a radical reorientation of life lived out in believing obedience (Mark 1: 15). This 'repentance' Jesus required is not just 'feeling sorry for your sin' or even 'changing your mind'; it is 'changing your way of living'. 'God's definitive revelation demands a radical conversion, a transformation of nature, a definite turning from evil, a resolute turning to God in total obedience . . . It affects the whole man, first and basically the centre of personal life, then logically his conduct at all times and in all situations; his thoughts, words and acts.'[30]

This radical reorientation of life in response to Jesus' proclamation is symbolically portrayed in the call of the first disciples (Mark 1: 16–20). The call was itself an act of grace, the beginning of a new community of God's people (Mark 3: 13–25), and a preparation for the mission of the disciples in which this grace was to be extended to others (Matt. 10: 8). The mission itself was to be carried out in the same way as the mission of Jesus — preaching the good news, healing the sick, exorcizing demons and calling people to change their way of living (Matt. 10: 7; Mark 6: 7–13).[31]

The way of discipleship, the response to the good news of the kingdom, is not to be thought an easy thing. Those who respond must count the cost of their allegiance (Matt. 8: 19–22), they must take up their cross and follow Jesus (Mark 8: 34), giving absolute priority to the work of the kingdom (Luke 9: 62). 'The cross is laid on every Christian . . . When Christ calls a man, he bids him come and die,'[32] he bids him write 'dead' over every desire and ambition which had previously determined his existence in order that he might come alive for God and his kingdom.

This radically reoriented life of obedience

is more than generalisations — it has to do with specific acts of self-sacrifice in concrete situations. To each one who becomes convicted by his message, John the Baptist has a fitting word, and in each case his ethical demand touches the point at which the man is enslaved to the powers of the old age and closed to God's action. To the people in general he says, 'He who has two coats, let him share with him who has none; and he who has food, let him do likewise.' To the tax collectors, 'Collect no more than is appointed you.' To the soldiers, 'Rob no one by violence or by false accusation, and be content with your wages.' (Luke 3: 11–14). This crisis created by the kingdom cannot be resolved by accepting concepts handed down by tradition ('We are descendants of Abraham'), but rather by obedience to the ethics of the kingdom.[33]

To the rich young ruler who asked, 'What must I do to inherit eternal life?', Jesus said, 'You lack one thing; go, sell what you have, and give to the poor, and you will have treasure in heaven; and come, follow me' (Mark 10: 21). In the presence of Jesus Zacchaeus, described as 'a chief tax-collector and rich' perceived this truth and declared: 'Behold, Lord, the half of my goods I give to the poor; and if I have defrauded any one of anything, I restore it four-fold.' To which Jesus responded, 'Today salvation has come to this house, since he also is a son of Abraham' (Luke 19: 9).

The disciple of Jesus refuses to lay up treasures on earth for he has learned the truth that 'where your treasure is, there will your heart be also' (Matt. 6: 19–21), and he has come to realise that discipleship involves a life of trust (Matt. 6: 25–33) and obedience (Matt. 7: 21) in which it is impossible to serve God and mammon (Matt. 6: 24).

The disciple's detachment from worldly cares and possessions contrasts with his concern for his brother (Matt. 5: 23–24), his neighbour (Mark 12: 31) and even his enemy and those who persecute him (Matt. 5: 43–48). His loving concern is shown not in mere pious activities and religious observances (Matt. 6: 1–18), but in forgiveness (Matt. 6: 14–15), in doing to others what you expect for yourself (Matt. 7: 12), in caring for the hungry, the thirsty and the naked (Matt. 25: 31–46). Because of his relationship to Jesus (Matt. 4: 17–21) he has become the salt of the earth and the light of the world (Matt. 5: 13–16).[34]

The Continuing Debate

The Planning Committee intended the Lausanne Congress to be 'a process, not just an event', and so the Covenant was not presented as 'the final word'. It sought to embody 'a consensus of the mind and mood' of the participants and so represents a crystallisation of evangelical thinking at that particular point in time.

At least three key issues relating to 'Christian Social Responsibility' still have to be faced: the primacy of evangelism, the relationship between reconciliation of man to man and reconciliation of man to God, and the precise nature of evangelical socio-political involvement.

The Primacy of Evangelism

Although the section of the Covenant dealing with 'Christian Social Responsibility' makes no mention of *priorities*, the subsequent paragraph on 'The Church and Evangelism' states quite categorically the traditional evangelical position: 'In the church's mission of sacrificial service evangelism is primary.' The issue, however, was not debated at Lausanne and none of the Scripture texts attached to the Covenant support the assertion.

John Stott acknowledged, 'Evangelism is an essential part of the church's mission', but did not ascribe it priority, observing that Jesus gave a Great Commandment ('love your neighbour') and a Great Commission ('go and make disciples').[35] Carl Henry insisted 'The church, under Christ's lordship is sent into the world to proclaim personal and social righteousness and redemption.'[36] René Padilla was forthright: 'I refuse, therefore, to drive a wedge between a primary task, namely the proclamation of the Gospel, and a secondary (at best) or even optional task of the church.'[37] The 'Response to Lausanne' was quite blunt: 'We must repudiate as demonic the attempt to drive a wedge between evangelism and social action.'

The difficulty of explaining the position adopted in the

Covenant can be observed in John Stott's 'Exposition':

> As we have seen, it [the church's mission of sacrificial service] includes both evangelistic and social action, so that normally the church will not have to choose between them. But if a choice has to be made, then evangelism is primary. Two reasons are given [in the Covenant]. The first is the immensity of the task: world evangelisation requires the whole church to take the whole gospel to the whole world ... The second is the biblical truth that the church is not a man-made society but, on the contrary, is at the very centre of God's cosmic purpose.[38]

The logic of this section is not immediately apparent and the reasons given would seem to support a dual emphasis on evangelism and social action rather than the primacy of evangelism.

The issue is not settled by stating that either evangelism or social action is primary, nor even that equal emphasis must be given to each. Both belong to the mission of the church in the world, and the situation in the church and the world at the particular time will determine the emphasis and the priority.[39]

Horizontal and Vertical Reconciliation

The relationship between *reconciliation with man* and *reconciliation with God* will be a continuing issue in ecumenical-evangelical relationships. The Bangkok Assembly placed heavy emphasis on reconciliation with man and tended to equate salvation with political and economic liberation, while the Lausanne Congress rejected this emphasis and, in reaction to it, emphasised reconciliation with God.

Once again, a polarising 'either ... or' must be replaced with a biblical 'both ... and'. The possibility of a middle way can be seen in the recorded discussion between Emilio Castro, Director of the World Council's Commission on World Mission and Evangelism, and Paul Little, Associate Director of the International Congress on World Evan-

gelization. Little's assertion that 'the Bible makes it clear
that the pre-requisite for reconciliation with man is reconciliation with God' was met by Castro's correction that
'the Bible also says that before you seek to reconcile yourself with God, you must first reconcile yourself with your
brother'.[40]

To be sure, Paul speaks directly only of 'reconciliation'
with God (II Cor. 5: 18–20, though cf. Eph. 2: 14–16), but
Jesus indicates that 'the way to God goes through a man's
neighbour' and stresses the necessity of forgiveness and reconciliation with man (Matt. 5: 23–24; 6: 14–15).[41] Willingness to forgive is the hand by which the disciples reach out
and grasp God's forgiveness. Yet it is precisely because they
are disciples of Jesus that they are able to reach out and
grasp their neighbour in love.

When the scribe asked about *the* greatest commandment,
Jesus replied with the twofold answer: 'You shall love the
Lord your God ... You shall love your neighbour as yourself' (Mark 12: 28 ff.). They are separate, but they can never
be separated. Again, it would seem, the emphasis will
depend on the situation in the church and the world.

Socio-Political Involvement

The Lausanne Covenant went far beyond its predecessor in
affirming socio-political involvement as part of our Christian duty, but it did not address itself directly to the form
that this political involvement should take.[42]

The traditional evangelical position has been that 'the renewal of the individual also reforms society',[43] but this
tragically underestimates the existence and the power of corporate evil. Changes in the lives of individuals do not automatically lead to changes in the structures of society. As one
Congress report expressed it, 'Institutionalised evil requires
institutional action.'[44]

Again, in recent years, evangelicals have traditionally
supported conservative political parties favouring the main-
tenance of the status quo. The Covenant, however, warns
that the church 'must not be identified with any particular
culture, social or political system, or human ideology'. The

affirmation that 'because mankind is made in the image of God, every person, regardless of race, religion, colour, culture, class, sex or age, has an intrinsic dignity because of which he should be respected and served, not exploited' clearly anticipates, in some situations at least, an outspoken opposition to the status quo.

But what form will this opposition take? 'The message of salvation implies also a message of judgment upon every form of alienation, oppression and discrimination, and we should not be afraid to denounce evil and injustice wherever they exist.' But are we only to denounce evil and injustice or are we also to work for justice? Is evangelical political involvement only a matter of words? What action is to be taken when the words of denunciation go unheeded and the poor are still oppressed? Will this lead evangelicals, in some situations, to support revolutionary movements, or is there some other way?

The discussion and the action must continue! Let the earth hear his voice!

CHAPTER VI

The Church and Evangelism

Peter Savage

'WE AFFIRM THAT Christ sends his redeemed people into the
world as the Father sent him, and that this calls for a similar
deep and costly penetration of the world. We need to break
out of our ecclesiastical ghettos and permeate non-Christian
society. In the church's mission of sacrificial service evangelism is primary. World evangelisation requires the whole
church to take the whole gospel to the whole world. The
church is at the very centre of God's cosmic purpose and is
his appointed means of spreading the gospel. But a church
which preaches the cross must itself be marked by the cross.
It becomes a stumbling block to evangelism when it betrays
the gospel or lacks a living faith in God, a genuine love for
people, or scrupulous honesty in all things including promotion and finance. The church is the community of God's
people rather than an institution, and must not be identified
with any particular culture, social or political system, or
human ideology.'
*(John 17: 18; 20: 21; Matt. 28: 19, 20; Acts 1: 8; 20: 27; Eph.
1: 9, 10; 3: 9–11; Gal. 6: 14, 17; II Cor. 6: 3, 4; II Tim.
2: 19–21; Phil. 1: 27)*

(LAUSANNE COVENANT, CLAUSE 6)

IN WESTERN SOCIETY at large, the very bastions of individualism are being shaken. 'Man desperately craves for love, for fellowship, for security, for belongingness, all of which he feels he has lost in modern society. Even the old and deep stability of the family unit is threatened.'[1] This widespread feeling has coincided with and probably contributed to the recent 'rediscovery of the church' in theological circles. Both are understandable reactions to the atomistic individualism of preceding years. The time is ripe for the church to show herself as a living community in the midst of society. As such, she can become in fact what she is already in God's design, that is, what paragraph 6 of the Lausanne Covenant calls 'the very centre of God's cosmic purpose and . . . his appointed means of spreading the gospel'.

However, as this paragraph of the Covenant implies, the church today falls far short of completing its God-given task. Many churches lack an evangelistic vision; they remain in what the Covenant labels 'ecclesiastical ghettos' where they cannot possibly 'permeate non-Christian society'. Others have a vision, but become stumbling blocks to evangelism when they 'betray the gospel or lack a living faith in God, a genuine love for people, or scrupulous honesty in all things including promotion and finance'. Finally, in mission work, too often we have forgotten that 'the church is the community of God's people rather than an institution, and must not be identified with any particular culture, social or political system, or human ideology'.

The critical question we face in our generation is, what is the biblical model for the church that will enable it to complete its task as the prime agent in the evangelisation of the world? This task can obviously not be completed simply by handing it over to church specialists or professionals. It requires, as the Covenant expresses it, that 'the whole church ... take the whole gospel to the whole world'. We must mobilise all the resources at our disposal: his people in the power of the Holy Spirit and under the direction of the Lord. This can best be done as we recapture the biblical vision of what the church should be.

Four Models of the Church Today

What forms has the local or 'gathered'[2] church taken today? I have selected four of the most common contemporary models to give us some idea of the nature of the ecclesiastical situation in which we find ourselves and how that compares with the biblical model for the church.

The Church as Lecture Hall

This model has characterised the Protestant Reformed tradition since the days of Luther and Calvin. The church is seen as the 'gathering of people who listened to the word of God being spoken to them'.[3] The key to the life of the church was the preaching, and the preaching emphasised doctrinal clarification. 'The ministers directed their sermons to the end of stimulating a right faith on the basis of a correct knowledge of evangelical doctrine.'[4] In this view, the preacher is endowed with an unusual power, a power which Calvin regarded as virtually divine: the preacher was the one who spoke and acted in the very name of God.[5]

While this model stimulates the development of fine biblical exposition, it fosters passivity in the congregation, making them more spectators and onlookers than active participants. They are continually on the receiving end and have little opportunity to give. This discourages the development of real disciples. 'The concept on which our meetings seem structured is that spiritual growth occurs as biblical information is digested and regurgitated in a three-point, alliterative message by one so trained.'[6]

The Church as Theatre

The congregation sits expectantly! Most are in a state of grace after going to confession the night before, and now await the central drama of their church. The priest appears, the choir sings, the congregation responds; all attention is centred around the drama which is about to be re-enacted on the altar. The bell tingles, responses are given and the sacramental moment is reached. The priest and then the congregation participate in the sanctifying grace that this 'body and blood' of Jesus Christ confers upon them. The drama over, the congregation scatter to their homes and social activities carrying with them the blessing of the sacraments.

The priest fulfils the critical function in this model, the administration of the sacraments. As with the previous model, the congregation is often reduced to passivity. In addition, it seriously limits the church's possibilities for evangelising. It is no wonder that within the medieval Roman Catholic church, special 'orders' had to be created to take the Gospel into the unevangelised sections of the world!

The Church as Corporation

Under this model, the church is in the business of retailing religion, much as any other commodity is marketed. Its goal is to make the goods and services of religion available to the people. Dr Robert H. Schuller has perhaps most clearly enunciated the operating principles for the church as corporation or supermarket:

I have sometimes described the Garden Grove Community Church [of which he is pastor] as a twenty-acre shopping centre for Jesus Christ. We are located right near a freeway interchange, with acres of surplus parking, with the buildings and the inventory in the form of programme and service designed to meet almost every conceivable need that an unchurched person might seek and expect from a church.[7]

He emphasises the importance of an ample church building to serve as a centre of operations; a trained laity to serve the community; and a good cash flow, if they are to expect God to do great things and enable further expansion and development.

The whole church is programme-oriented, the full-time pastoral team functioning as corporation executives. Management principles forged on the anvil of the successful business world are easily transferred into this model. Profit is measured in numerical figures, whether in first-time decisions, membership or offerings. The team is highly qualified and professional. The undergirding goal is 'find the hurt and heal it!'[8]

This model raises some serious questions as to the extent to which it may have accommodated the Gospel to this expression of the consumer society. Furthermore, how much biblical discipleship can be carried on in this setting?

The Church as Social Club

This model is one of the cultural side-effects of an affluent society. A person may choose to join the church as club if he desires to identify himself with the social interests it represents and the services it provides. Often he is only qualified for membership if he satisfies certain conditions regarding his social status, etc.

A church may be joined and used . . . for the religious good to be had from religious association, rather than out of love of a common Lord for the sacrificial service for his kingdom. It may be composed of a number of people who have been persuaded that it would be for the good of their souls . . . Such a group does not exist for a cause, but for a comfort. Nor is it created by any Gospel in which self is lost. Nor is it tenanted by one indwelling, overruling, organising presence.[9]

This club caters to the 'inner needs' of its members, demanding involvement only in its activities, not its community. In fact, the member's 'keenness' is measured by the amount of time expended in the many activities, regardless of the quality of that involvement.

The religious club becomes a socialising centre where the pastor is either the co-ordinator of activities, a counsellor or janitor. Success is measured in the status, value and social security it affords its members. In many cases, the church caters exclusively to a select group in society, having little commitment to evangelism and less desire to move outside its own social group.

Many other models for the church, of course, can be found today, but these four suffice to give us an idea of the variety in the current scene. The question now is how these models appear in the light of the biblical teaching on the church.

The Biblical Model for the Church

Paragraph six of the Lausanne Covenant singles out one basic characteristic of the biblical model for the church: 'The church is the community of God's people.' It is around this concept of 'community' that I would like to centre my discussion of the biblical model for the church, and its responsibility to carry out the task God assigned to it to be 'his appointed means of spreading the Gospel'.

An Overview of Community

The Christian community, according to Scripture, must be characterised by both *comprehensiveness* and *cohesiveness*, that is, it must extend itself to include all kinds of people while at the same time maintaining a strong bond of unity.

The club model for the church which we mentioned above violates this principle most flagrantly by limiting its membership to certain types of 'acceptable' people. It is not easy to avoid this danger, however. Rather than build community out of diversity we often tend to let each sub-group form its own church and grow as an isolated 'homogeneous unit'.

Scripture, however, teaches that the community that is alive in the Spirit must struggle to live out the reconciliation of all men to each other and to God — the reconciliation which is inherent in the Gospel — by uniting black and white, intellectual and action-oriented businessmen, new believer and mature believer, etc. We see the apostle Paul struggling with the problems caused by this comprehensiveness in the early church. Time after time he stresses the need for community harmony, for 'being of the same mind, having the same love, being in full accord and of one mind' (Phil. 2: 2); 'I appeal to you . . . that all of you agree and that there be no dissensions among you, but that you be united in the same mind' (I Cor. 1: 10). Problems of immature Christians threatened to disrupt community (I Cor. 3: 1–3). The most serious problem, however, was the presence of both Jews and Gentiles, who came from radically different backgrounds, in the church. Many naturally wanted the new Christian 'movement' to be divided down cultural and racial lines, and some demanded that the other side conform to their cultural patterns. To these Paul spoke his remarkable declaration of their new unity in diversity: 'There is neither Jew nor Greek, there is neither slave nor free, there is neither male nor female; for you are all one in Christ Jesus' (Gal. 3: 28). In Acts 15 we see the Apostles working out the practical implications of this principle of comprehensiveness in the life of the church. The same principles are binding on the church today.

If then the community is to be so radically comprehensive, how is it to maintain its cohesiveness? Through its submission to the lordship of Christ. Alan Stibbs describes it this way:

A large orchestra and choir are able to realise elaborate harmony and performance, not when separate individuals or groups copy each other, but when each plays or sings his own distinctive part. What unites them all is their willing submission to the control of one conductor. What enables them to contribute various parts harmoniously, is obedience to the printed score, response to the conductor's guidance and attentive awareness of the stage reached by the contributions of others.[10]

The basis of the Christian community as described in Scripture is the *covenant* that God has established with his people. They are a 'chosen race, a royal priesthood, a holy nation, God's own people' (I Pet. 2: 9) who have entered into a relationship with God through the finished work of Jesus Christ. They are bought and sealed with the blood of Jesus Christ, the 'new covenant', and in this way are brought into a living relationship with God (Rom. 5: 1, 2) and are clothed in the righteousness of Christ himself which has been imparted to them (Rom. 3: 25). God initiates the covenant with his people 'which sets them aside against the rest of the world for the sake of the world'.[11] As the Lausanne Covenant points out, the church has a mission of 'sacrificial service' and must break out of its 'ecclesiastical ghettos and permeate non-Christian society'. The church has been called out so 'that you may declare the wonderful deeds of him who called you out of darkness into his marvellous light' (I Pet. 2: 9).

While the basis of the Christian community is God's covenant, its operating principle, the heart of its action, is its obedience to the lordship of Christ. This is only proper since by virtue of his death and resurrection Christ is the head of the church; Scripture calls it the 'church of the Lord which he obtained with his own blood' (Acts 20: 28). The members are instructed to 'grow up in every way into him who is the head, into Christ, from whom the whole . . . makes bodily growth and upbuilds itself in love' (Eph. 4: 15, 16; cf. I John 1: 3, 7). As each member obeys and participates in Christ, he is enabled to participate in and enjoy his fellowship with other believers.

The proper name of any member of the community is 'Christian' for he is 'in Christ' by virtue of his participation

in the covenant and his obedience to his Lord. They are the
saints 'in Christ Jesus'. God makes every blessing theirs 'in
Christ'. Baptism is a sign and a seal of initiation into Christ
Jesus. They have 'put on Christ'; henceforth all of life is to
be lived 'in Christ'. They are to work 'in him' and be 'rooted
and built up in him'.

The binding and animating force in the community is the
ministry of the Holy Spirit.

> Such possession of the indwelling Spirit of God by
> every individual is likewise the decisive mark and seal of
> every man's participation in Christ, and of his mem-
> bership in the community of his people. For on the one
> hand, 'no man can say that Jesus is the Lord, but by the
> Holy Ghost'; and on the other hand, 'if any man has not
> the Spirit of Christ, he is none of his'. It is, too, this same
> Spirit who not only brings new life, but also guarantees to
> all whom he has given, endurance to the end and ultimate
> participation in the full inheritance.[12]

It is the Spirit who distributes gifts, functions and ministries
within the community so that they complement each other,
strengthening the complex of interlocking relationships that
make up the body. As Paul points out in I Corinthians
12: 14–24, this gives each member a sense of his own value as
well as that of his fellow brother or sister. Each has a role to
complete, but no one can complete his role without the support of the others. Each person's role is valuable; no one is
strong enough or, for that matter, was meant to stand on his
own. We need each other.

For this reason, the community expresses itself in love
that stimulates its members to growth. In fact there is a
direct correlation between a person's growth in Christ Jesus
and his growth in ministry. In Romans 12 Paul links the need
to grow as a person, to perceive one's identity and value,
with the discovery of one's gift, function and calling within
the community (cf. vv. 3–21). Growth as an individual and
growth as a functional unit of community go hand in hand.
Only as gifts are discovered and exercised can there be the
full participation in community that the Bible described.

This love also expresses itself in meeting the totality of needs of the community. Some feel that the only mandate given to the church is to minister to the needs of the soul of man. This, however, presupposes a false dichotomy in man, who is a material-spiritual unity. Furthermore it finds no resonance with the experience of the early church which, though populated by the poor, cared for all in such a way that there were no needy among them (Acts 2: 45, 4: 32–35). Nor does it resonate with the apostle John's words, 'If any one has the world's goods and sees his brother in need, yet closes his heart against him, how does God's love abide in him?' (I John 3: 17). Our ministry to the whole man must spring from the presence of God's love in us, as John points out. It meets people at their point of need. In the early church, again, the concern was so deep that when the young churches heard of the famine in Jerusalem, they offered material help to the mother church there (cf. Acts 11: 27–30).

Acts 6: 1–6 records a dispute between the Jews and Greeks in Jerusalem. The latter brought the complaint that the Greek widows, people with no financial resources, were being neglected in the distribution of the community's goods. The problem of need here was aggravated by the accusation that one group was being discriminated against. But the church did not hesitate to face this problem head on: it appointed leaders to oversee the distribution, to correct the error, while at the same time not neglecting the ministry of the word and prayer. We have much to learn from their firm understanding of the real social situation in which the community was living.

This kind of caring involves not only material help, but also standing up to dangers for the sake of the community. The early Christians did not fail in this as they aided and protected the apostle Paul when his ministry ran into heavy opposition.

Scripture teaches that the community is essentially an organic entity, as opposed to an institutional one. We see this most clearly in the metaphors used to describe the church: body, marriage, family, brotherhood. At the same time, however, it must express itself in some concrete, organised fashion. 'No community exists without some institutions that give it form, boundaries, discipline and the possibilities of expression and common action. On the other hand, no institution could long exist without some common mind and drive that expressly defines itself in institutions.'[13]

The problems generally come when the external structure begins to take undue precedence as both age and spiritual arthritis begin to set in. There must be balance between the two. In most cases, the living community requires only a minimum of organisation and a structure borrowed from the immediate cultural setting.[14]

The leadership of the community tips the balance between its being a mere structure or a living organism. If the leaders see their role in terms of offices, status and prestige, it will be nothing more than an institution. If, however, they see their role as servants, they will have found the secret of the early church in Acts:

> The ministries had as yet not acquired the character of offices. The command given by the Master Himself — 'whoever should be great among you, let him be your servant' — is lived out as the essential truth of things. Even the Apostle who founded the community at Corinth and who received most explicit instructions on these matters, thinks it not beneath his dignity to strive to win the approval of his congregation and declines to exercise dominion over them. He wishes to prove anew to them his apostleship, which in fact, needed no further authentication, by the manifestation of the signs of an apostle. And those in Corinth who were marked out as leaders by their possession of the charisma and diakonia of governing are recalled to the community as persons who have proven themselves by faithful service, and who therefore have shown by their service that they are worthy to be obeyed when necessary.[15]

In the last analysis, it is the involvement in and commitment through the Holy Spirit to mission — which features evangelisation — that will determine the community's proper balance. As the community is mobilised under the Holy Spirit within the real world, its throbbing vitality will be sustained.

With this overview of the biblical community in mind, let us consider separately several of its distinctive components: the eschatological dimension, discipleship and the sacraments.

The Eschatological Community

The Christian community lives in the tension of the 'already' and the 'not yet'. That is to say, it lives in expectation of the kingdom of God which will be fully established in the future, but it also lives the reality of the presence of the kingdom which had broken into history with the coming of Jesus Christ. Not only that, but in all its activity it works towards the establishment of that kingdom. In a real sense it is involved in 'making history'.

For the early church, God's 'breaking into' their daily lives in the person of Jesus Christ was the living evidence of the presence of the kingdom (cf. Acts 5: 19; 7: 52; 10: 36–43; 13: 28–41; 14: 3; 17: 13). The community not only enjoyed these 'irruptions' of God into history, but actually sought them so that the 'times of refreshing may come' (Acts 3: 19) and they might experience now a foretaste of the kingdom that was to be fully realised in the future. The kingdom was something to be known in the present, not merely some distant, nebulous reality.

This sense of participating in and making history drove the early church forward in evangelism. Michael Green describes it this way:

> They proceeded to announce these joyful tidings with tireless zeal and boundless enthusiasm. It spread like wildfire precisely because the first hearers well understood that this was the Messianic salvation which was at issue. It was not merely a matter of the atoning death of a great man: since the days of the Maccabees they understood that the death of a hero for his people had expiatory significance. Nor was the resurrection, by itself, the fundamental thing. John the Baptist was rumoured to have

risen from the dead; Jesus himself had on occasion, it appears, raised folk from the dead without anyone supposing that there was anything Messianic about them. But when Jesus, Jesus who claimed to bring in the eschatological salvation rose from the tomb, that was a different matter. It was, as they put it, seen to be 'according to the scriptures'. It was the vindication of the Suffering Servant, the ascension in glory of the Son of Man, the fulfilment of the prophecy to David through Nathan long ago that 'he shall build a house for my name and I will establish his kingdom forever. I will be his father and he shall be my son'. And that was something to shout about. That was good news.[16]

The eschatological nature of the kingdom gave the early church its missionary identity in the world. They had a mission in time and history which, far from closing them off from the world, thrust them into it. Their mission was born out of Christ's Great Commission (Matt. 28: 18–20) and meant working to establish the kingdom — which had already come but which was still yet to come — in all the nations of the world. The Christian community was of the 'new age', they were the 'new humanity' in Christ Jesus. They were pilgrims awaiting their new land, but at the same time pioneers of the faith who were going forth to establish the kingdom. A vibrant, exhilarating sense of destiny filled the entire community in the times of the early church, and must continue to characterise the church as it carries on the same task today.

The Community of Disciples

The Christian community is basically a learning community that is observing and growing in response to all that the Lord has taught and continues to teach through the Holy Spirit. We may describe discipleship in two ways, or rather, speak of two aspects of discipleship. The first is a relationship with the Lord (Mark 3: 14 records that Jesus appointed twelve disciples 'to be with him'). Paul Minear has summarised the relationship in the following terms: 'To die with him [Christ] — to live with him. To suffer with — to be glorified with. To be crucified with — to be raised with. To be baptised with — to be made alive with. To be buried with — to sit with. To be placed with — to rule with. To be conformed to — to come with.'[17]

The complementary aspect of discipleship is submission and obedience to the will of the Lord. 'Not every one who says to me "Lord, Lord," shall enter the kingdom of heaven, but he who does the will of my Father who is in heaven' (Matt. 7: 21). A Christian community that lacks the radical discipleship which Jesus demanded (a commitment so strong that our ties to our families and even our own lives could be called hatred by comparison, according to Luke 14: 26–33) can easily deteriorate into a religious club. Furthermore, when this dimension of submitting to the lordship of Christ is lacking, the unconverted usually hear what John Yoder has called a 'para-message', instead of the Gospel, emanating from the Christian community. 'You are often saying something worse than you mean to say because of the context in which you act. You tell people about stewardship and sacrifice for the sake of Jesus, but they see your automobile and house. They get some notion about the place of affluence in the Gospel other than the one you meant to be talking about . . .'[18]

The church as a learning community, in which all are becoming disciples and are making disciples, has as its goal 'building up the body of Christ, until we all attain to the unity of the faith and of the knowledge of the Son of God, to mature manhood, to the measure of the stature of the fullness of Christ' (Eph. 4: 12, 13). While there are some in the community with special gifts and functions in this task, all are responsible to edify each other through healthy conversation (Eph. 4: 29), mutual exhortation and meaningful worship (Col. 3: 16), etc. Those with the special gifts must carry out their functions as good stewards, leading others to growth by their example (I Tim. 4: 12) and their teaching (I Cor. 2: 1, 16).

This edification also includes discipline where necessary, not always by means of overt instruction, but also through community example and social pressure. The whole community was called to bring social pressure against the brother caught in scandalous sin — sexual perversion, materialism, idolatry, drunkenness, oppression — so that the evil leaven did not corrupt the community (I Cor. 5: 11). This is the responsibility of the 'gathered community' (I Cor. 5: 4, 5), for we must remember that Jesus gave the awesome responsibility of 'binding and loosing' to the community, not to individuals. A spiritually mature person who is aware of an offence in a brother has the responsibility to go to him and lead him to repentance and restoration. If the offender resists, this becomes the concern of the whole community (Matt. 18: 15–17; Gal. 6: 1). This is never a judicial matter, but is always done in a pastoral spirit (cf. Paul's attitude in II Cor. 2: 1–8). The heart of the community of disciples is that the members submit to one another as they also submit to the Lord, conscious of their responsibility to maintain the purity of the community which is the Lord's and which must bring glory to his name.

This discipleship is also an evangelistic medium. In the early church, those whom the Lord did not add to their number, did not dare add themselves (cf. Acts 2: 47). The outsiders were aware that joining the Christians meant the radical commitment they saw in the community, not some airy promise of peace and plenty. They saw the true nature of the Christian life lived out in front of them.

The Sacramental Community

The essence of the sacramental community is its offering spiritual sacrifices or worship to God. Individually and corporately, the community offers the central sacrifice: the dedication of their lives to God (Rom. 12: 1). Every member therefore shares in the priesthood of believers (I Pet. 2: 9) and all the members together offer spiritual sacrifices acceptable to God. The covenant refers to this dimension by pointing out that 'a church which preaches the cross must itself be marked by the cross.' Let us look more closely at three facets of the sacramental community.

First, the sacramental community is, as we have mentioned, a worshipping community. The church regularly remembers God's great intervention in Christ Jesus as she celebrates the Lord's Supper. Worship and gratitude spring from the community that has experienced and continues to experience the goodness of the Lord. The gratitude leads the community to a rededication of their life to God. These acts of worship and sacrifice are not only verbal, but concrete as well. Paul calls the gifts the Philippians have sent him 'a fragrant offering, a sacrifice acceptable and pleasing to God' (Phil. 4: 18). The writer of Hebrews later exhorts his readers 'to do good and to share what you have, for such sacrifices are pleasing to God' (Heb. 13: 16).

Second, the sacramental community is an intercessory community. She pleads with God that his name may be glorified, his will done, his kingdom established (Matt. 6: 9–10). She also pleads for her fellow believers and fellow men in general, that needs be met; that they may grow, receive comfort in sorrow, be reconciled to God through the Gospel. She prays for government, that their leaders may work for justice and harmony in society.

Third, the sacramental community is a suffering community. Her full sacramental nature is not fulfilled until she suffers for the sake of others (II Cor. 1: 6) and the Gospel so that she participates in the very suffering of 'The Way', the suffering of Christ himself (I Pet. 4: 13–16). Suffering is often an evangelistic medium as well, for in it the community is beaten on the anvil of life and can become, under the Spirit of Jesus, the true expression of the Gospel to a people in a given culture.

The Lausanne Covenant affirms that 'the church is the community of God's people'. I have tried to outline the basic components of that community as given in the Scriptures: it is a comprehensive community that extends itself to all persons, regardless of their social status or their cultural background; a community based upon the finished work of Christ and bound together by the ministry of the Holy Spirit; a community that lives together in a love that seeks to build up each individual and the group as together they exercise the gifts which the Holy Spirit gives to them. It is a community which voluntarily submits itself to the lordship of Christ. In it we see now the reality (albeit imperfectly expressed) of the kingdom of God which erupted into history in the person of Jesus Christ. The church is the community which is learning to 'flesh out' the meaning of being the body of Christ in its age and culture as it lives and learns together as disciples of Christ. It is a community that worships the living God, that sacrifices to meet the needs of others, that intercedes on behalf of God's interests and those of her neighbours, that willingly participates in the sufferings of Christ.

It goes without saying that each of the four contemporary models which we examined at the beginning of this chapter falls far short of being the biblical community as taught in Scripture and so well exemplified in the early church. Lecture hall, corporation, club and theatre all lack the profundity and life that the biblical community demands.

The Church and Evangelism

Can we, therefore, take seriously the Covenant's affirmation that 'the church is at the very centre of God's cosmic purpose and is his appointed means of spreading the gospel'? If we are working with the four models previously described, or others like them, we certainly cannot. They simply are not equipped to undertake the task. If, however, we take the biblical model for community, we find a completely different situation. This model is well able to face the challenge Christ gave of sending 'his redeemed people into the world as the Father sent him' to carry on that 'costly penetration of the world' which he had personally exemplified in his ministry.

The question of whether the church is adequate to the evangelistic task is being widely debated today. Many feel that in its place, the so-called para-ecclesiastical structures should carry on the work. Dr Ralph Winter has analysed various ecclesiastical and para-ecclesiastical structures in order to better understand their place in the Christian mission. He sees the church as a vertical structure with the advantages of a greater internal diversity, objectivity and

overall perspective, but the disadvantage of limited mobility. It is often bogged down with bureaucracy as a result of
the distance between those who support the work and those
who finally carry it out. It may have difficulty gaining a
broad support for projects, especially enterprises beyond its
immediate internal needs. On the other hand, the para-
church organisation is a horizontal structure with a more
narrowly defined objective and the direct support of those
who back it. It has the advantages of mobility and efficiency;
but also has the disadvantages of seeing only its own goals
and therefore lacking the overall perspective. The rest of the
church may even need protection from the para-church's
oversell of its cause. Nevertheless, it does offer a healthy
outlet for the divergent visions and concerns of different
elements in the heterogeneous church structure.[19]

In this discussion, Dr Winter seems to imply that the para-
church structure is really best suited to undertake evangelisation. However, although his analysis may be helpful
within the traditional western ecclesiastical set-up and may
explain the inability of many churches to evangelise, it
misses the heart of the problem: the model of the church
with which Dr Winter is working. It certainly does not
appear to be the Christian community we described earlier.
Furthermore, other contemporary models of the church
outside the North American context prove quite the opposite of what he is saying. The greatest outreach in evangelism has often sprung from community churches. In his
discussion of the Chilean Pentecostal Church, Christian
Lalive D'Epinay helpfully isolates the community dynamics
of that church as evidence of the church's ability to complete its role as the chief agent for evangelisation. There, as
in the Independent Churches of Africa, winning people to
Christ is the central focus of the meaningful community life.
'Pentecostalism offers to the masses faith in a God of love,
the certainty of salvation, security in a community, and a
sharing in responsibility for the common task to be fulfilled.
It thus offers them a humanity which society denies
them.'[20]

Furthermore, we must affirm that the presence of the
'community of saints' is not only an option, but an integral

part of the message of Good News. Can the Gospel *really* be proclaimed if there is no authentic exhibition of its fruit, that is, if there is no living community?

The communication of the Gospel is by seeing as well as hearing. This double thread runs all through the Bible; image and word, vision and voice, opening the eyes of the blind and unstopping the ears of the deaf. Jesus is the Word of God and the Image of God. The Word became visible, the Image audible. The Apostle John, writing of Christian origins at the start of his letter, refers to 'that which was from the beginning, which we have heard, which we have seen with our eyes' (I John 1: 1). Paul describing his experience on the Damascus Road said: 'I saw a light ... I heard a voice' (Acts 26: 13, 14). We are familiar enough with the verbal element in evangelism. Where is the visual?[21]

We might well ask, what attracted the ordinary man to Christianity in the early church? From what we see in Acts, it must have had a lot to do with the life of the community as well as the proclaimed message — their warm fellowship, their great enthusiasm, their care for each other, their joy in the Lord. As Leighton Ford has stated, 'The world is not looking for perfection. It is looking for a substantial demonstration of the peace of God — a community where shalom is really to be found.'[22]

As we trace the history of the proclamation of the Gospel through the pages of the New Testament, we see that it is vitally linked with the community of disciples that lived the eschatological reality of the 'breaking in of God'. They were the authentic living epistles written to the world by Jesus not in isolation, but as members of a dynamic community that was truly God's workmanship (Eph. 2: 10) and which collectively exhibited his wisdom to the whole universe (Eph. 3: 10). Our western accommodation of the Gospel has so emphasised the individual aspect of salvation and evangelisation that it has all but lost sight of the truth that it is only as the Gospel is expressed collectively in the biblical community that it can be perceived in its entirety. Proclamation of the Gospel will be aided by the godly life of one individual, but its many-faceted impact can only be fully felt when seen in a living community in a concrete socio-economic setting. The church is the body of Christ in a very literal sense. All the members must be involved if it is to adequately reflect his glory and make his name known among men in our generation.

It is helpful once again to observe the model of the early church. The community in Jerusalem was the context from which the first missionary movement sprang. Michael Green notes[23] that from its earliest beginnings Christianity was a lay movement and maintained that character for a remarkably long time. In Acts 8 we find that it was largely anonymous 'lay' Christians, forced to leave Jerusalem in the wake of persecution, who carried the Gospel with them wherever they went. Their communication must have depended heavily on informal conversations in their homes and places of work, as they related to their friends and acquaintances the message which had brought liberation and joy to them. Their spontaneous witness embodied a natural credibility — they weren't being paid to spread the message. Their message was taken seriously and the movement encountered widespread acceptance, especially among the working classes. That movement which had sprung from the living community in Jerusalem naturally, in turn, stimulated the birth of many new communities where its dispersed membership had settled.

This naturally raises questions about the validity of the corps of professional evangelists and teams and missionary societies which so dominate the current church scene.

All of this makes it abundantly clear that in contrast to the present day, when Christianity is highly intellectualised and dispensed by a professional clergy to a constituency increasingly confined to the middle class, in the early days the faith was spontaneously spread by informal evangelists, and had its greatest appeal among the working class.[24]

We need to devote much more thought to what this example

means to us today in our situation. What should the Christian community as a whole be doing instead of depending exclusively on the professional?

Going back to the question of the professional, the person who has special evangelistic gifts, what should be his relation to the community? Scripture teaches that such persons were in a very real sense free to follow the leading of the Holy Spirit (Acts 16: 16,7) and required to preach 'in the sight of God' (Acts 10: 33), which gave them the measure of autonomy they needed as they carried out the task of pioneering the Gospel message in new areas (Acts 8: 36; 10: 23–28). Scripture, however, also teaches that they can only exercise their special ministry as members of the body which has authority over them, the authority which Jesus Christ himself invested in the church. In view of his special gifts and functions, such a person is commissioned by the community to carry out his ministry. He is accountable to both God and to the community for his actions, his objectives and strategy in evangelism; his submission to God (Acts 14: 26, 27); and the purity and effectiveness of his message (Acts 15). Is there not, in view of scriptural warrant, a place for the accountability of evangelistic agencies to living communities?

Evangelisation and the Cultural Setting

Although this topic is undertaken more fully in Chapter X, we must make several comments on its relation to the subject of the church and evangelism. The Covenant declares that the church 'must not be identified with any particular culture, social or political system, or human ideology'. As is widely recognised today, too often our proclamation of the Gospel in cultures foreign to our own has been marred by our adding cultural elements to the Gospel as though they were part of the essence. In planting churches, missionaries have often demanded that they take on forms that are extraneous to the cultural setting. This, however, is not in accord to Scriptural teaching.

As a biblical community is born in a new culture, the overseas evangelist must be ready to accept forms of church life that meaningfully express to those Christians the reality of the Biblical community. That new church must discover its true Spirit-given identity within that cultural and socio-economic setting. As a community in worship, it must express eschatological joy in musical forms that will naturally come from their contemporary culture. As a gathered community, both the church structure as well as the forms of leadership will be strongly conditioned by the cultural framework in which they live. Teaching and preaching may take on new forms of communication familiar to the people. They may well perceive the biblical concept of the community in such enriching ways that they will either excite or threaten the visitor from overseas. In the end, all of this will allow the Holy Spirit to live in an 'earthen vessel' that truly expresses the identity of the community of saints in that culture. The result will be the kind of authentic Christian community that by its life and proclamation is truly able to communicate the Gospel in and to that cultural setting. Only the Christian born in that culture and 'un-domesticated' by any other[25] can provide the leadership needed to work out the full implications of the Gospel for that community. The foreigner must not be threatened by this, but must realise that he is but a servant and co-worker with God in working out his purposes with his people in that place.

Conclusion

The church today finds itself faced with two great inter-related challenges: the challenge of the massive task of world evangelisation and the challenge of being the truly biblical community described in Scripture that is capable of carrying out that task. May we work and learn together as we undertake this double challenge that the name of the Lord might be glorified and the earth might hear his voice!

CHAPTER VII

Co-operation in Evangelism

Howard A. Snyder

'WE AFFIRM THAT the church's visible unity in truth is God's purpose. Evangelism also summons us to unity, because our oneness strengthens our witness, just as our disunity undermines our gospel of reconciliation. We recognise, however, that organisational unity may take many forms and does not necessarily forward evangelism. Yet we who share the same biblical faith should be closely united in fellowship, work and witness. We confess that our testimony has sometimes been marred by sinful individualism and needless duplication. We pledge ourselves to seek a deeper unity in truth, worship, holiness and mission. We urge the development of regional and functional co-operation for the furtherance of the church's mission, for strategic planning, for mutual encouragement, and for the sharing of resources and experience.'
(John 17: 21, 23; Eph. 4: 3, 4; John 13: 35; Phil. 1: 27; John 17: 11–23)

(LAUSANNE COVENANT, CLAUSE 7)

PARTICIPANTS AT LAUSANNE rejoiced in the felt unity of fellowship they experienced together for ten days. Diverse cultures, languages, and ecclesiastical traditions were temporarily blended as Christian believers shared in worship, study, and dialogue, united by the same vital faith in Jesus Christ.

That very real and valid joy of being together, however, should not blind us to three fundamental facts that bear on the whole question of co-operation in evangelism: (1) This experience was made possible because flesh-and-blood believers came together at a particular time and place — in other words, within history. (2) The unity, while real, was temporary; it continues to exist more as memory than as present fact. (3) This unity, while based in the transcendent Gospel, was made possible by a specific, man-made, space-time structure, the International Congress on World Evangelization. The unity was experienced because a specific enabling structure was created.

It is well to bear these observations in mind as we consider the problem of co-operation in evangelism. The Congress affirmed through the Lausanne Covenant that 'the church's visible unity in truth is God's purpose'. It stated the need for Christians to be 'closely united in fellowship, work and witness', while emphasising that 'organisational unity may take many forms and does not necessarily forward evangelism'. More specifically, the Congress called for 'the development of regional and functional co-operation' in evangelism for mutual encouragement, planning, and the sharing of resources. These affirmations were related to several New Testament passages, especially Jesus' prayer in John 17.

The purpose of this chapter is to reach back behind the discussion at Lausanne to spell out some fundamental issues involved in the question of co-operation in evangelism, and then to carry the discussion forward beyond the Lausanne Covenant, indicating the directions to which these issues point for the future.

Unity as an Expression of the Gospel

Oneness is an essential and fundamental fact of the Gospel. Biblical faith rests on this fundamental assertion: 'The Lord our God is one Lord; and you shall love the Lord your God with all your heart, and with all your soul, and with all your might' (Deut. 6: 4–5; cf. Mark 12: 29). The Bible insists that there is but one God and God is one, and all that exists comes from his hands. Scripture radically rejects any ontological dualism (whether between good and evil or between spirit and matter) by beginning with God and making the entire universe dependent on God's creative Word. God and the universe are distinguishable, and only God is eternal.

In contrast, all non-biblical philosophy and religion is fundamentally dualistic.[1] Man in rejecting revealed truth pushes the present problem of evil clear back to eternity and makes an eternal dichotomy of all reality. Such dualism is behind all non-biblical thinking and has often infected Christian theology.

The fact that God is one provides the foundation for the New Testament emphasis on the unity of the Gospel and of the church. 'There is one body and one Spirit, just as you were called to the one hope that belongs to your call, one Lord, one faith, one baptism, one God and Father of us all, who is above all and through all and in all' (Eph. 4: 4–6). There is thus a certain 'givenness' to the church's unity. The

Gospel *is* one, and there is but one Gospel, for it is the re-vealed truth of the one God. And yet this very fact that the church is, by its nature, *one*, if not understood biblically, can easily lead right back to a Platonic dualism between an ideal church (which is truly and safely one) and the real church on earth (which is in fact fragmented but need not be concerned about this because, after all, the ideal, 'spiritual' church is unalterably one, and that is what really matters).

Because there is one God, there is but one Gospel. And because there is but one Gospel, there is but one church. Jesus Christ is one, and the church is his own body. Faced with factions in the Corinthian church, Paul asked, 'Is Christ divided?' (I Cor. 1: 13). He is not, either in head or body. And yet the space-time reality of the church too often fails to confirm this unity, just as happened in first-century Corinth. Many groups 'profess to be followers of the Lord but they differ in mind and go their different ways, as if Christ himself were divided.'[2]

Evangelicals have no trouble affirming the unity of God and even of the Gospel, but we get into difficulty with the church. What does 'one Lord, one faith, one baptism' mean in practical terms when we are confronted with the reality of the church in history?

I suggest that evangelicalism's difficulty at this point attests to a fundamental theological problem which evan-gelicals have yet to deal with adequately: the problem of the church. The fact is that Protestantism has never developed a fully biblical doctrine of the church. Hendrik Hart observes 'It is becoming more evident to many of us that even though the leaders of the Protestant Reformation sincerely intended to break with the traditional Roman Catholic conception of the church, nevertheless the tradition arising from the Re-formation did not succeed in making that break.'[3] In other words, Protestantism — and thus contemporary evan-gelicalism — operates with a somewhat confused and often scholastic/Platonic view of the church which *a priori* cancels out the possibility of arriving at a biblically sound solution to many problems related to the nature and mission of the church — whether the problem be unity, evangelism, social witness, or whatever. The only solution therefore is to return to Scripture and self-consciously dig out a biblical ecclesiology that does not conflict with biblical soteriology, which sees ecclesiology and soteriology as one, and the church as part of the Gospel.

Roman Catholic ecclesiology is based on the twin pillars of Scripture and Tradition. But Tradition has generally meant the predominance of the institutional over the charismatic in the experience and doctrine of the church.[4] Too often evangelicals have uncritically and unconsciously accepted this Roman way of conceiving the body of Christ. The result is that we get hung up over the question of organisational versus spiritual unity, and conceive of these as almost mutually exclusive categories. Because of the excesses of Roman Catholicism and of the ecumenical movement, evangelicals tend to reject *a priori* any talk of organisational unity and are satisfied to accept a vague, indefinable 'spiritual' unity *which has very little practical significance within space-time history*. Henri Blocher was right to observe in his paper for Lausanne that 'invisible unity must be expressed in a visible way'; his question, 'Haven't we fallen into an easy self-satisfaction when we have acclaimed our spiritual unity?' can be answered in the affirmative.[5]

The recovery of a biblical understanding of the church will mean the ability to see that spiritual unity and organisational (or better, structural) unity are different but not necessarily antithetical. The options aren't merely either to accept the church as essentially institutional (the traditional Roman Catholic view) or else to reject the validity of (and thus the need for) all organisational unity. As I suggested in my paper on 'The Church as God's Agent of Evangelism', the Bible sees the church essentially in charismatic-organic terms, as the community of God's people. This is the church. But organisational-institutional structures have their functional validity, provided they are seen as para-church structures and are not 'sacralised'.

The fact that there is but one God and one Gospel means there can also be but one church of Jesus Christ. But the affirmation 'one church' must be understood biblically. There is but one people of God on earth, and it is as the people of God that the church is one.[6] This is much more than an invisible spiritual unity. It exists (although imperfectly) in space and time, and for both theological and practical reasons it must be given some structural expression.

The unity of the church and unity in evangelism are therefore required as an expression of the Gospel itself.

There is, of course, a very real and practical sense in which the church has, and must maintain, spiritual unity. The church must in fact be 'one in the Spirit'. Twice the statement on Co-operation in Evangelism in the Lausanne Covenant uses the phrase, 'unity in truth'. What is this unity which is God's purpose and which we seek to make manifest?

Unity in truth is unity in Jesus Christ, who is the Truth. He is, in fact, the incarnate truth. So the church's unity in truth means the incarnation of the truth of Jesus Christ in today's world and cultures.

It is here that John 17 is especially helpful. Several things stand out in Christ's prayer for the unity of the church.

1. *The primary purpose of the unity of the church is that God may be glorified.* Jesus prays, 'Glorify thy Son that the Son may glorify thee' (v. 1). Christ's overarching concern — here as always — is that God the Father may be glorified. Jesus refers to this eight times in his prayer. Everything Christ prays for here — both the unity and the witness of his disciples — is in order that God may receive glory. Jesus says of his followers in verse 10, 'I am glorified in them' — or, as the New International Version has it, 'Glory has come to me through them.' This is, above all else, the purpose and aim of the church. God's people are called 'to live for the praise of his glory' (Eph. 1: 12); 'to him be glory in the church and in Christ Jesus' (Eph. 3: 21). As Peter Beyerhaus reminds us, 'today it is extremely important to emphasise the priority of this doxological aim before all other aims of mission'.[7]

2. *The secondary purpose for the unity of the church is the authentic communication of the Good News.* This is stated most clearly in verses 21 and 23. Jesus prays that his followers 'may all be one; even as thou, Father, art in me, and I in thee, that they also may be in us, so that the world

may believe that thou has sent me ... I in them and thou in me, that they may become perfectly one, so that the world may know that thou hast sent me and hast loved them even as thou hast loved me.' The church must demonstrate 'unity in truth' so that the Good News may be made credible.

3. *Unity in truth is unity with Christ and thus with the Trinity.* Jesus' prayer is 'that they may be one, even as we are one' (v. 11). This unity is 'I in them and thou in me' (v. 23). Further, the same *kind* of unity that exists between the persons of the Trinity is to be found within the church and between Christ and the church. The church is to be one 'even as thou, Father, art in me, and I in thee' (v. 21). Key words in this whole prayer are 'even as'. We should especially note verse 18, 'As thou didst send me into the world, so I have sent them into the world' (c.f. John 20: 21). The church is to demonstrate within itself and in relation to Jesus Christ the same quality of relationship that exists between Jesus Christ and God the Father. This is unity in truth, true unity.

4. *This unity in truth means both unity of belief and unity of life; both orthodoxy and orthopraxy.* It is significant that both are included in Jesus' prayer.

Unity in truth means unity of belief. Christians share the same hope, the same faith (Eph. 4: 4–5). Christ prays for his disciples because they have received and kept his *words* (vv. 6–8). The key statement is verse 17: 'Sanctify them in the truth; thy word is truth.' Unity in truth is unity in the Word of God and the words of Christ. Four times here Jesus speaks of *the word* he has received from the Father and transmitted to his disciples. What Christ shared with his followers had *true content* that could be communicated; it was not merely existential, supra-rational experience. Finally, Christ prays 'for those who are to believe in me through their word' (v. 20), not just through their life. *Evangelism would involve communication of a message.* And unity in truth must be grounded in basic agreement as to the content of that message. The Lausanne Covenant took pains to emphasise this side of the question of evangelical unity.

But unity in truth also means unity of life. It means orthopraxy, or what Francis Schaeffer has called 'orthodoxy of community'. Incarnation means nothing if not the living out in daily experience of the implications of biblical truth. This also is involved in the prayer, 'Sanctify them *in* the truth' (v. 17). Christ's followers are sent into the world as Jesus himself was: as incarnated truth (v. 18). His disciples are to be known by the love (v. 26) and joy (v. 13) they demonstrate. The church being one in Christ as Christ is one with the Father certainly means more than mere doctrinal agreement. The cross must be taken as the basis not only of soteriology but of ethics as well.[8]

All evangelicals should be able to concur with these words from the document, 'A Response to Lausanne', which grew out of the Sunday night 'radical discipleship' seminar at Lausanne: 'There is no biblical dichotomy between the word spoken and the word made visible in the lives of God's people. Men will look as they listen and what they see must be at one with what they hear.' Both unity and evangelism involve much more than merely transmitting what Samuel Escobar has called 'verbal summaries' of the Gospel.

Co-operation in evangelism, especially on a broad scale, may not involve agreement at every point of doctrine, practice, or methodology. But it certainly must be based on unity in truth in both its verbal and incarnational dimensions. It must be founded upon the truth as regards the church. That is, such co-operation must be related to the church as the community of God's people. The Christian community must be both a demonstration of the Gospel and the goal of evangelism.

Unity as a Requirement for Evangelism

As already noted, Jesus himself underlined the pragmatic importance of unity for evangelism when he prayed, 'that they may all be one . . . so that the world may believe that thou has sent me' (John 17: 21).

Strangely, evangelistic and missionary concern among

evangelicals has often tended more towards fragmentation than towards unity. Those most deeply concerned about evangelism are often most adamantly opposed to, or else indifferent towards, the practical question of unity. Have we taken Jesus' prayer for unity *for evangelism* sufficiently seriously?

If both evangelism and the glory of God summon us to unity, this question must take a higher place on the evangelical agenda than it has until now. Evangelicals would do well to consider what Donald G. Bloesch has written in his chapter on Christian unity in *The Reform of the Church*: 'The goal of authentic ecumenism is not a super-church with power and prestige but rather a world-wide fellowship of believers united under the Word and dedicated to the conversion and salvation of mankind. What we should aim for is ... an evangelical ecumenism which places Christian mission above institutional survival.'[9]

The goal of such an 'evangelical ecumenism', says Bloesch, 'would not simply be the unity of the church but also and above all the conversion of the world'.[10] The missionary motive, rather than being an excuse for continuing fragmentation, must be the reason for evangelical convergence.[11] At present, most ecumenists seem concerned with unity for its own sake and unconcerned about evangelism (in the biblical sense), while too many evangelicals appear concerned with evangelism in itself but are little preoccupied with evangelistically necessary unity and co-operation. Bloesch's call for an 'evangelical ecumenism' is timely.

It would appear that most evangelicals are not *really* convinced that co-operation and unity are essential for effective evangelism. If they are convinced, we may legitimately ask, where is the evidence? There are few visible signs of evangelical evangelistic unity that can be pointed to today, other than evangelistic crusades or similar efforts which are essentially exceptional and short-term and are usually only marginally connected to the church. The tendency, of course, is to dismiss this lack by affirming the church's 'invisible, spiritual unity'.

I suggest that the problem here is, again, *the problem*

of our understanding of the church. Lack of a sufficiently biblical view of the church produces two results: (1) the tendency to limit the whole question of unity to the invisible-spiritual dimension, and (2) the tendency of efforts at co-operative evangelism to be little related to the actual edification of the church.

We might ask here: Is the essential question for effective Gospel proclamation one of the co-operative evangelistic efforts, or is it the visible unity of the church? Which is more crucial — unity in evangelism or the unity of the people of God? Will the world be convinced more readily by united evangelistic efforts or by the corporate unity of the church as God's people?

This is not an either/or question, of course. Certainly co-operative evangelism is to be encouraged. *But such evangelism must be integrally related to the life and edification of local communities of believers.* The principal problem with co-operative efforts up to now has been that such efforts have been largely unrelated to the daily on-going community life of the church. They have been a special, extraordinary, intensive added-on programme that could not be integrated into the daily experience of specific local Christian communities. It is now generally recognised that this was a major weakness of the early Evangelism-in-Depth crusades.[12]

I would suggest that the evangelistic-missionary mandate summons the church today *both* towards more effective co-operative efforts in evangelism *and also* towards some form of visible unity of the church itself.

It is significant that in his high priestly prayer Jesus does not only pray for the oneness of all believers for the sake of 'co-operation in evangelism'. Jesus was concerned about the unity of the church in itself, and evangelicals must share this concern. Any valid 'evangelical ecumenism' must be based not only on evangelistic pragmatism but, even more fundamentally, on a clear biblical understanding of the church.

Neither evangelism nor ecumenism are things in themselves. They are both aspects of the church's life in the world, and are both defined by the biblical mandate of the church and the Gospel. When evangelism and ecumenism are defined on the basis of the biblical understanding of the church (i.e. of ecclesiology and not just soteriology, narrowly conceived), then the essential interrelatedness of these two concerns will become apparent.

I suggest, therefore, that both the evangelistic mandate and the ecumenical motive summon contemporary evangelicalism to a new quest for the biblical understanding of the church.

The question of the church — in relation either to evangelism or to unity — was scarcely touched upon at Lausanne.[13] Yet it is fundamental to much of the discussion that took place there. I argued in my Lausanne presentation that the Bible sees the church (1) in cosmic-historical perspective, (2) in charismatic rather than institutional terms, and (3) as the community of God's people. There are aspects of these affirmations that have direct bearing on the question of co-operation in evangelism. The ecclesiological question needs to be investigated further to provide an adequate basis for the future development of evangelistic and ecumenical concerns within evangelicalism.

Unity as a Problem of Structure

As previously noted, the International Congress on World Evangelization was a specific, man-made structure. Further, it was made possible in large measure by the existence and resources of another major evangelical structure, the Billy Graham Evangelistic Association.

Co-operation in evangelism doesn't just happen apart from enabling structures. God works today, as he has throughout history, not only through human beings but also through human structures. Yet man-made structures are subject to the sociological pressures of institutionalism and must be seen as secondary and supportive, not as of the essence of the church.

Co-operation in evangelism and the oneness of the church are, therefore, also problems of structure. There is growing evangelical awareness of this. Calls are increasingly heard for some form of post-Lausanne structure, and steps are being taken in this direction. The key word appears to be 'fellowship'. Billy Graham has called for 'a fellowship of some kind', principally for information exchange.[14] Harold Lindsell believes that 'the participants at Lausanne want a fellowship of true believers created as an instrument for world evangelisation. But they do not want an ecclesiastical machine or hierarchical structures.'[15]

The essential question is, what kinds of structures can and should be created to further the oneness of the true church and the effective proclamation of the Gospel? The following observations may be made.

1. *Structures for the co-operation and unity of the various communities of the one people of God should be created at various levels.* Cultural diversity dictates considerable variety in the worship and community lifestyle of the church, but at each level this diversity should be transcended by some visible structures for unity. Cultural diversity must not be made an excuse for the lack of some visible demonstration of reconciliation and true oneness.

2. *The structural principle for the expression of the unity of the church is that of the body.* The church is the body of which Christ is the only head. This principle holds good at every level of the church. Thus valid structures for unity must be based on an organic-charismatic model, rather than a hierarchical-institutional model. In practice, this means that such structures should be flexible and functional, and should be considered as para-church structures for the expression of oneness, not as an essential part of the church itself.

3. *Priority should be given to the expression of Christian unity in today's urban centres.* Jacques Ellul suggests that 'the city is man's greatest work. It is his great attempt to attain autonomy, to exercise will and intelligence.'[16] The modern city is the locus of the clash between the church and the principalities and powers. Therefore it is the primary context in which unity needs to be demonstrated today.

Wherever possible in cities around the world, large public rallies should be held regularly, uniting all the people of

God in the city who will co-operate. If in major cities around the world all true Christians could unite regularly in a 'great congregation' to joyfully praise God, hear the Word, and bear witness, the impact would be incalculable. Such rallies would give public, visible testimony to the unity of the body of Christ and put the faith in the centre of the public arena once again. They should be *regular* and *frequent* (probably once a month), and they should unite all who are willing to confess that Jesus Christ is Lord and Saviour. They should be held in large public arenas wherever possible. Here the church in each city could recover some sense of peoplehood that would cross denominational and confessional lines, and here the world could be made to see the visible reality of the unified church.

4. *Some form of world-wide structure for unified fellowship and witness is necessary.* This structure should serve principally as (a) an information 'nerve centre' to monitor what is happening world-wide in the growth and witness of the church; (b) a point of contact and communication between the many evangelical structures around the world, such as evangelistic and missionary structures, denominations, Bible societies, seminaries, colleges, and the newly-forming evangelical communes; (c) an enabling structure or catalyst to bring about direct communication between like structures in various parts of the world. Its function should be primarily one of information, communication, and co-ordination, rather than one of initiating new programmes of its own which would only tend towards institutionalisation and the duplication of existing ministries.

Such a world-wide structure should probably be based on some form of the Lausanne Covenant and on the concept of 'unity in truth' which we have been discussing. On the other hand, it should not be so narrowly formulated as to exclude evangelicals in non-Protestant Christian communions.

If such a structure is based on a clear understanding of the church, it will succeed in giving some visible, organised expression of the church's unity without tending towards a 'super-church'. The structure will be seen as essentially *para-church* rather than *super-church*; as standing alongside of and serving the true body of Christ, rather than being over it or appropriating to itself the prerogatives of the head, Jesus Christ. It will promote a unity that is both spiritual *and* visible.

Conclusion

Lausanne was both an expression of unity and a call for unity. As an expression of unity it demonstrated the growing strength, cohesion, and universality of the evangelical movement. As a call for unity, it pointed to both the pragmatic and theological need for the visible oneness of the church. If this call is to have universal meaning, emerging world-wide evangelicalism must increasingly heed the Lausanne Covenant's summons to 'visible unity in truth'.

What is evangelicalism today? It is more than a group of theologically conservative churches. It is decreasingly a specific branch of Western Protestantism and increasingly a trans-confessional movement for biblical Christianity within the world-wide church of Jesus Christ. It is a world-wide movement which is beginning to hold out the hope for transcending Western evangelicalism's bondage to American and European 'culture Christianity'.[17] Lausanne, in fact, may in the future serve as a convenient reference point for marking the emergence of evangelicalism on a truly world-wide scale.

This is a time, therefore, not for triumphalism — evangelicalism's imperfections, both present and potential, are too serious for that — but rather for the emergence of what Donald Bloesch calls 'a catholic evangelicalism'. 'The kind of theology that we should seek', says Bloesch, 'is one that is both profoundly evangelical and authentically catholic.' Biblically, 'one cannot be fully evangelical without at the same time being truly catholic. And one cannot be catholic without also being evangelical.'[18]

The time may be ripe around the world for the emergence of a thoroughly biblical evangelical movement that includes both Catholics and Protestants. Arthur Glasser notes that 'evangelical Protestants are beginning to encounter evangelical Catholics' and are discovering that 'many loyal Catholics know and love Jesus Christ with an intimacy and devotion surpassing their own'.[19] The biblical and charismatic emphases within Roman Catholicism in the wake of Vatican II are rapidly invalidating many traditional Protestant criticisms of the Roman Church. The charismatic movement already is bringing many Catholics and evangelicals together. And in some countries where Catholics are witnessing renewal it is already an open question as to who is really doing more for evangelism — Catholics or Protestants.

The Lausanne Covenant is a non-sectarian document. It is, in fact, not even a specifically Protestant document! By seeking to be both evangelical and biblical, it also succeeded in being surprisingly catholic. It could well serve as the basis for a world-wide Christian fellowship that is at the same time evangelical, catholic and charismatic.

Should not these, in fact, be the 'marks' of evangelicalism's emerging 'unity in truth'? For the church of Jesus Christ must be *evangelical* — solidly based on the pure biblical Gospel and its demands — for witness and discipleship. The church must also be *catholic* — concerned with the unity, universality, and holiness of the church. And it must also be *charismatic* — living in close community through the indwelling love, grace, and power of the Holy Spirit as a present reality. It is thus that 'the whole body, joined and knit together by every joint with which it is supplied . . . makes bodily growth and upbuilds itself in love' (Eph. 4: 16).

CHAPTER VIII

Churches in Evangelistic Partnership

Orlando E. Costas

'WE REJOICE THAT a new missionary era has dawned. The dominant role of western missions is fast disappearing. God is raising up from the younger churches a great new resource for world evangelisation, and is thus demonstrating that the responsibility to evangelise belongs to the whole body of Christ. All churches should therefore be asking God and themselves what they should be doing both to reach their own area and to send missionaries to other parts of the world. A re-evaluation of our missionary responsibility and role should be continuous. Thus a growing partnership of churches will develop and the universal character of Christ's church will be more clearly exhibited. We also thank God for agencies which labour in Bible translation, theological education, the mass media, Christian literature, evangelism, missions, church renewal and other specialist fields. They too should engage in constant self-examination to evaluate their effectiveness as part of the church's mission.'
(Rom. 1: 8; Phil. 1: 5, 4: 15; Acts 13: 1–3; I Thess. 1: 6–8)
(LAUSANNE COVENANT, CLAUSE 8)

We have seen the end of one missionary era; we are beginning a new one in which the idea of world mission will be fundamental.[1]

WHEN EMILIO CASTRO first made this statement almost two years ago in Bangkok '73 (World Conference on Salvation Today), no one would have dared predict that a year and a half later evangelicals from all over the world would make a similar affirmation. Indeed, the original version of Castro's statement caused evangelicals all over the world to raise their eyebrows. But as he later clarified his point in the *International Review of Mission*, he was pointing to a phenomenon that evangelicals also had to recognise at Lausanne '74: the missionary enterprise was at last becoming the business of the whole church.

Lausanne was not another Bangkok. Both events had their own unique styles, their own strengths and weaknesses. Each could learn from the mistakes of the other. Nevertheless, they both recognised the dawning of a new missionary era and the fact that 'the dominant role of western missions is fast disappearing'.[2] Each emphasised different aspects of this new era. For Bangkok '73, it was the new situation of missionary interdependence.

In Mexico City the phrase was coined: Mission in six continents. Now we realise that the missionary situation in Sweden is also the responsibility of the Christian

Church in Africa, Asia or Latin America, and that when
we come to reflect on the possibilities open to us in the
local situation we must remember that we have at our
disposal the resources of the world church.[3]

Lausanne '74 stressed, on the other hand, the responsibility
of all the churches not only to help each other in the evangelisation of their respective areas, but to send missionaries
to other parts of the world to the 2,700 million who have yet
to be evangelised. Both recognised, nevertheless, the need
for greater co-operation in a world-wide evangelistic partnership.

Why an Evangelistic Partnership?

Let us specify the main reasons, as I see them, why an evangelistic partnership between the churches around the world
is needed today.

The Fact of World Mission

There is, first of all, the plain fact of a *world* mission. Contrary to the fears implied in several recent publications,[4] the
missionary enterprise is not coming to an end. It is very
much alive, not as the private possession of the Western[5]
churches, but as an intercontinental phenomenon.

According to a recently published study,[6] there were in
1972 2,971 *reported* missionaries from the Third World,
representing 203 sending agencies. These figures are very
conservative, however, if one considers the fact that out of
697 letters and questionnaires that were sent out, only 245
responded (or 34.1 per cent). Even so, they were sufficiently
potent to permit Michael Griffith to state:

The striking fact brought out by this book is that there
are now far more Asian missionaries today in 1972 (quite
apart from those from Africa and Latin America) than

there were missionaries from Europe in the whole of the Third World in 1810.[7]

1810 was the year for which William Carey proposed a World Mission Conference at the Cape of Good Hope. But if such a conference had been held, not only would there have been no indigenous representatives from Africa, Asia and Latin America, but even North America, which in 1971 had 27,000 missionaries (out of a total of 43,000), would probably not have had any representatives, since in that year the first missionary society (the American Board of Commissioners for Foreign Missions) was organised in Anglo-Saxon America.[8]

There are those who might say, what are 3,000 plus missionaries from the Third World compared to 43,000 from the First World?[9] To which one must respond, not much if one limits oneself to cold statistics. But considering the fact that these new missionaries are coming out of the lands of exploitation and oppression, poverty and backwardness, representing churches which did not even exist 164 years ago; and considering that not only the number of missionaries from the Third World but also the number of new indigenous societies is increasing at a tremendous rate, then its significance can be fully appreciated. Little wonder that Virgil Gerber has referred to this phenomenon as being 'no longer a "snowballing" development', but reaching ' "avalanche" proportions!'[10]

The Biblical Imperative of World Mission

An evangelistic partnership, secondly, is required by the biblical imperative of world mission. The fact that God's redemptive mission to the world constitutes the central thrust of the economy (plan) of salvation puts world evangelism in the centre of the life and action of the church. This has at least two implications.

On the one hand, it implies a necessary awareness of God's redemptive commitment to man not as an abstract concept, but as a historical being. This is the only perspective from which Jesus of Nazareth the historical person can be understood. He is *Emmanuel*, God with us, God becoming man (specifically a Jew), and identifying himself with the sufferings and woes of men and women in order to redeem them through his death on the cross.

As the centre of God's redemptive action, Jesus Christ comes through the Holy Spirit to all men and women in their concrete human situations. This is so because sin (man's alienation from God and neighbour) is revealed therein. Redemption (man's liberation from his alienating situation), must, therefore, also be manifested in the concrete human situation.

God's mission is no spiritualistic, escapist, non-historical enterprise. Rather, it is oriented towards and realised in the concrete situations of sin. It wants to transform man *historically*, that is, not only religiously (in his relationship to the transcendent God), but socially, psychologically and culturally as well. Little wonder then that the New Testament describes the ultimate goal of God's purpose in Christ in terms of the creation of a new humanity.

The centrality of God's redemptive mission in the message of the Bible also underscores the importance of the church as a missionary agent. Indeed, the church herself is a direct result of the missionary enterprise and by her very life a living witness of God's redemptive action in Christ. She is called not only to be a living word (cf. 'living stones', I Pet. 2: 5, but to proclaim 'the wonderful deeds of him' who called her 'out of darkness into his marvellous light' (I Pet. 2: 9).

The church is in her very essence a missionary (sent-out) community. Given her multiple expressions in the world, however, she is exhorted to witness to the oneness of the Gospel by maintaining 'the unity of the Spirit in the bond of peace' (Eph. 4: 3). This is no forced ecumenical reading of the New Testament, but rather a fundamental aspect of the church's participation in God's mission. The church is called to be one in mission because the God whose name she speaks is *one* God (John 17: 21), the faith that she proclaims is *one* faith (Eph. 4: 5) and the world to which she is sent is broken, divided and disintegrated. How then is the church to be a sign of reconciliation (cf. Eph. 2: 11 ff.; II Cor. 5: 16 f.)

if she is herself divided in her witness? The church must be one in mission so that the world may believe that Jesus Christ is indeed the Son of God and, consequently, the hope of mankind (cf. John 17: 21; Col. 1: 15 ff.).

Millions Beyond the Frontiers of the Faith

Thirdly, partnership is needed because of the millions around the world who have not yet had the opportunity of receiving the Good News and responding favourably or unfavourably to its call to repentance and faith. One cannot 'pay lip service' to the biblical imperative of world mission and remain unmoved by the fact that after 2,000 years two thirds of mankind have yet to have a chance to consider the Gospel as an option for their lives.

I am referring not only to the millions who have literally never heard, but also to the millions who are geographically near, but live on distant socio-cultural frontiers. To say, for example, the de-Christianised masses of the West have had ample opportunity to reasonably consider the option of the Christian faith is to oversimplify the complex reality of western society, with its fantastic input from the mass media, the socio-cultural road blocks in the clusters of men and women that make up the western mosaic and the psychological distance which syncretistic religious tradition has brought about between them and the faith of the New Testament.

I am also referring to those who confess to be religiously Christian, but who have never personally experienced the Gospel. This includes for instance, the masses of nominal Christians who go to church once or twice a year at the most: the so-called popular Catholic and Protestant masses; and the thousands in hetero-Christian religious bodies in Latin and Anglo-America, Europe, the Philippines and parts of Africa.

When all of these millions are put together, we begin to realise that much more than two thirds of mankind still needs to be evangelised. Who is going to accomplish this tremendous task? How? With what resources?

Of course, these questions can be brushed aside by simply

answering, the church. But the church is scattered in little communities all over the world (the churches) which much too often spend more time bickering with one another about the faith than living and sharing it with the world! Obviously, in order for the church to live up to her calling and rise up to the challenge of the millions who are beyond the frontiers of the faith, the *churches* have got to join in a world-wide evangelistic partnership.

The Mutuality of Gifts

Fourthly, the Holy Spirit has endowed the churches with manifold, complementary gifts. He has not only given to each church the saving gifts (faith, love, hope), the traditional ecclesial gifts (evangelists, apostles, teachers and pastors; cf. Eph. 4: 11ff.) and the many operational gifts listed in I Cor. 12–14 and Rom. 12ff; he has also endowed them with complementary socio-economic and cultural gifts. To some, he has given an effective manpower which is able to penetrate frontiers closed to the rest. To others, he has given financial resources able to make possible the strategic endeavour of the former. To all of them, he has given many collective and individual talents capable of mutually enriching the life and ministry of one another.

Properly exercised, these gifts should be more than adequate to enable the churches to get the task done. Given the varieties of situations in which the churches find themselves, they could engage in a world-wide evangelistic effort that would surpass the impressive impact of the Christian faith upon the Roman world.

Tragically, however, the churches have yet to mobilise their *mutual* resources in a joint evangelistic partnership. To be sure, there have been and are impressive co-operative efforts. But they fall short, qualitatively and quantitatively, of the potential and the need.

Earlier in this chapter I referred to the fact that world evangelism is increasingly becoming the business of the whole church. But is it not an equally impressive fact that this is taking place under a tremendous burden, on the one part, and alongside a tremendous waste on the other? Can the fact go unnoticed that while younger, financially poor, but humanly rich churches in the Third World spend all they have to send a *limited* number of missionaries to places where they are better received and for whose evangelisation they are better equipped, older, financially rich, but humanly impotent (due to their historic-cultural backgrounds) churches spend millions on their own pet projects at home and on sending thousands from among their own, even though they may be *evangelistically* ineffective?

The issue is not whether or not the younger churches should be commended for their sacrifice of love. It is not whether the physical presence of the whole church is needed as a testimony to the unity of the church; nor whether the churches should or should not be equally responsible for the evangelisation of their respective areas; nor the historical fact that the Christian faith has tended to expand faster when the churches have had limited financial resources at their disposal. The issue is rather whether such a disproportionate missionary endeavour is an adequate response to the imperative of world mission; whether it is a responsible exercise of the manifold gifts which the Holy Spirit has given the churches; and whether the churches can ever expect to get the job done so long as they have such a poor stewardship of the gifts that God has entrusted to them for the fulfilment of his redemptive mission to the world.

On What Basis?

It is obvious, therefore, that an evangelistic partnership is not only necessary but imperative. The question is, however, on what basis can such a partnership take place? This is a very important question, for a partnership is basically an agreement between two or more parties in relation to a particular enterprise. We have already defined the nature of the enterprise. We have indentified the partners. We have even touched upon the theological and historical content of the partnership. We must now consider the operational requirements.

A Dynamic, Multifaceted Vision

All human enterprises respond to a particular vision of reality. This vision is, in turn, the result of a previous analysis of that reality. This may or may not be consciously recognised by those caught up in the action, but it is not enough to rest on a general vision of the lost. Let me explain why.

As I suggested above, the lost are not an abstraction. They are concrete human beings in varying historical circumstances. Their so-called lostness varies quantitatively as well as qualitatively.

Lostness varies quantitatively because, as the Church Growth movement reminds us, people live in 'homogeneous unity'. To be sure, these units are also heterogeneous, multiplying content-wise in an incredible number of forms. Thus, within an ethnic group there may be sub-units of an economic, family, political-ideological or educational nature which may have direct or indirect links with other ethnic units or sub-units. Yet, when we pose the quantitative question (how many are lost), we have to look around for these units and sub-units, because that is where people are to be found. The personal lostness of the people is linked to their socio-cultural context. When people are lost, they are lost as members of particular groups; when they are saved they are saved as members of their respective groups. Thus Jesus commands us to teach the 'nations' (Matt. 28: 19). And it is in this same context that we must understand the mourning of the tribes of the earth at the second coming of Christ (cf. Matt. 24: 30) and the worshipping multitude 'from every nation, from all tribes and peoples and tongues' (cf. Rev. 7: 9ff.).

The question, then, is not merely how many persons are lost, but how many are lost *within the specific segments* of the human family.

We immediately encounter the qualitative dimension. People are lost not only in their socio-cultural contexts, but also in degrees. This does not mean, of course, that we lose sight of the sharpness of the biblical notions of 'being' and 'not-being' in Christ. There is a cutting, radical difference between being lost and being saved that does not allow for any degrees. One is either saved or he is not.

At the same time we must not forget Rom. 1: 24ff, and II Cor. 3: 18. There are levels of the experience of perdition just as there are degrees of experiencing salvation. There are those who are 'near' and those who are 'far off' (cf. Eph. 2: 17), just as salvation is experienced as a constant change into the likeness of Christ 'from one degree of glory to another' (II Cor. 3: 18).

What does this mean in the context of evangelism?

It means, on the one hand, that we need to be *aware* of the state of people's lostness. We need to understand their situations of sin, for 'sin ... brings forth death' (Jas. 1: 15) There is a correspondence between sin and repentance just as there is between sin and lostness. The forms which repentance from sin takes vary in accordance to the situation of sin. To the adulterous woman Jesus said, 'Go, and do not sin again' (John 8: 11), but to the rich young ruler he said, 'Sell all that you have and distribute it to the poor ... and come, follow me' (Luke 18: 22). Likewise, there are those whose sins have so blinded them that their hearts have become hardened, so that seeing, they do not perceive, and hearing, they do not understand (John 12: 38ff.).

This means, furthermore, that some groups are harder to reach than others. Their situation is much more complicated, their level of religious understanding denser and their resistence to the Gospel, therefore, stronger, so that one must have much patience, endurance and faith in their evangelisation.

Moreover, the qualitative question relates to the various unreached areas in the church's very life. In the Old Testament, the prophets were constantly calling Israel to renew her vows, to repent from her sins and be *converted* to Yahweh! In the New Testament, while the term conversion is primarily used in reference to the new birth, it is also used, together with other similar terms (*e.g.* repentance), in relation to believers. Why? Because there is a sense in which the church has to be constantly evangelised. As Al Krass has suggested, there are many in the church 'who have (partially) heard the gospel and (partially) accepted Christ as

Lord'.[11] In fact, all confessing Christians in one way or another fall into this category. Accordingly, we 'always need to be listening for "more light and truth to break forth from God's holy Word" '.[12]

A Spirit of Mutuality

This comprehensive vision both produces and is the result of a spirit of mutuality between the churches. On the one hand, as the churches begin to see the immense number of the unreached; as they discover their own unevangelised sectors; as they become aware of the multifaceted evangelistic situations, they realise the need for partnership in order to tackle the challenge. On the other hand, their mutual willingness to learn from one another, to search for and understand the present evangelistic frontiers, enables them to see in perspective the challenge of world evangelism.

The lack of this spirit of mutuality is produced in part by the churches' inadequate awareness of the world and of themselves and in part by their provincialism and self-centredness. It is keeping many churches separate from one another and, consequently, from sharing their God-given gifts in a world-wide evangelistic partnership.

A Continuous Re-evaluation

This is why the churches need to continuously evaluate themselves. They need to lift up their eyes to analyse the world, to better understand each other, to discover their weak points as well as their strengths. This effort alone can guarantee the growth of a dynamic, multifaceted vision and a spirit of mutual respect and love which will, in turn, lead to and fortify a partnership in mission.

This brings us to another question: if this partnership is not only necessary but imperative for the advance of the Gospel, how can it be realised? In which direction must the churches move in order to set it in motion?

In Which Direction?

Right away it must be confessed that there are no easy answers. Nevertheless, the following principles can help open the way for a more effective, world-wide, co-operative evangelistic action.

Multiple Strategies for Varying Situations

First, to fit the varying situations in which people find themselves, the churches need to develop multiple evangelistic strategies. This involves not only methods, but also goals, manpower, materials and tactical approaches.

The question of goals is of utmost importance, because without them an enterprise can lose its sense of direction, and also because they are the fundamental prerequisite for a sound process of evaluation. In evangelism, we need to distinguish between two kinds of goals: *ultimate* goals have to do with the comprehensive objectives of God's redemptive mission to the world; *penultimate* goals are those things which the churches feel they must do as missionary communities sent out to witness in word and deed to the Gospel among the peoples of the earth, to invite them to accept the salvation which it proclaims and to integrate into their fellowship those who respond affirmatively.

Since people live in different contexts, penultimate goals vary from one place to another. The churches must first analyse their specific areas of endeavour in the world and set their goals according to the needs of the particular situation. At the same time the churches must also analyse their own internal discipleship needs and set appropriate evangelistic goals in response to them. There will be, then, a multiplicity of goals whose realisation will require people with varying skills, multiple materials and many tactical approaches.

To effectively make disciples in the world, the churches need to be developed evangelistically. They must be constantly on the lookout for internal inconsistencies, continuously making disciples in their own constituencies and training them for mission. They must engage in never-ending analysis and evaluation of their stewardship performance and potential. They must always try to discover the manifold gifts which the Spirit bestows upon the individual believers and the churches as a whole, praying for and looking up to the Spirit's guidance as to the best way of distributing these resources for their maximum effectiveness in the evangelistic enterprise. The traditional separation between Christian education, social concern, worship, pastoral care, stewardship (or church administration) and evangelisation will thus be broken down as the churches develop multiple strategies to meet the challenge of each situation in faithfulness to the comprehensiveness of God's mission.

Multiple Ministries for a Multi-dimensional Task

This leads to the second principle. Given the comprehensiveness of the task, there needs to be not only a complete understanding of the church's life in mission, but a pluralistic approach to the Christian ministry. In other words, the activities of the churches need to be integrated so as to contribute to the fulfilment of their witnessing vocation. The ministry must also be understood in relation to the whole of God's mission. Accordingly, multiple ministries need to be developed to fit the multiple dimensions of the task.

If, as James Hopewell has said, 'Ministry is the gift received in mission',[13] then the churches must seek to discover and cultivate the gifts that the Spirit entrusts to them so that they may implement the strategies for their missionary engagement that are developed in response to the varying needs of life. The search for and the cultivation of new ministries is as endless as the need to develop new strategies and as dynamic as the operations of the Spirit.

The very idea of new ministries, however, has always constituted a touchy point in ecclesiastical circles, as is illustrated by the notion of specialised ministries. In many ways, all ecclesial ministries are specialised because they are special gifts of the Spirit. The ministries outlined in Ephesians 4: 11ff. are given in order to help the church fulfil the multiple dimensions of her witnessing vocation. These gifts, however, have too often been rigidly defined. Even though the gifts have always had multiple and dynamic expressions in response to the challenges of history, stereotypes have been formed which overshadow and push them aside. These varieties of ministries have thus been labelled 'specialised' agencies, because the churches have been too committed to traditional definitions of what constitutes a pastor, an evangelist, a teacher and a modern apostle (missionary).

We need to recapture the multifaceted nature of the ministry and recover its place within the church's witnessing vocation. We must recognise that as the gift of the Spirit in mission, the ministry cannot be bound to the needs of past historical situations, nor to the limited missiological conceptions of past generations. As God's redemptive mission is oriented to the multiple situations of the human family and is, therefore, multi-dimensional, so the ministry is oriented to the changing situations of life and must have, accordingly, multi-dimensional manifestations.

Such a rediscovery and acknowledgment of the so-called 'specialised' ministries of our day — Bible translation, theological education, youth work, Christian literature work, radio, TV, film and other aspects of the mass media, mass evangelism, counselling, foreign missionary service, Christian social action, etc. — will enable us to understand them as contemporary forms of the ministries outlined in Ephesians 4: 11ff., as witnessing resources of the church. It will also help remove the fear that so many ecclesiastical bodies have about competition from the 'specialised' agencies (*i.e.*, that the latter will take away human and financial resources). The rediscovery of the pluri*formal* reality of the ministry will make possible the rediscovery of the pluri-*structural* manifestations of the church. This, in turn, will unveil the ecclesiological character of the para-ecclesiastical agencies as supplementary manifestations of the church in mission and witnessing partners of the churches which are to be taken into account in any evangelistic partnership.

Multiple Forms of Evangelistic Partnerships

Thus we come to the third principle: if the task is multi-dimensional, requiring multiple ministries and strategies to fit the varying situations of life, then it follows that multiple forms of evangelistic partnerships are needed.

One of the erroneous missiological assumptions of the church in the twentieth century has been the idea that the biblical imperative and the practical need for a partnership in mission can only be expressed organisationally. Thus early in this century mainline Protestants began to organise local and regional councils of churches. In 1948, the World Council of Churches was formed. In 1958, the International Missionary Council, which brought together para-ecclesiastical agencies in a missionary partnership, was integrated into the WCC to give the latter a missionary perspective. Evangelicals, for their part, have organised their own local, regional and world fellowships, but have not limited them to ecclesiastical organisations. In fact, some (*e.g.* the Evangelical Alliance of Great Britain) do not have any organisational members; they are fellowships of individuals. Not being sufficiently satisfied with the structural possibilities of the World Evangelical Fellowship,[14] however, a continuing committee was formed at Lausanne '74 to attempt to carry on the Congress's vision of an evangelistic partnership between the churches.[15]

It must be asked, however, whether this concept of partnership is comprehensive enough to embrace the dynamics and multi-dimensions of the task and the need for a pluri-formal ministry to execute multiple evangelistic strategies through pluristructural expressions of the church. Even the WCC's Commission on World Mission and Evangelism (heir of the former IMC) had to realise that partnership does not depend on any form of ecclesiastical organisation. Rather, it depends on the willingness of believers, persons and collectivities, ecclesiastical and para-ecclesiastical entities, to work together for the evangelisation of the world in concrete human situations through the exercise of particular ministries and in accordance with strategies designed for these specific ends. Isn't it time that evangelicals learn the same lesson?

We need, therefore, not one but multiple forms of evangelistic partnership. These forms will vary in scope and orientation. Some of them will be geographical in scope, bringing together churches and agencies for the evangelisation of particular regions. Others will be socio-cultural, focusing their co-operative efforts on specific socio-cultural frontiers where the Gospel has not yet penetrated. Others will be *intra-ecclesiarum*. They will be oriented towards the evangelisation of lost areas within the churches, the renewal and transformation of not only those who claim to be in Christ yet show a shallow faith, but also of the lifestyle of the total community.

Such partnerships will also vary time-wise. Some will be for short periods of time; others will be more permanent.

They will also need to be cross-cultural and use multiple resources. In other words, they will need to represent co-operative efforts between continents and between churches and agencies with different types of resources, gifts and needs. This will accentuate not only the inter-dependence of the church, but also the mutuality of responsibilities.

Given the technological propensity of our world, however, a question is bound to emerge: Who is going to see that all of these different forms of partnership are carried out? My answer is very simple yet profound: God! Since the mission is his, he is actively involved through the Holy Spirit in the planning and outworking of its particular dimensions.

This is no simple pietistic reductionism; it is a profound affirmation of faith. No evangelistic effort is outside the boundaries of the Spirit. It is he who from of old has stirred up the church, dispersed in mission, to join in co-operative efforts of evangelisation. And it is he who today is making all sorts of Christians from different regions, cultures, ecclesiastical traditions, socio-political contexts and professional backgrounds aware of the need for pluriformal evangelistic partnerships. He is, furthermore, helping them to form such co-operative enterprises. Some of these may directly involve one *or more* of the existing inter-ecclesiastical, inter-agency or inter-personal-national or interpersonal-global organisations (*e.g.* WEF, WCC, EFMA-IFMA, *Deutscher Evangelischer Missions-Rat*, etc.). Some may have only an indirect relationship; others may have no relation whatever.

There is, for example, the Evangelical Community for Apostolic Action (CEVAA — *Communauté Evangelique d'Action Apostolic*). This consortium of churches in Africa, the Pacific, France, Italy and Switzerland was formerly associated with the Paris Evangelical Missionary Society, and has now come together for the purpose of bearing a united African-Pacific-European witness. Thus far they have been engaged in two missionary projects in Dahomey and France and are preparing to open up a third 'front' in the Pacific.

A Latin American counterpart of CEVAA is the Latin American Community of Evangelical Ministries (CLAME — *Comunidad Latinoamericana de Ministerios Evangélicos*). It also has taken over the work of a missionary society. Unlike the former, however, where the parent organisation went out of existence, in CLAME the Latin American Mission-USA and -Canada did not cease to exist structurally. Rather they became members of the Community with specific tasks assigned to them. Moreover, CLAME is a consortium of para-ecclesiastical agencies *and* churches. Its work, though oriented towards the evangelisation of Latin America, is more diversified and not as tightly organised. Some of its member entities have already formed or are beginning to form more specifically evangelistic partnerships between themselves and/or with other entities not related to the Community.

This is the case of the Institute of In-depth Evangelism, which has invited a team from Africa Enterprise, a South and East African evangelistic organisation dedicated to mass evangelism, to collaborate in an evangelistic effort among the Afro-Caribbean communities of Costa Rica and Nicaragua. Africa Enterprise will also be collaborating in the near future with an Indian evangelistic association in a series of evangelistic efforts in Central India.

Other examples could be cited: the International Fellowship of Evangelical Students, one of the oldest international co-operative ventures in student evangelism; the inter-Asian

missionary association that was formed as a result of the All
Asia Mission Consultation in 1973 to help promote and co-
ordinate the missionary cause among Asian evangelical
Christians, and many others. These suffice, however, to illustrate how in our day the Holy Spirit is bringing together
church bodies, para-ecclesiastical organisations and groups
of individual Christians in concerted efforts of evangelisation.

Instead of spending endless energy and precious resources
on setting up additional expensive global machinery to promote the cause of world evangelisation and to stimulate co-
operative evangelistic efforts between the churches and
para-church agencies, we should all concentrate our efforts
on searching the Lord's mind to see where his Spirit is draw-
ing us *all* to participate with other believers in the evangelisation of the world. For it is 'Not by might, nor by
power, but by my Spirit, says the Lord of hosts' (Zech.
4: 6).

CHAPTER IX

The Urgency
of the Evangelistic Task

John Gatu

'MORE THAN 2,700 million people, which is more than two
thirds of mankind, have yet to be evangelised. We are
ashamed that so many have been neglected; it is a standing
rebuke to us and to the whole church. There is now, however, in many parts of the world an unprecedented receptivity to the Lord Jesus Christ. We are convinced that this is
the time for churches and para-church agencies to pray
earnestly for the salvation of the unreached and to launch
new efforts to achieve world evangelisation. A reduction of
foreign missionaries and money in an evangelised country
may sometimes be necessary to facilitate the national
church's growth in self-reliance and to release resources for
unevangelised areas. Missionaries should flow ever more
freely from and to all six continents in a spirit of humble
service. The goal should be, by all available means and at
the earliest possible time, that every person will have the
opportunity to hear, understand, and receive the good news.
We cannot hope to attain this goal without sacrifice. All of
us are shocked by the poverty of millions and disturbed by
the injustices which cause it. Those of us who live in affluent
circumstances accept our duty to develop a simple life-style

in order to contribute more generously to both relief and evangelism.'

(*John* 9: 4; *Matt.* 9: 35–38; *Rom.* 9: 1–3; *I Cor.* 9: 19–23; *Mark* 16: 15; *Isa.* 58: 6, 7; *Jas.* 1: 27; 2: 1–9; *Matt.* 25: 31–46; *Acts* 2: 44, 45; 4: 34, 35)

(LAUSANNE COVENANT, CLAUSE 9)

ARTICLE 9 OF THE Lausanne Covenant recognised the urgency of the evangelistic task by quoting statistics showing the number of people who have yet to be evangelised (2,700 million), admitting that this is a standing rebuke to the whole church. It also acknowledged the unprecedented receptivity to the Lord Jesus Christ at present, a phenomenon that is being widely echoed in Africa today. In declaring the need for prayer that the church should be enabled to meet the challenge, the Covenant stated, 'We are convinced that this is the time for churches and para-church agencies to pray earnestly for the salvation of the unreached and to launch new efforts to achieve world evangelisation.' The article was not reluctant to refer to the problem of foreign missionaries and funds which is today characterised by the famous 'Moratorium Debate'. It could, however, only recommend 'a reduction' of foreign missionaries and funds, instead of the debated issue of 'withdrawal'. Thus, although the problem of foreign missionaries and funds was recognised, it was not fully dealt with in the Congress. Nevertheless, I felt that this showed a promising change in attitude on the part of the evangelicals. I hadn't really expected them to face the issue, at least not during the first few days of the Congress.

The article went on to say, 'The goal should be, by all available means and at the earliest possible time, that every person will have the opportunity to hear, understand and receive the good news. We cannot hope to attain this goal without sacrifice.' This paper is an attempt to further investigate the situation and, in the light of today's experience, to see where we go from here.

Urgency and Mobilisation

Christians need to be reminded of the urgency of the evangelistic task as many times as possible. We must recognise that this was the motivation that kept the early church alive. There was urgency and therefore the need to mobilise all possible resources; this included the sharing of property about which we read in Acts. This urgency also marked their commitment to the Great Commission, 'Go ye,' and the Great Command, 'Love your neighbour.' (It is important that these two go together: if not, our concern will be in vain.) But while all this is true, the Christian must have the inspiration which is only found in the risen Christ whose Gospel we proclaim. The joy of that proclamation is our commission.

'When Christians keep silent instead of speaking about the tremendous experience of the risen Christ, they withhold from men the very best thing that they can give them.'[1] This is not to say that evangelism is 'speaking only', for the 'proclamation of the good news of Jesus Christ' should be by word and deed to the whole world and to the local man to the end that all may believe in him and be saved.

In attempting to meet this need, many methods are now being employed in various parts of the world. These range from the normal missionary concept of western personnel going to areas of the Third World to Third World missionaries going to the countries of the West. There is also the ecumenical sharing of personnel designed by the World Council of Churches, the coming together of mission boards and churches in Francophone Africa, Guellilar for Christ, Campus Crusade for Christ, as well as such large-scale organisations as the Billy Graham Association and Africa Enterprise. One must thank God for the enthusiasm that motivates these organisations and the challenge they feel to proclaim the Good News. But in the context of a situation already bedevilled by denominational rivalries and competition, the coming of yet 'another label' onto the scene too often means further division and a weakening of our Christian witness in a world that has never before so needed the Good News. Consequently, the reaching of the unreached is delayed. The solution, therefore, must not be seen in inviting more groups to participate but rather in mobilising the potential that the church already has. Whatever methods that are found to be appropriate can be used. These may well be borrowed from other people's experience, but adapted to the needs of the locality where the mission of God is taking place. What we are recommending is the responsibility of the local Christian community to rise to the challenge before it, instead of importing further theological and denominational differences. Consequently, our first priority must be to 'evangelise' the church.

The experience of the East Africa revival is a good example. After the church was challenged about its coldness and self-complacency, evangelism became not only the duty and responsibility of the pastor or the full-time evangelist employed by the church, but the urgent task of every committed Christian who had now come to know the Lord afresh. Evangelism then continued in the buses, market places, prison and detention camps, hospitals, etc. People did not need to be enlisted into the preaching mission, but each one in his own corner was a proclaimer of the good news.

The Situation Today

We certainly need such an outpouring of the Spirit before we can talk about proclaiming the Good News. But we must realise that the situation is very complex. Speaking to the All Africa Conference of Churches assembly at Lusaka, Zambia, the General Secretary, the Rev. Canon Burgess Carr, had this to say:

Never before have we been able to speak about the reality

of the church in Africa with as much confidence as we do today. The phenomenal growth of Christianity now taking place on our continent and the pervasive influence of the church upon every aspect of our societies, certify that, this time, Christianity has come to stay in Africa.

But there are several disturbing paradoxes. At the same moment that we welcome the spreading of Christianity throughout Africa, we are also painfully aware that the acceptance of the Faith has meant outright rejection of Africa's soul. As a consequence there is a deep spiritual crisis, indeed a crisis of faith, in the church in Africa just at the time when we are witnessing the most rapid growth of the Christian faith ever recorded in all its history. Second and third generation Christians are rebelling against the illegitimate and un-Christian violence done to our traditional customs.[2]

The enthusiastic missionary of the nineteenth century assumed that the African had no history and therefore no religion. This made him forget the African past and introduce the 'European present' clothed in the religious garb of the day. In a book describing the early times in Mashonaland, a missionary writes:

The religious notions of the Mashonas in these parts . . . are very vague. When a person dies he is interred just outside the kraal and over his grave a low hut is built and this becomes the place of prayer for the friends and relatives of the deceased. At certain seasons of the year they bring beer and meal as an offering and hope by this means to gain his favour and help in their daily life. But religion as a controlling, power-giving comfort in sorrow, victory over sin, and hope for the future — of all this, they are totally ignorant and only the light of the gospel can disperse their darkness.[3]

One would have thought that instead of disregarding this religious tradition, the missionary might have realised this opportunity to follow the basic teaching principle of moving from the known to the unknown. That is, he might have seen that the Mashona death traditions provided him with a wonderful starting point to speak about the Man who died 'at the gate', Jesus Christ.

The total blindness to indigenous factors which characterised this approach is once again expressed by another writer:

It was no use beginning with the profound truths of theology. These people with centuries of barbarism behind them, and with the bias of their moral nature so set against godliness, are at first incapable of comprehending even those plain religious facts which appear so self-evident to every Christian child. I told them the 'old, old story' of redemption, but even this was above their grasp. I spoke of sin and repentance and forgiveness; they only smiled and looked puzzled.[4]

One must ask if the missionary had bothered to look for another 'old, old story' indigenous to the Mashonas of Rhodesia which would have made his 'new story' more comprehensible.

In Asia there were written records of both a religious and secular nature. Africa, however, was presumed to have had no culture since 'writing' as known in the West, did not exist. Neither time nor effort was expended to discover and understand the African background. The evangelical zeal was such that everything was wiped out in order, as it were, to start with a clean slate. Yet in doing so African referential and expressive symbols were ignored. Broom and Selznick have defined these kinds of symbols as follows:

Referential symbols are denotative, they are words or objects that have a specific reference, they are instrumental. *Portable typewriter* is a referential symbol, it is a convenient way of referring to a specific class of objects. Expressive symbols are connotative. They evoke associations that are diffuse and open-ended rather than specific and limited. The word *professor* denotes one who holds a position on faculty but the same word connotes a wide range of associations, not fully specified, suggesting authority, knowledge and wisdom ... A symbol invested with connotation evokes responses that are personally meaningful, that is, the connotations are experienced by the persons as comforting or threatening, uplifting or degrading.[5]

Had these symbols been utilised, they would have made the Gospel very much at home in Africa. As it is, however, the Gospel has been made so foreign as to create the all too prevalent crisis we see among third-generation Christians who consider Christianity a foreign religion. These symbols still exist in Africa: tonal music and proverbs and idioms which although varying from tribe to tribe represent the cultural heritage of the African people are two examples. Our task today is to uncover and utilise these symbols so that the Gospel may truly take root in Africa.

Under the acculturalisation programme being carried out by the Mobutu regime in Zaire, everyone is asked to renounce his western baptismal name. While we may disagree with the programme we must admit that the giving of western names for baptism brought with it another kind of 'colonisation'. In many cases the baptismal name was turned into the surname, and consequently family connections were religiously and psychologically severed. These may not be very major issues to discuss here, but they definitely show us some of the hypotheses formulated in previous missionary enterprise which make the proclamation doubly difficult. That is, we must not only proclaim, but also try to put right the former hypotheses and misconceptions.

Pressing Issues

In this light, we see that there must be a total revolution in the life of our churches to enable them in good conscience to go out to others. This brings me to some of the issues that must be tackled immediately. The past relationships between mission boards and the local churches have left us with certain legacies. Some of these are good, but others very questionable. Those that are questionable must be faced before it is too late. In his book, *The Missionary Factor in East Africa*, Roland Oliver discusses the influence of the colonial government on the colonies, and the relationship of those governments to the missionary movement, and the dangers inherent in such relationships. In his Introduction he states:

> Superficially at least, it would seem that there has been a remarkable contrast between the institutional stability of the churches in East Africa and the rapidity of political change within the African states. In the political field the scene has changed since independence almost beyond recognition ... It is not merely that colonial governments have been replaced by African ones. It is that the political model presented by the colonial power has been deliberately cast aside. Democracy on the Westminster pattern has been abandoned even as a goal. The current political philosophy is that of the single revolutionary party, dominating the central legislative, permeating the civil service and the armed forces and exercising through party officials a detailed control over the provincial and district administration. The churches however, have undergone no such drastic changes. Africans have progressively taken the places of Europeans, but have continued to do the same jobs and to teach the same doctrines.[6]

For Oliver, the fact that the African church continues to teach the same doctrines and that Africans are doing the same jobs as Europeans were doing, seems to be a sign of health in the East Africa Church! However, without giving a value judgment on the present trend of African political developments or questioning individual interpretations of democracy, one must admit that the church as a human organism cannot remain stagnant while the environment around it is changing so very rapidly. True, we shall not change the doctrine of the Trinity, but we must find a way of interpreting such doctrines in the form, method and approach which are most meaningful to the local people of God in that given area. Old structures will therefore have to disappear for new ones to be born. We shall have to lay aside all that hinders us, all that makes it difficult for us to be fully engaged in the total mission of the people of God and, particularly, in evangelism.

For example, hospitals and schools and other specialised activities in many parts of the Third World have for many years been the concern of the churches. While there may yet be some places where this church involvement may be required, the church must never continue certain programmes just because 'they are part of our organisation', whatever that organisation may be. It might be important to maintain a school with a strong evangelical tradition in a dominantly Muslim country, but the church would not stand to lose in a situation where a government can run these schools and yet allow the church to be involved in character and conduct formation as well as the pastoral care of both the teachers and the pupils in any given area. This has already happened in some countries, yet it is a very well known fact that we have continued to hold on to traditional activities in order to keep 'our flag', and thus, our pride. We must examine ourselves to see whether in such cases we are acting upon and living good stewardship principles. 'Christ's evangelists must humbly seek to empty themselves of all but their personal authenticity in order to become servants of others,' says article ten of the Covenant, and this emptying must also occur in the churches which hold to prestigious institutions and positions instead of going out to proclaim Jesus Christ.

In the Third World, too many churches have become and remained 'receiving' churches. We are very fond of receiving personnel and their salaries, gifts of old clothing, equipment, theology and even church organisations and structures. We believe the churches overseas to be wealthy and better off while on the other hand we are poor and need help. While we must reject any attitude of triumphalism and self-sufficiency on our part (about which the apostle John accused the Laodicean church in Revelation 3: 14–22), we must at the same time affirm that when we commit God's work to his own hands and direction, he will find not only money, but also the other necessary resources to complete the task. We must re-read the story of Abraham more seriously these days, especially those of us who call ourselves evangelicals. Abraham left his homeland knowing only that God had told him to do so. He even came to the point where he obeyed God's command to sacrifice his son, and then saw God come to his rescue and provide the needed sacrifice. The point here is not that when a certain person feels he has been called to Africa or Latin America, he should just pack up and go, especially where there is a church already in existence. Rather Abraham's story demonstrates the necessity of the local church to be so determined as to sacrifice all else for the sake of the Gospel. We must move forward with whatever we have before stretching begging hands elsewhere. For too long we have been a sitting church, expecting people to come to us; the disciples of our Lord, however, were an active group involved in a movement of the Holy Spirit, the same Spirit that moves people today. The long-cherished assumption that the churches of the Third World are poor is a fallacy that must be discarded. Efforts must be made to convince our followers of the tremendous wealth of resources we already have that will remain untapped as long as we continue to depend too much on the help from overseas.

In this connection, the paternalism of the so-called sending churches and the subserviency of the receiving churches must also go, along with the imperialistic tendencies that characterised the years of the western colonisation. This is where the selfhood and self-reliance of the local churches comes in, for until we are in a position to see ourselves as an essential part of the body of Christ and not an appendage — which, as we say, is neither in the meat nor in the skin but lives off the main animal — we shall never feel able to participate fully in the mission of God in the world as we see it today. Third World churches have a unique mission in a world of totalitarianism where we face man's possible annihilation and total self-destruction through nuclear warfare, the lack of personal liberty because of the colour of one's skin, the reality of hunger while some are dieting, etc. Only Japan can tell the rest of the world what it means to be faced with nuclear deterrents, having suffered and continuing to suffer the aftermaths of the malady. Only countries like India can effectively talk about problems of teeming millions. We must, therefore, participate in the world mission as those coming from peculiar backgrounds in order to save our brothers of the West, most of whom have already forgotten what it is like to be under the yoke of foreign regimes and governments.

Partnership and its Problems

Article 8 of the Lausanne Covenant dealt with the partnership of the churches in evangelism in saying, 'God is raising up from the younger churches a great new resource for world evangelisation, and is thus demonstrating that the responsibility to evangelise belongs to the whole body of Christ. All churches should therefore be asking God and themselves what they should be doing both to reach their own area and send missionaries to other parts of the world.' The first sentence of that article states that domination by western missions is fast disappearing and that a new era is dawning. It is very easy to think of partnership as a good philosophical change from domination by foreign mission boards, but the practicability of the proposal demands the patience of the dove and the wisdom of Solomon. We could easily use a different terminology but continue the same outdated patterns. For example, attempts have been made to send missionaries from the Third World back to the First World, but some very serious questions have risen in the process.

1. In sending these men and women, are we simply reversing the process, but committing the same mistakes as in the era of great missionary enterprise? This question arises from the suspicion that those from Europe and America feel guilty about the past and in order to make up for it now ask the younger churches to send missionaries to the West. In reality the climate there is far from being truly receptive to these people. The person so sent is in many cases used merely to interpret what the mission board has been doing

in his home country, not to engage in the prophetic evangelistic call that arises from the commission 'Go ye.' Is this fair on the part of the individual?

2. This has acted as a 'brain drain' upon the younger churches at a time when we have the greatest need to use every possible resource to do God's work in the local situation. There have been cases of people holding very responsible positions in their home churches being used in some very minor assignments overseas. This is not a question of status but rather of usefulness and the stewardship of God's talents in the present situation in our countries. One must not forget that even if he does not become a victim of the brain drain, such a person will have serious readjustment problems when he returns to his country. Unlike the missionary from the West who may find it impossible to readjust into society because he is perhaps considered too primitive, outdated or old-fashioned, the person from the Third World has difficulty in adjusting because he is too advanced and sophisticated for the local church. Many have returned home only to resign from the ministry or from the church in order to take secular jobs. The adjustment of a foreign missionary to his own cultural situation may be easier than the other way round. What must we do to eliminate this situation? The problem becomes more pointed when you remember that this affects the witness of the church both locally and overseas, and at the same time robs the local church of the cream of the leadership which is so scarce and therefore very precious.

3. How can there be real partnership in a situation of inequality? It has been argued, and rightly so, that whatever any church possesses in terms of talents, personnel or money belongs to the people of God everywhere. Therefore, in the sharing between two churches that may not be of equal status in terms of wealth, there must not be a continuing domination by the rich churches of the West. This is indeed theologically right, but our historical hang-ups are so entrenched that they make this theological base a very weak foundation. Is there a way in which this partnership can be made more real without undertones of patronage?

4. Although we are all committed to world evangelisation,

it would be unthinkable to proceed blindly today while there is a wealth of information available which those who were involved in early missionary enterprises did not possess. Such problems as the acceptance of contrary value systems which distort the Gospel, our concern for counting heads and writing reports on conversions, forgetting societal and institutionalised sins both in our countries and abroad must be investigated. This is a time of great search for the truth; we cannot continue to give simplistic answers and evade the cardinal problems.

In conclusion then, while we must give praise to God for the achievements of the missionary enterprises of the earlier century, the complex situation of the present one raises serious questions which we must face. We have not reached the point where we can provide a cut and dried answer. The 'Moratorium Debate' is just one way of facing up to such problems and one that has been widely misunderstood. Some have even termed the proposition a denial of the Lord's commission 'Go ye'; others have said it is satanic in that it calls for separation rather than togetherness. We must accept the fact that the debate raises some very fundamental questions which demand a complete revolution in our thinking and approach to mission. The urgency of the evangelistic task demands that we be both honest with each other and honest with God in our attempts to find his guidance for our involvement in his mission. We do so in confidence, for although our world is so different from that of previous centuries we are led by the same changeless God whose instruments we are.

CHAPTER X

Evangelism and Culture

Jacob A. Loewen

'THE DEVELOPMENT OF strategies for world evangelisation calls for imaginative pioneering methods. Under God, the result will be the rise of churches deeply rooted in Christ and closely related to their culture. Culture must always be tested and judged by Scripture. Because man is God's creature, some of his culture is rich in beauty and goodness. Because he has fallen, all of it is tainted with sin and some of it is demonic. The gospel does not presuppose the superiority of any culture according to its own criteria of truth and righteousness, and insists on moral absolutes in every culture. Missions have all too frequently exported with the gospel an alien culture, and churches have sometimes been in bondage to culture rather than to the Scripture. Christ's evangelists must humbly seek to empty themselves of all but their personal authenticity in order to become the servants of others, and churches must seek to transform and enrich culture, all for the glory of God.'
(*Mark 7: 8, 9, 13; Gen. 4: 21, 22; I Cor. 9: 19–23; Phil. 2: 5–7; II Cor. 4: 5*)

(LAUSANNE COVENANT, CLAUSE 10)

'WHAT IN THE world does our attitude towards money have to do with religious syncretism?' a righteously indignant western theologian snorted.

Similar demonstrations of our western blindness to our own cultural hang-ups still raised their ugly heads from time to time at the Lausanne Congress on World Evangelization, but, thanks to God, such outbursts were few. On the whole the Congress was characterised by a new concern for the whole man and by a repentant recognition that we had been failing to appreciate the multiplicity of cultural milieus in which men from different tribes, races and colours feel at home. This more open attitude, still relatively new in evangelical circles, stepped out boldly from the very beginning when in his opening address Dr Billy Graham publicly confessed that in the past he had often failed to separate the Evangel from its American cultural wrapper, and that all too often he had addressed himself only to the needs of men's souls, forgetting the needs of the whole man. It is thus most gratifying to see how often aspects of this new 'whole man' concern are reflected in the Lausanne Covenant (see paragraphs 5–11).

Evangelicals have not always had these attitudes in the past, and their guilt in serious disrespect towards other peoples and their differing cultures, especially in so-called 'mission fields', is clearly spelled out in the Covenant (see paragraphs 5 and 10). Lest some of us still fail to recognise the importance of this new awareness, and others, while having become aware of some of our past failures, fail to appreciate the gravity of these shortcomings in our cross-cultural evangelism, the writer of this paper has been asked: (1) to spell out some of the most critical shortcomings of the past (if not of the present) in our world evangelism efforts; (2) to propose ways of correcting or overcoming these failures; and (3) to suggest some guidelines for indigenous churches on how they can insure that they are reflecting faithfully the instructions of God's Word within their own specific cultural framework.

Past [and Present (?)] Shortcomings

Probably the most serious error, and one which will be very hard for us evangelicals to 'own', is the fact that for all the wonderful things God achieved through the post-Reformation missionary movements, they were really born and nurtured in the imperialistic empire-building atmosphere that permitted western white man to believe he not only had the right, but actually the sacred duty to conquer the world and to civilise it. The link between this empire-building drive to conquer and urge to evangelise the world is, of course, most readily seen in the expansion of the Hispanic-Catholic empires. The conquistador with the sword was habitually accompanied and blessed by the priest with a cross and the baptismal font. To be conquered by the armies of Spain or Portugal was the first step in becoming 'civilised and christianised'. In fact, Catholic theologians of that day constructed elaborate theologies that urged kings to conquer and to christianise the barbarians the world over.

For evangelical missions the link between the expansion of empires and the spreading of mission is not as readily apparent, but it was just as real. In fact, its lesser visibility made it more subtle and possibly even more dangerous. In a recent thesis presented at the University of Amsterdam, a Latin American theologian who studied the thinking on missions of the Reformers and the Puritans reports that they, like their Catholic counterparts, believed and preached that conquest and civilisation must precede evangelisation because 'God cannot dispense his grace to barbarians.' Their model was: conquer, civilise, and evangelise. It is only now — after World War II and the end of colonialism — that the missions themselves have begun to realise just how extensive the symbiosis between them and the conquering and colonising forces of their respective countries actually was.

In fact, it is precisely this comprehensive and highly intricate inter-linking between empire establishment and church-building of the past that today makes it so hard for the people of the many newly independent countries of Africa to extricate the essentials of the Gospel from the colonial-culture wrapper in which they received it. In fact, to many it still seems so much a single package that they are tempted to throw out the 'Gospel baby' together with the 'colonial bath water'. As much as we may hate to admit it, we cannot deny the fact that western evangelical Christianity did its full share in providing the supernatural rationale for colonial domination.

In order to drive home the gravity of this all-pervasive interaction between western Christianity and its western cultural setting, this paper will illustrate two specific areas of culture blindness in some detail. It goes without saying that the two problems discussed are merely examples of a whole host of similar cultural 'exports'. Others include the replacing of consensus decision-making with majority vote, the introduction of the paid pastor, over-dependence on verbal symbols, etc.[1]

Blindness to the Problems Produced by the Missionary's Own Culture

Only rarely have missionaries become adequately aware of the fact that they too were products of a culture that was not totally congenial to the outworking of the Gospel. As a rule they have never realised that the world view and value systems of their own home cultures could seriously prejudice the Gospel in the eyes of another culture, or even that their own understanding of the biblical message and their personal experience of salvation could, in fact, be limited by them. It came as a very rude shock to me when I suddenly realised that my western naturalistic and materialistic view of germs and illness actually made it next to impossible for me to 'believe' sufficiently for faith to heal, and that my South American Indian Christian brothers, who operated on an animistic world view — one much more akin to that of the Bible — could much more readily appropriate the power of God than I could. In fact, they had to 'kick me out' of the prayer circle in order to achieve healing, as the following experience illustrates.

Nata, a Chocó Indian woman, was deathly sick with pneumonia and the believers decided to save her life through prayer. In the first attempt, in which they asked the missionaries to join, they were only partially successful. When Nata had a relapse and was about to die, the Indian Christians made a second and successful attempt, but this time they excluded the two missionaries. Here now follows the leader's explanation of why:

'Isn't it wonderful! This morning Nata was dying, and here she is well and making supper.'

'Yes,' Aureliano rejoined. 'God is good: God is great! His Spirit is more powerful than all the fever spirits and he has truly healed her.'

'Yes,' I said, 'I noticed that you anointed her with oil again this morning and prayed over her.'

'We did. And this time God really healed her.'

'I notice that you did not invite David nor me into the circle.'

'I'm sorry, Tiger [the author's local nickname], but we couldn't invite you. You two fellows really don't believe, and you cannot heal by God's power when you have unbelievers in the circle.'[2]

An equally unsettling experience made me aware of a closely related problem which Claude Stipe has already called 'usurping the authority of the Holy Spirit by missionaries'.

Trying to set a good example for the Chocó believers after their first communion service, which the leader ended with an appeal for testimonies on what God was asking individual believers to do for him during the next week, I had said that he had asked me to teach each Christian home in the community how to have a family worship service. However, already after the first successful lesson God's Spirit broke through and showed me that I was usurping an Indian believer's task. When I confessed my failure and asked:

'Did God tell anyone here to do this?' One of the men said: 'God told me to do it. But when you got up in the communion service and said he had called you, I decided that I must have heard wrong. You know so much more about the Bible than I.'

I went to my Indian brother and apologised for having led him to disbelieve the voice of the Spirit and having lied when I said that the Spirit of God told me what to do. I asked him to forgive me. And he did. But then came the 'crunch'. The Indians had a prayer meeting on my behalf that morning and they prayed as follows: 'Lord, *Imama* "Tiger" doesn't listen to your Spirit very often, but this experience shows that he can listen when he tries. So we pray, Lord, help him to listen to you more.'[3]

I must personally confess that since this experience I can no longer glibly say God wants me to do this or that. I am deeply aware now that my western 'spiritless' culture has given me an acute hearing defect to the voice of the Holy Spirit.

Blindness to the Debilitating Syncretism of our Own Christianity

Missionaries have been aghast at certain practices of African Independent Churches and in righteous indignation have cried: 'That's pure Christopaganism!' But the very same people have been busy teaching Africans to use the Christmas tree and to celebrate Christ's birthday in the third week of December. In fact, these elements are so usually accepted as Christian that few people stop to think about their pagan Germanic origin, and the fact that the time actually corresponds to the celebration of the winter solstice by the peoples in Northern Europe.

Likewise, Easter, the great celebration of the resurrection of Christ which we often celebrate with a sunrise service, got its name from none other than the teutonic goddess of fertility called Eostre, and the sunrise service had its origin in the sun worship associated with this cult.

But frankly, I am not at all concerned about this type of syncretism. It is relatively harmless. It merely represents the borrowing of an old form which has been filled with a *new* and *Christian* meaning. And it is a 'healthy' type of syncretism. There is a dangerous kind of syncretism, however, and that is the syncretism of meaning. Here the form may have all the appearances of being Christian, but its meaning is not. Permit me to recall the opening quote on money and syncretism and to illustrate it with the account of an experience described in a book which is at the press:

> 'Every tribe and culture uses one or more of these . . .' — as I was speaking I was pointing to the blackboard on which a simplified listing of Wissler's cultural universals had been written — '. . . as heart, the most important centre or hub of their way of life. It is like the axle of a wheel which forms the centre around which the whole wheel turns. You say that you have known the missionaries for about twenty years. Can you suggest one of the items in this list which you would consider to be the axle of the missionary's way of life?'
>
> 'Money!' the group of teachers from a South American tribe exclaimed unanimously and unhesitatingly.
>
> 'But do missionaries really teach about money?'
>
> 'No, they usually talk about God and religion, but money is still the most important thing in their way of life,' the Indian teachers — all Christians — affirmed with obvious conviction.

The missionaries present were beginning to fidget and I noticed several of them shift towards the edge of their chairs as I continued.

'How can you be so sure that money is the axle of the missionary's way of life?'

'Because ...' and then with devastating accuracy the Indian Christians one after another recounted personal experiences that showed how money was the ultimate yardstick in both the material and spiritual areas of the missionaries' life and culture.

[Now followed a lengthy — here irrelvant — discussion on communism and the preconquest Indian culture which the teachers defined as having the quest for spirit power as its highest value.]

'And now,' I continued, 'that all of you here are Christians, is the Spirit of God the axle of your Christian way of life too?'

'No,' they responded, obviously subdued, 'our axle now is ... is money.'

'How come? Are you not children of your ancestors? If the axle of their Christian life would have been the Spirit of God, why is it not yours?'

'Money is our axle now because that is what we have learned from the missionaries.'[4]

If the Bible states that mammon and God are mutually exclusive, is not the replacement of the Holy Spirit by money as the axle of our way of life a subtle but devastating kind of syncretism that has occurred in western Christianity? Is it not one which all of us westerners, including missionaries, have learned and are practising totally unawares? Are we missionaries also the 'blind guides' of whom Jesus spoke so cuttingly? (Matt. 23: 16ff.).

The importance of our awareness of this kind of syncretism is so crucial that I feel constrained to include a second example. Those of us who have been missionaries or pastors in other cultures anxiously watching over new believers have discovered that we tend to trust those believers who behave externally like ourselves. We accept it as desirable when local believers act like we do. But what if the meaning of this behaviour is not the same in the new setting as in the missionary's own culture? Let me try and illustrate what I mean.

Recently I spoke on conversion from an anthropologist's perspective at a conference made up of missionaries and African believers. I pointed out that conversion involves a fundamental restructuring of values and that genuine conversion will make Africans better Africans. I further pointed out that conversion usually follows a model. This model can be indigenous as in the Toba of the Argentine Chaco who have reconstructed their traditional puberty ceremony for the conversion experience;[5] or it can also be imported as in the case of many believers who were taught to be converted according to the pattern of the denomination of the missionary; or it can be newly developed.[6]

Finally, I added that conversion in its spiritual dimension means the presence of the Spirit of God in human life as the source of all guidance and power. As soon as the meeting was opened for discussion, a leading national believer got up and confessed:

'Sir, what you have said about conversion deeply moves me because, I must confess: I have not been converted that way. My deeper African values have not been changed. I have merely become an imitation European on the outside. I have not learned to listen to the Holy Spirit. I have been trained to listen very carefully to what the missionary who controls the purse wants.'[7]

Have we missionaries in cases like this denied true spiritual renewal to the Africans by exporting and implementing our own model of conversion and producing a church that has the form of religion but denies the power thereof (II Tim. 3: 5)?

Avoiding or Correcting the Errors of the Past

We are well aware that there are thousands of missionaries working in cross-cultural evangelism in the world today, and many more are preparing to do so. If the people now working or those intending to work in the future want to avoid the errors of the past, I would like to suggest at least four concerns as crucial:

1. They will have to make a serious effort to understand the culture in which they themselves were raised, and discover how it influences, if not weakens, their faith and their witness.

2. The missionary evangelist crossing a cultural boundary must learn to appreciate the new culture. In fact, he must be ready to be taught as much by the people to whom he goes as he expects to teach them. If God in Christ had to be born as a babe divesting himself of his divine prerogatives and learning to become a Jew in a specific cultural setting, how much more then must we, finite human creatures, be ready to empty ourselves of our own culture and be ready to be taught by the people to whom we want to minister! (Phil. 2: 5–8; Heb. 5: 8).

3. Since total emptying is a relative impossibility for us human beings, the missionary evangelist must recognise that the further away from his home base he goes to witness, the more temporary his personal involvement in the development of the church will usually be. At great distances God can usually use him only as a mirror, a catalyst, or as a source of alternatives; never as a long-time fixture.[8]

4. The missionary evangelist must constantly be on the alert for ethnocentric, imperialist attitudes in new guises; and once discovered, he must resolutely reject them. One such new attitude that I often meet as I go about my work with the Bible Society could be called 'translational imperialism'. The majority of the Bibles now in print were made by missionary experts who spent long and tedious years in preparing them. But no matter how many years they may have spent in learning the language, these translators were

translating not into their mother tongue but into a second language. And in fact, since it was foreigners who carried the responsibility for the new translation, the local believers were by that same token being robbed of their personal encounter with the inspiration. It is for this reason that the Bible Society today has gone on record to say that it will publish translations made by second-language speakers only under very extenuating circumstances. All new translations must be made by mother-tongue speakers as translators.

Some Guidelines for Biblical Church Growth

If truly indigenous churches are to grow meaningfully in their respective cultures, it is imperative for national believers in each culture to assume several fundamental responsibilities. We need to underscore here that each of these responsibilities applies as much to the churches of the West as to the developing churches in the Third World. Among these are:

1. The responsibility for the Scriptures in their own language. If the Bible is to be the eternal, infallible record of God's will for all men, then it becomes important that all cultures 'wrestle' with the 'birth' of this message in their own language. Mother-tongue speakers as translators must develop a deep awareness that they are dealing with more than merely a word that is purported to be from God. They must experience the fact that God's Spirit is at work in this Word. This responsibility carries at least two dimensions with it: (a) Mother-tongue speakers as translators must ask: 'God, how would you have said this if you had spoken only in our language?' The result will be the birth of a translation that will read like an original. (b) Furthermore, since more or less every language exhibits specific grammatical and semantic categories for which there are no equivalents in the Greek or Hebrew original texts, the translator must have specific guidance from the Holy Spirit in order to make the proper choices. This is essential if the Bible in those translations is to be as valid as the original. This has been detailed

in another paper from which we quote briefly below.[9] For churches with a longer history this may mean that each generation must again grapple with the inspiration and the translation of the Scriptures.

2. The responsibility for responding to the Spirit of God in the development of hymns, rituals, and worship patterns. Needs in different cultural settings vary, and unless the church meets all the needs, it will be providing a partial and therefore dangerous religion. Furthermore, we have to recognise that believers who have grown up in an animistic world-view with a lot of spirit-world experience, actually have a far better listening capacity for direction from the Holy Spirit than most westerners do. I remind readers again of the confession I had to make to the Chocó believers.

3. The church should seek to expose itself to the sympathetic scrutiny of responsible believers from other cultures. Frequently in such encounters the foreigner's sympathetic questions will serve as mirrors that make local flaws stand out visibly. Once having recognised the imperfection, the church must then obey Christ, its head, in correcting it. An example of such an experience among the Toba of the Argentine Chaco was reported in *Practical Anthropology*.[10] But it could just as well have happened that Toba Christians could serve as mirrors to western churches, as the example on money orientation shows.

I am personally confident that when a church will seek to know and obey God's Word, enlightened by the Holy Spirit, it will grow, and no power of men, angels, or devils can stop or overcome it.

CHAPTER XI

Education and Leadership

Jonathan Chao

'WE CONFESS THAT we have sometimes pursued church growth at the expense of church depth, and divorced evangelism from Christian nurture. We also acknowledge that some of our missions have been too slow to equip and encourage national leaders to assume their rightful responsibilities. Yet we are committed to indigenous principles, and long that every church will have national leaders who manifest a Christian style of leadership in terms not of domination but of service. We recognise that there is a great need to improve theological education, especially for church leaders. In every nation and culture there should be an effective training programme for pastors and laymen in doctrine, discipleship, evangelism, nurture and service. Such training programmes should not rely on any stereotyped methodology but should be developed by creative local initiatives according to biblical standards.'
(*Col. 1: 27, 28; Acts 14: 23; Titus 1: 5, 9; Mark 10: 42–45; Eph. 4: 11, 12*)

(LAUSANNE COVENANT, CLAUSE 11)

THE FRAMERS OF the Lausanne Covenant are aware of missiological issues developing in the Third World, although as a document it basically reflects a western perspective. In regard to education and leadership, the framers, and hence the signers as well, have taken the following positions:

1. There should be no dichotomy between evangelism and Christian nurture. The church growth mentality has been partially responsible for this abnormality.

2. Western missions have been too slow to train national leaders and transfer authority and responsibility to them.

3. The present structure of theological education needs renovation, so that it will be geared towards the development of church leadership.

4. The framers and signers are committed to indigenous principles in leadership development, the attaining of indigenous leadership being the supreme goal.

5. Leadership training programmes should be developed according to local, indigenous cultural situations.

6. Such training programmes should not be limited to ministerial training aimed at producing an élite professional group but should extend to the laity as a whole. In both the training should be total, including doctrine, discipleship, evangelism, nurture and service.

7. There should be flexibility and adaptability in the creation of training models and methods which arise out of local creative initiatives and are in keeping with biblical standards.

These principles are keys that can unlock Third World evangelicals from their prisons of western, particularly Anglo-American, evangelical confinement. Keys are useless unless they are actually used: likewise, these concepts in the Lausanne Covenant are worthless unless they are implemented in real-life situations, particularly in the Third World churches that are awaiting liberation.

Several crucial issues and questions raised by this section of the Lausanne Covenant must be answered so that the above-mentioned liberating keys can be utilised. The most basic question is, how can indigenous Christian leadership be developed in the Third World, and how is theological education related to this process? Let us begin by analysing three aspects of this question.

The Failure to Develop Indigenous Leadership in the Third World

While the Lausanne Covenant acknowledges that 'some of our missions have been too slow to equip and encourage national leaders to assume their rightful responsibilities', and while it claims to be committed to indigenous principles, it fails to recognise that, generally speaking, *all* missions have failed to develop adequate indigenous leadership. Further, development of indigenous leadership is understood only as the transference of responsibility from the missionaries to nationals. This concept reflects a traditional understanding of indigenity as self-government, self-propagation, and self-support, which means no more than securing independence from missionary control and financial and ministerial independence. We shall discuss the inadequacies of this view later. The point is, however, that the mission boards have not realised even this traditional ideal of indigenity. The mission boards certainly have not lacked *time* for transference of responsibilities to national leaders. Neither do the missionaries and mission executives lack willingness to implement this policy. What factors have contributed to this world-wide failure? Generally speaking, national churches attribute the failure to missionary dominance, while missionaries deplore the lack of 'qualified' national leaders. But these are only symptoms of the problem rather than causes. The latter must be found at a deeper level.

1. *The western model of ministry imposed upon the Third World churches is the overall context for the failure to develop indigenous leadership.*

The pattern of the Protestant ministry as practised in most Third World churches is basically a replica of the Catholic and Reformation model of ministry developed within the context of western church history. It has been faithfully transplanted to the mission fields through the various mission agencies. Until very recently it was accepted as the standard model for emulation in the Third World, seldom being questioned by either national leaders or missionaries. The continuous dependence of the Third World churches on this western pattern has determined the shape of their ministry. There is, however, an inherent contradiction between the biblical pattern of the ministry through exercise of spiritual gifts and the western model based on professional clericalism. There is also a contextual contradiction between the shape of indigenous leadership as a cultural phenomenon and the type of leadership that emerged from the West. Only a specific form of leadership modelled upon the western ministerial pattern was permitted to develop. Other forms, however biblical and indigenous, have fallen short of the standard norm, and hence have not had an opportunity for development or recognition. The western denominational structures only reinforced this confinement.

2. *The western model of ministerial training has been a means of preserving that pattern of ministry, and hence has contributed to the failure to develop indigenous leadership.*

The development of an indigenous ministry has been the goal of practically every mission, and the 'training of a native clergy' has always been their top priority. But the models of training have been western theological schools, be they Bible schools or seminaries. Missionaries seldom questioned this transference or were even aware that such transplantation is a questionable one.

Models of ministerial training are conditioned by the pattern of ministry. The pattern imported from the West has been that of a full-time professional pastor of the Catholic and Anglican parish or congregation; the goal of theological schools has been to train such pastors or 'evangelists' under missionary supervision and pay. But even the evangelists have ordination as pastors as their ultimate goal. Thus the western ministerial pattern determines the model of training, which in turn reinforces the pattern of ministry for which students are trained. This endless cycle has moulded Third World churches into the western pattern of ministry, and, over a long period of time, has consolidated them into it through the system of theological education initiated and maintained by western missions. Even after a church has attained its independence in the three-self manner, it usually remains dependent upon the mission in its theological education. Missionaries find a theoretical basis for retaining control of theological schools on the grounds that it is their responsibility to train national pastors and that the native church is not capable of operating a seminary due to its lack of qualified personnel and finances. The result of this situation is that the western model continues to dominate the theological schools, which in turn conserve both the western pattern of the ministry and the style of ministerial leadership.

3. *The western form of ministerial leadership recognition reinforces the western type of leadership and inhibits the development of indigenous forms of leadership.*
Generally speaking, there are two types of leadership: *charismatic leadership* which is recognised by the people through the actual exercise of both spiritual and natural gifts, and *official leadership* which is usually recognised through official means, such as ordination or holding office as chairman of a certain committee.

Within the western pattern of ministry, ministerial leaders

are usually produced in the second manner. A young man declares himself called to the ministry, is admitted to the seminary, and upon graduation is usually appointed to a church and ordained. As an ordained minister he is considered one of the native ministerial leaders. In this pattern, leadership recognition is dependent upon the western model of theological education (degrees) which usually guarantees qualification for ordination. A man may obtain the status of leadership because he is ordained, but lack the real gifts of leadership and hence suffer from an illusion of prominence accompanied by frustrations arising from a sense of false professionalism. This form of leadership recognition has, on the one hand, preserved the western model of ministry and training, and, on the other hand, prevented biblical and indigenous forms of leadership from being recognised as authentic and legitimate. Foreign missionaries exercised their control through the theological schools and ordination, effectively insuring the process of domestication through these two handles of control. As a result, the kind of leadership developed is moulded after the image of the western pastor, as the missionaries conceive of him.

4. *Over-emphasis on evangelism and the misuse of Christian schools contributed to the failure to develop solid Christian nurture, the bedrock of indigenous leadership.*

Evangelicals' over-emphasis on evangelism, usually conditioned by a zeal to report statistical success in terms of 'church growth', has produced a superficial evangelism characterised by cheap discipleship. Christian education has often been confined to Sunday school activities, not in-depth Christian nurture in the homes and churches. Often teenagers and young adults are lost to the world due to the missionaries' and pastors' inability to cope with their problems.

Mission schools, as was the case in China, have been used as either a means to introduce western civilisation or a ground for evangelism. Instead of educating Christian youths for indigenous leadership, mission schools have often discredited national cultural heritages, thus uprooting the students from their cultural background in a process of domestication through westernisation.

Strong and influential Christian leadership usually comes from second or third generation Christians. The failure in Christian nurture and education, therefore, has contributed to the failure to prepare national leadership.

De-Westernisation of the Ministry

The ministry is the goal and context of leadership development. As a goal it determines both the model of training and the style of leadership development. Thus any attempt to renovate theological education or leadership development must begin with a redefinition of their goal, the ministry. It is not possible to 'improve theological education', as suggested by the Covenant, in isolation from its ministerial context. Rather, a complete, integrated approach to the development of indigenous leadership within the overall context of the church and her ministry must be undertaken.

De-secularisation and Christologisation of the ministry

If dependence on the western model for the ministry is the context of the failure to develop indigenous leadership then two mandates are given to Third World Christians: (1) a critical examination of the western model of ministry and (2) the de-westernising the ministry. These mandates should be approached from the biblical perspective, taking into full consideration the local indigenous factors. This should be the common task of all Third World Christian leaders. I believe it to be the initial and most crucial task before us if we desire a radical reformation in Third World theological education that will pave the way for true indigenous leadership development. Anything short of this will be (in the words of a Chinese saying), 'Changing the soup without changing the medicine.'

A critical and historical analysis of the traditional missionary model of the ministry exported from the West shows that it is built on an administrative structure reflecting the Roman mentality rather than on a functional structure of service as found in the New Testament. The administrative structure depends upon the creation of an élitist group of professional clergy whose authority is invested in its administrative status. This is especially obvious in the Roman Catholic, Episcopalian and Methodist systems. As a power structure of imperial magnitude, it basically reflects a secular model. Higher ecclesiastical bureaucrats, armed with the authority of promotion and ordination, control lower clergies, lower clergies in turn, armed with the sacraments and the rights of interpreting the Word, subjugate, if not exploit, the laity. In the mission fields western missionaries usually enjoy these positions of authority over their 'native helpers' and exploit them, at least financially, as their subordinates. Many of the mission executives in the West who hold the final word of decision in both ideology and administration are not immune from the practice of exploitation.

To correct this abuse of power and to transform church officials into true servants of the Lord, Third World churches must initiate a process of de-secularisation, followed by a Christologisation and pneumatisation of the ministry. That is to say, Third World ministry must be reshaped to become Christ-centred and Holy Spirit-oriented within the biblical context of the life and function of the body of Christ. This is a task that should be pursued not only by Third World churches, but also by all churches throughout the world, especially those in the West. The churches in China have already completed the task of de-secularisation and de-westernisation and are enjoying a new freedom of pneumatic ministry.

De-westernisation and indigenisation of the ministry

The second aspect of ministerial reform in the Third World is de-westernisation, combined with indigenisation of the ministry. The task is a cultural one: how can we open ourselves to the free working of the Holy Spirit in the exercise of our ministry within our socio-cultural context? This implies that we must initiate a critical process of de-culturalisation whereby we may be enabled to discover the alien cultural impositions that are hindering the free movement of the Holy Spirit among the people. It also implies the need for wisdom regarding acculturalisation or indigenisation. We must discover local forms of thought and styles of work which facilitate the ministry of the Spirit in concrete situations, thereby creating authentic indigenous pneumatic ministry.

What does this process imply? It implies that Third World churches must no longer take the western model for granted. We must rethink our western inheritance; we must rebuild our foundations, and reshape our ministry. We must resist the illegitimate imposition of western concepts and practices, just as Paul resisted the Jewish imposition of circumcision upon the Gentiles. It means that we have to reduce missionaries and full-time clergy to their functional value. It means that we have to allow a wide variety of ministries to express themselves in untraditional forms and acknowledge them as equally valid. It means that we have to reorient our concepts and standards of recognition or ordination along pneumatic lines, rather than merely along educational or official lines. It means that we might have to practise what we have preached since the Reformation: the priesthood of all believers and the parity of the clergy and the laity. The reshaping of the ministry will immediately force us to restructure the form of theological education and the style of indigenous leadership development.

Innovations in Theological Education

If the form of the ministry determines the style of ministerial leadership, the style of leadership also determines the character of leadership training or theological education. While theological education may establish the form of the ministry, as has been the case thus far, it must not be allowed to dictate what the ministry should be. Rather, theological education must aim to reproduce a form of the ministry consonant with that of the servant role, as described in the New Testament.

New style for the development of indigenous leadership

The biblical pattern for the ministry is that of extending the ministry of Christ and the Holy Spirit. The true leader or activator is Christ through the Spirit, while man becomes an earthen vessel through which the Spirit acts. The model of leadership development is Jesus Christ, the true servant of the Lord; the apostle Paul was the closest human imitator.

Biblical leadership is servanthood, not domination or control. Christian leaders are basically powerless and weak, like Jesus and Paul were, but become powerful and lead because they are filled by the Holy Spirit. The new style of leadership development is different from the old secular style in its weakness and servanthood.

If Jesus is our model, then the goal of leadership development and theological education is nothing less than equipping believers to *be* like Jesus, to *know* the redemptive work of God in Christ Jesus and to *do* the works of Jesus. Here we have three types of training goals: 'be-goals', 'know-goals', and 'do-goals'.

Body-ministry: the context of leadership development

These goals cannot be adequately developed by the traditional approach through classroom instruction and fixed curriculum. While a certain amount of know-goals may be transmitted through this system, spiritual leadership after the model of Jesus and Paul or Peter cannot be developed in isolation from the life situation of the living body of Christ. This new style of leadership must be developed through a communal approach within the biblical framework of 'life together', where the gifts of the Holy Spirit are exercised according to what each has received from the Lord. This implies that indigenous spiritual leadership must be developed within the life and ministry of the church.

The ministry of the church as a whole, therefore, becomes the schoolground for training in servanthood. Whatever other para-institutional agencies there may be, they become secondary and supplementary. Otherwise the academic system will dominate the ministry again. The be-goals, know-goals and do-goals set forth in the Bible cannot be developed outside the church ministry context. It is like swimming. One cannot become a good swimmer without getting into the water. Nor can one become a good field marshal without battle experience. How can one learn the biblical be-goals — like loyalty to Christ and faithfulness to his ministry, love for his flock and compassion for the unregenerate, willingness to forgive, humility, self-denial, sensitivity to the leadings of the Holy Spirit, etc. — without active participation in the living ministry of the church? How can one develop know-goals, such as the work of the Holy Spirit, the nature of the Gospel, and the defence of the faith, without becoming actively engaged in life-changing spiritual exercises, evangelism, and actual apologetical tasks? How can one develop one's gifts without exercising them in the ministry of the church? It is in this grassroots ministry that students will experience both spiritual power and indigenous forms of ministry. The gradual growth that they experience will constitute the development of a new style of indigenous leadership development.

Implications of innovations in theological education

This kind of rethinking, although by no means new, implies that any attempt to 'improve' the present form of theological education is not enough. What we need is not renovation, but innovation. The whole philosophy and structure of theological education has to be completely reshaped. Radical innovation in the Third World theological education implies the following:

(1) Theological education should be integrated with the ministry of the church, both locally and nationally. This further implies that the whole church as the body of Christ, as a functional unity, should condition the style of corporate leadership, training, allowing for considerable diversity rather than the uniformity along denominational lines which has been imposed by the West.

(2) Theological education should be conceptualised in terms of be-goals, know-goals, and do-goals which are in-

tegrated into a living whole, rather than as mere indoctrination or classroom transmission of certain information.

(3) Third World theological education should develop along biblical and indigenous lines, freeing itself from western super-power imperialistic theological captivity. This implies that we should reject the liberal-conservative or ecumenical-evangelical dichotomy. Third World theological education should aim at training indigenous leaders to think critically and independently.

(4) Third World theological education should develop a multi-level and multi-programme approach in order to meet the diversified needs of the church. If we question the paid-pastor model of the ministry, then we should develop programmes consistent with the body-ministry model.

(5) Third World theological education should be conducted within the context of the church and the local culture. This means we should emphasise not only the doctrinal aspects of the ministry, but also the practical; not only biblical content, but also the cultural context; not only selective adaptation from the West, but also selective adaptation from the living situation. We should not swallow everything that is developing in the West, such as the 'church growth' fad. Third World theological educators must help their churches free themselves from continuous dependence on the West for ideas and forms of ministry.

This means a shaking of foundations and a collapse of existing structures. It is going to cost a great deal.

The cost of indigenising theological education

Revolution is always costly. To do the will of God cost John his head, to obey God's commandment cost Jesus' life. Not a few lives were sacrificed in the wave of the Protestant Reformation. A revolution in Third World theological education is going to be equally costly.

To missionary boards it is going to mean a loss of power and control over their theological schools in the Third World. What will hurt them most will be the loss of their control over doctrinal orthodoxy and church policy in their mission churches. The Third World churches might have to face the eventual termination of financial subsidies from the West, which would be a great blessing in disguise. Innovators will be misunderstood by both missionaries and fellow workers who are not yet liberated from their servile mentality. But the day has come for Third World theological leaders to rally themselves together to form a united front in a theological liberation movement, a movement whose voice was already heard in the Radical Discipleship Caucus at Lausanne.

If we reshape the ministry and restructure leadership training along biblical lines in the Third World, I believe that we will see the release of a spiritual dynamic in the churches that could produce a great awakening for world evangelisation. Once the laity is freed for 'body-ministry' the power of the Spirit will be unleashed. Come, Holy Spirit, come!

'Revive thy church, oh Lord, beginning with me' (C. Y. Cheng, 1881–1939).

CHAPTER XII

Spiritual Conflict

C. René Padilla

'WE BELIEVE THAT we are engaged in constant spiritual warfare with the principalities and powers of evil, who are seeking to overthrow the church and frustrate its task of world evangelisation. We know our need to equip ourselves with God's armour and to fight this battle with the spiritual weapons of truth and prayer. For we detect the activity of our enemy, not only in false ideologies outside the church but also inside it in false gospels which twist Scripture and put man in the place of God. We need both watchfulness and discernment to safeguard the biblical Gospel. We acknowledge that we ourselves are not immune to worldliness of thought and action, that is, to a surrender to secularism. For example, although careful studies of church growth, both numerical and spiritual, are right and valuable, we have sometimes neglected them. At other times, desirous to ensure a response to the gospel, we have compromised our message, manipulated our hearers through pressure techniques, and become unduly preoccupied with statistics or even dishonest in our use of them. All this is worldly. The church must be in the world; the world must not be in the church.'
(*Eph. 6: 12; II Cor. 4: 3, 4; Eph. 6: 11, 13–18; II Cor. 10: 3–5; I John 2: 18–26, 4: 1–3; Gal. 1: 6–9; II Cor. 2: 17, 4: 2; John 17: 15*)

(LAUSANNE COVENANT, CLAUSE 12)

THE LAUSANNE CONGRESS might have been nothing more than an enormous (and expensive) launching platform for a vast programme of world-wide evangelisation which avoided the theological problems posed by evangelisation for the church today. There is reason to believe that a high percentage of the participants shared the pragmatic viewpoint expressed in the editorial of a well-known, evangelical magazine in North America shortly before the Congress. It stated that since the Berlin Congress (1966) had established the theological framework for evangelisation (the key word had been evangelism), the 1974 Congress would concentrate on the practical aspects of that task (the key word would be evangelisation). Fortunately, as this vast gathering developed the theological problems imposed themselves upon the discussions and resulted in the Lausanne Covenant, a document which questions positions traditionally entrenched in the evangelical churches.

The twelfth paragraph of the Covenant warns against worldliness in the church, placing this warning in the context of the spiritual conflict to which the New Testament often refers. It points to the subtle ways in which the world conditions the church, even to the extent of shaping its message and evangelistic methods. It concludes with an echo of John 17: 16: 'The church must be in the world; the world must not be in the church.' In this chapter we will take this paragraph as an invitation to reflect upon the meaning of the world in its negative sense (to which the Covenant refers), the influence which the world exerts upon the church, and the role which the Gospel must play in the church if she is to be faithful to God in her confrontation with the world.

The World Today

The dominant factor of the modern world is the rapid growth of a new type of society — the consumer society — as the culmination of the technological revolution which began in the nineteenth century. The phenomenon of internal migrations has been an accomplice of the dizzying world-wide growth of an urban civilisation whose defining feature is the all-importance of technological products. Virtually all humanity today participates in the life of the city. As Jacques Ellul has observed, 'We are in the city even if we are in the country for today the country (and soon this will be true even of the immense Asian steppe) is only an annex of the city.'[1] His affirmation not only points out a statistically verifiable fact, that is, the tremendous demographic expansion of the urban centre,[2] but also embodies a perception of the global character of the 'consumer mentality' which characterises modern society in both the developed and underdeveloped countries.[3]

The consumer society is the offspring of technology and capitalism. Historically it appeared in the West when the bourgeoisie assumed political power and made technology the instrument of its own enrichment. Private property, which in pre-industrial society had given security to the common people, no longer fulfilled a social function but was transformed into an absolute right.[4] The great capitalistic industries emerged. Their watchword would be an ever-increasing production rate, although a good part of it would consist of trivialities — 'articles which, though reckoned as part of the income of the nation, either should not have been produced until other articles had been produced in sufficient abundance, or should not have been produced at all.[5] Any activity not directly related to industrial development would be relegated to a lower plane. Labour relations would be governed by personal convenience for the industrial proprietors, for whom property would be a means of personal enrichment rather than an instrument of service to society. The mass media (especially radio and television) would be utilised to condition the consumers to a life-style in which they work to make money, make money to buy things, and buy things to find value for themselves. As Jacques Ellul has demonstrated, 'Lifestyle is formed by advertising.'[6] Advertising is controlled by those whose interests are aligned with a constant increase in production, which in turn depends upon a level of consumption possible only in a society where to live is to possess.[7] In this way, technology is placed in the service of capital in order to impose the ideology of consumerism.

Analysts of contemporary society generally consider that the developed countries are in the transition from the first to the second technological revolution. If in the first revolution man's work was replaced by that of the machine, in the second man's very thinking is being replaced by the machine. The era of automation and cybernetics is beginning. Today as never before we have at our disposal the technological resources to put an end to one of the most pressing problems haunting the masses in three fourths of the globe: hunger. Nevertheless, technology maintains its ties with the economic interests of a minority who remain untouched by the misery of 'the disinherited of the earth'. The emergence of huge multi-national industrial conglomerates has perhaps been the most important factor in the exportation of the consumer ideology to the Third World. The urban centres are not merely the operational base for these industries: their very existence depends upon their capacity to become a co-ordinated system and organise all of life as a function of production and consumption. For this reason, the city gradually presses man into a materialistic mould, a mould which gives absolute value to 'things' because they are status symbols, a mould which leaves no room for questions about the meaning of work or the purpose of life.

The present industrial system serves capital, not man. As a result, it turns man into a one-dimensional being — a cog in the massive machinery which operates on the laws of supply and demand and is the principal cause of environmental pollution. It creates a yawning and ever widening chasm between the haves and have nots on a national level, and between the rich countries and the poor countries on an international level. Today, despite technological advances and industrial expansion unprecedented in human history, the underdeveloped nations are further away than ever from the solution to their problems. The technological age, which brought in the harnessing of atomic energy and the conquest of outer space, is paradoxically the age of hunger.[8] In general, the rich nations refuse to recognise the relationship between their own economic development and the underdevelopment of the poor nations.[9] International organisations find their hands tied because they have no means of eliciting the co-operation of the great industrial countries.[10] As Josué de Castro has affirmed, 'the official doctrine of development of the great western powers is very narrow, and is dominated by selfish concerns derived from an unadulterated colonialist inspiration'.[11] Avarice is the very cement of the economic system that has engendered the consumer society.

In the modern world, consumerism has even invaded the areas where poverty reigns. In both the wealthy zones and the poverty belts of the large urban centres, the mass media spread their image of happiness — the *homo consumens*. The whole world, as a result, is becoming a 'global village', united around the principle of consumerism. Although the under-developed countries are consumers on a much lower level than that of the developed countries, the mentality which gives a preferred status to consumer goods prevails in both. The obsession of the wealthy is what Josué de Castro has aptly described as 'ostentatious consumerism': 'the consumerism of imported luxury items with little or no usefulness in the collective social and economic development and which in fact substantially impairs the progress of the economy'.[12] On the other hand the poor desire the upward social mobility that will enable them not only to satisfy their most basic needs (food, clothing and shelter), but also to acquire all those goods advertised as status symbols (especially a car and electrical appliances). The so-called 'revolution of rising expectations' has an ambiguous value: although clearly a search for respect and human dignity on the part of indigenous peoples, it also reflects their conditioning by the mass media with their concept of the *homo consumens* as the ideal for mankind.

Behind the materialism which characterises consumer society lie the powers of destruction to which the New Testament refers. The apostle Paul perceived that the principalities and powers of evil were entrenched in the ideological structures which oppress men. Although this is not the place to elaborate upon this subject,[13] I believe that the two following observations regarding the Pauline concept of the relation between 'the world' (in its negative sense) and demonic powers are relevant:

(1) The world is a system in which evil is organised in opposition to Good. Nevertheless, it is its connection with Satan and his forces which gives it that character. Satan is 'the god of this world' (II Cor. 4: 4; cf. John 12: 31, 14: 30, 16: 11; I John 5: 19); his forces are 'the powers that rule this world' (I Cor. 2: 6 TEV), 'the cosmic powers . . . the authorities and potentates of this dark world' (Eph.6: 12 NEB), 'the elemental spirits of the universe' (Gal. 4: 3, 9; Col. 2: 8, 20).[14] This apocalyptic vision of the world permeates the Pauline epistles and points to a cosmic dimension of not only sin, but also Christian redemption. The work of Jesus Christ cannot be understood apart from this background.[15]

(2) The demonic powers enslave man in the world through the structures and systems which he treats as absolutes. In an important article on 'The Law and This World'[16] Bo Reicke has shown that in Galatians 4: 8 ff. the apostle Paul is warning his readers not only against legalism, but against a return to their slavery to spiritual powers which exercise their dominion over men through organised religion, against a return to gods who in their essential nature are no-gods (*tois phasei mē ousin theois*).[17] This interpretation concurs with the best reading of I Corinthians 10: 20, where the idea is *not* that pagan sacrifices are offered to the demons 'and not to God' (RSV) but rather that they are offered to the demons and 'that which is not God' (NEB). In the words of

C. K. Barrett, for Paul idolatry 'was evil primarily because it robbed the true God of the glory due to him alone ... but it was evil also because it meant that man, engaged in a spiritual act and directing his worship towards something other than the one true God, was brought into intimate relation with the lower, and evil, spiritual powers'.[18] The same relation between the demonic powers and the idolatrous making absolute of a man-made system appears in Colossians 2: 16 ff. and is not unrelated to the references to the 'wisdom of this world' in the first two chapters of I Corinthians. To speak of the world is to speak of an oppressive system governed by the powers of evil who enslave men through idolatry.

The relevance of these Pauline concepts today is obvious once we understand the consumer society's idolatrous character and power to condition men. Translated into the language of modern sociology, the apostle's vocabulary describes institutions and ideologies which transcend the individual and condition his thought and life-style. Those who limit the workings of the evil powers to the occult, demon possession and astrology, as well as those who consider the New Testament references to those powers as a sort of mythological shell from which the biblical message must be extracted, reduce the evil in the world to a personal problem, and Christian redemption to merely a personal experience. A better alternative is to accept the realism of the biblical description and understand man's situation in the world in terms of an enslavement to a spiritual realm from which he must be liberated. As A. M. Hunter affirms, 'There is no metaphysical reason why the cosmos should not contain spirits higher than man who have made evil their good, who are ill-disposed to the human race, and whose activities are co-ordinated by a master-strategist.'[19] In his rebellion against God, man is a slave of the idols of the world through which those powers act. Today, the idols which enslave man are those of the consumer society.

Both technology and capital can put themselves at the service of either good or evil. From their union, which recognises no ethical principle, has emerged the society which worships economic prosperity and the consequent material well-being of *homo consumens*. The consumer society is the very social, political and economic situation in which the world dominated by the powers of destruction has taken form today: the blind faith in technology, the irreversible reverence for private property as an inalienable right, the cult of increased production through the irresponsible sacking of nature, the disproportionate enrichment of the multinational corporations which further impoverishes the 'disinherited of the earth', the fever of consumerism, ostentation, and fashion. This materialism is the ideology which is destroying the human race. The church of Jesus Christ is engaged in a spiritual conflict against the powers of evil entrenched in ideological structures which dehumanise man, conditioning him to make the absolute relative and the relative absolute.

The Worldliness of the Church

The church is an eschatological reality — it belongs to the era of fulfilment introduced by Jesus Christ; it is the first fruits of the new humanity. It is, however, also an historical reality and, as such, it is subject, along with the rest of humanity, to the conditioning influence which the world exerts upon human life in all its dimensions.

In the period between the resurrection and second coming of Christ the new era supersedes the old and eschatology operates in the very stream of history. The resulting eschatological tension colours the whole life and mission of the church. The Lausanne Covenant refers to one of the most important aspects of that tension: 'we believe that we are engaged in constant spiritual warfare with the principalities and powers of evil, who are seeking to overthrow the church and frustrate its task of world evangelisation.' Later in the same paragraph, the Covenant points out that the activity of the powers of destruction is perceived not only in terms of 'false ideologies outside the church', but also in terms of the church's accommodation to the world in thought and action. This explicit recognition of the church's vulnerability before the world constitutes in itself one of the most praiseworthy notes of the whole document, all the more significant when its contrast to the usual triumphalism of evangelicals is taken into account. In his book *Acción pastoral latinoamericana: sus motivos ocultos* ('Latin American Pastoral Work: Its Hidden Motives'), Juan Luis Segundo has pointed out the mechanisms operating in Latin America — a traditionally Roman Catholic continent — which have made the church opt for an accommodation with consumer society, rather than choosing the biblical message with its demands for personal conviction. His thesis may be summarised as follows:

(1) *Urban society demands that the basic questions of human life are not discussed.* For this reason its unity depends not upon a common participation in universal values or a common vision of the world (as was the case with traditional societies) but rather in consumerism. Values and world views are relegated to the sphere of private life and, ultimately, considered purely relative.

(2) *Christianity can no longer count upon the help which closed societies provided in the past.* Without this help, an open society maintains a vague attachment to Christianity, related to man's uprootedness in the city, and this rootless attachment makes room for religious rites. The transmission of Christianity from one generation to another, however, no longer can be left to the social milieu.

(3) *In consumer society, being a Christian depends upon personal conviction.* Any profound idea which challenges the 'massification' of man is revolutionary, and only an heroic minority holds to it.

(4) *Pastoral work, therefore, must choose between a minority which accepts the demands of the Gospel and a 'consumer majority' which is falsely committed to Christianity.*

(5) *Pastoral work has substituted 'artificial consumer majorities' for true Christianity and, therefore, has had to reduce its demands to a minimum.* The main reason for this is a three-fold fear: (a) A fear of freedom on the part of the priests, since 'the step from pressure to liberty, a key step for a new orientation in pastoral work free from traditional

vices, would cause profound psychological and material anguish for the majority of the clergy.'[20] (a) A fear for the destiny of the masses since 'if pastoral work changes from the protective majority to the committed minority, the majority will remain without protection and, in all probability, without the basic essentials of Christianity.'[21] (c) A fear for the Gospel as, it is reasoned, the Gospel *alone* cannot achieve what the church, through its alliance with the system, can. In other words, the church is not ready to depend exclusively upon the Gospel.

This is the incisive analysis of the situation of Christianity within the consumer society as seen by a Latin American theologian. I have considered it useful to summarise it point by point because he clearly delineates the motivation behind *any* kind of Christianity which has stronger ties to the Constantinian mentality than to the Gospel of Jesus Christ. What Segundo says about Latin American 'culture-Christianity' can also be applied to the 'culture-Christianity' to which I referred in my paper 'Evangelisation and the World' which was presented at the International Congress on World Evangelisation:[22] the Christianity which is identified with the 'American Way of Life' and whose influence has spread to almost all the countries of the world. Like traditional Roman Catholicism, it has accommodated itself to the world in its eagerness to reach the majority so that there are more Christians. As a result the church, far from being a factor for the transformation of society, becomes merely another reflection of society and (what is worse) another instrument that society uses to condition people to its materialistic values. Its accommodation to the world is seen in the two spheres which the Lausanne Covenant points out in referring to the danger of worldliness in the church in 'thought and action'.

(1) In the *sphere of thought*, the church's accommodation to the world is realised mainly through the reduction of the Gospel to a purely *spiritual* message — a message of reconciliation with God and salvation of the soul. In accord with this, the mission of the church is defined exclusively in terms of evangelisation, which in turn is understood as the proclamation that by virtue of the death of Jesus on the

cross, the only thing a man must do to be saved is to 'accept Jesus as his all-sufficient Saviour'. This separates faith from repentance, the 'essential' elements of the Gospel from the non-essential, the *kerygma* from the *didache*, and salvation from sanctification. On its most basic level, it means a separation between Christ as Saviour and Christ as Lord. This produces a gospel which permits a man to maintain the values and attitudes prevalent in a consumer society and at the same time enjoy the temporal and eternal security which religion provides. His life will be clearly divided between his 'religion' compartment and his 'secular activities' compartment. God has something to say with regard to the first, but not the second: he will be a God interested in the worship service, but not in social problems, politics, business or international relations.

This version of the Gospel is custom made for the 'artificial consumer majorities'. It is another easy product to market in the consumer society. It represents one of those 'false gospels which twist Scripture and put man in the place of God', to which the Lausanne Covenant refers. This can only be corrected through a return to the biblical Gospel, to the Gospel which centres upon Jesus Christ as Lord of the universe and of the whole of life, to the Gospel which 'A Response to Lausanne' clearly defines in the following terms:

The Evangel is God's good news in Jesus Christ; it is good news of the reign he proclaimed and embodies; of God's mission of love to restore the world to wholeness through the cross of Christ and him alone; of his victory over the demonic powers of destruction and death; of his Lordship over the entire universe; it is good news of a new creation, a new humanity, a new birth through him by his life-giving Spirit; of the gifts of the messianic reign contained in Jesus and mediated through him by his Spirit; of the charismatic community empowered to embody his reign of shalom here and now before the whole creation and make his good news seen and known. It is good news of liberation, of restoration, of wholeness, and of salvation that is personal, social, global and cosmic.

(2) In the *sphere of action*, culture-Christianity reflects the conditioning of the consumer society. Only this can explain the obsession with numbers mentioned in the Lausanne Covenant: 'At other times, desirous to ensure a response to the gospel, we have compromised our message, manipulated our hearers through pressure techniques, and become unduly preoccupied with statistics or even dishonest in our use of them.'[23]

This expresses one of the most obvious forms in which the church has adjusted herself to the world. To accompany a truncated Gospel, we have an evangelistic methodology which mechanises the addition of people to the church. If in consumer society the constant increase of production is the only interest, it is quite understandable that consumer religion would give priority to the numerical increase of the church.

Some might object by saying that keeping a numerical count of believers is a legitimate concern for any person whose heart is quickened with the very desire of God 'who desires all men to be saved and to come to the knowledge of the truth' (I Tim. 2: 4). Juan Luis Segundo provides the answer:

> There is an obvious fact: there are two ways to count Christians. One begins, for the sake of statistics, with the bare minimum: baptism, some attendance at the sacraments, claimed Christian allegiance for a census, and refraining from heresies expressly condemned in the Denzinger. The other counts only those Christians who are ready to take their message to the rest of society, to emerge victoriously from their contact with other ideas and philosophies of life and to commit themselves to a global transformation of society in accord with the revelation of Christ.[24]

In the last analysis, these two methods correspond to two conceptions of the Gospel, the mission of the church and the Christian life. If our evangelical churches have given primacy to an accounting on the basis of the bare minimum (the only exception being that the denominational manual, not the Denzinger, provides the criteria for defining heresy), this demonstrates that they have not been able to escape from the conditioning of consumer society and, in their interest to find more converts, have accommodated their message to this society. The necessary reform demands a total reconstruction of the local church so that it may embody the demands of the Gospel.

The Gospel, the World and the Church

The church has only two alternatives in its confrontation with the world: either it adapts itself to the world and betrays the Gospel, or it responds to the Gospel and enters into conflict with the world.

The world (in the negative sense of the word) is a system in which evil is organised against God. The life-style which it imposes upon men is a slavery to the principalities and powers of evil. It cannot tolerate the presence of values or criteria which challenge its powerful conditioning influence. Its influence is so subtle that it can be detected even in the one dimension of life where man would like to believe himself most free: religion. As the Lausanne Covenant clearly indicates, satanic activity can even be present within the church in the message which it preaches and the methodology which it uses to spread its message.

The Gospel is the good news of the victory of Jesus Christ over the powers of darkness. The Saviour whose death was an atonement for sin is also the Lord who 'disarmed the principalities and powers and made a public example of them, triumphing over them' (Col. 2: 15), his salvation provides not only freedom from the consequences of sin, but also freedom from the power of sin. It deals not only with man's reconciliation to God, but also a complete re-structuring of life according to the model for the new man provided by God in Jesus Christ. In other words, the Gospel offers not *only* a religious experience, but also a new creation, a new life-style under the rule of God.

The church is called to incarnate the Kingdom of God in

the midst of the kingdoms of this world. The Gospel leaves it no other alternative. Committing itself to it, however, means entering into conflict with the world. One dare not think that the church can resist the conditioning of the world without that very resistance plunging it into conflict with the powers of destruction. When one takes into account the origin and history of the church, it is not surprising to find that in their confrontation with the world Christians are caught up in a conflict; it is, rather, surprising that Christians would *not* expect this to happen. The church derives its meaning by virtue of its connection with Jesus Christ, the Suffering Servant whose rejection of the establishment of his time brought him to his death. The apostle Paul affirms that it was 'the powers that rule the world' (NEB) — the forces of evil — who crucified the Lord of Glory. From that point on, the way of the church is stamped with the cross. In the words of Martin Luther King, 'If the church of Jesus Christ is to regain once more its power, message, and authentic ring, it must conform only to the demands of the Gospel.'[25]

The epistle to the Galatians illustrates the practical meaning of the cross of Christ in the church's confrontation with the world. In the very first verses Paul places his ideas in a cosmic context by affirming that Christ 'gave himself for our sins, that he might *deliver us from this present evil world*, according to the will of God and our Father' (1: 4 AV). In a later passage he uncovers the hidden motives of the false teachers who had infiltrated the church in Galatia to deform the Gospel message: they wanted to maintain their good standing before men and avoid the conflict. Paul's very questions suggest that this was indeed the case: 'Am I now seeking the favour of men, or of God? Or am I trying to please men?' From the perspective of the Gospel, there is only one alternative: 'If I were still pleasing men, I should not be a servant of Christ' (1: 10). The radical nature of the option reflects the great distance between two life-styles: that which corresponds to the present evil world, being subject to the powers of destruction, and that which corresponds to the new creation, being under the lordship of Jesus Christ. The false teachers had wanted to avoid the conflict and that had led them to adulterate the Gospel: they wanted to compel the believers to submit to the rite of circumcision so that they might 'make a good showing in the flesh ... that they may not be persecuted for the cross of Christ' (6: 12). For his part, Paul understands that if Christ died to free us from the present evil world, the cross of Christ stands between him and the world: it is the cross 'by which the world has been crucified to me, and I to the world' (6:14).

Conflict is inevitable when the church takes the Gospel seriously. It is just as true today in the consumer society as it was in the first century. From the perspective of the Gospel it is not a matter of a man leaving time in his schedule — already full of secular activities — to give his dues to God, to devote some time to religion and thus make himself worthy of the inner peace and material prosperity that religion provides. What *is* important is that he be liberated from his slavery to the powers of destruction and integrated into the purpose of God to place all things under the lordship of Jesus Christ, into the new creation which is made visible in the community which models its life upon the Second Adam. When, in its desire to avoid the conflict, the church accommodates itself to the spirit of the age, it loses the prophetic dimension of its mission and becomes an agent of the status quo. The salt loses its savour. It is a thermometer instead of a thermostat. As a result, it opens itself to the criticism exemplified in the words of Pierre Bunton:

> It has all but been forgotten that Christianity began as a revolutionary religion whose followers embraced an entirely different set of values from those held by other members of society. Those original values are still in conflict with the values of contemporary society; yet religion today has become as conservative a force as the force the original Christians were in conflict with.[26]

Consumer society has imposed a life-style which makes property an absolute right and gives priority to money over men, and production over nature. This is the form which 'the present evil world' has taken, the system in which the powers of destruction have organised human life. The danger of worldliness against which the Lausanne Covenant warns us has a concrete form: it is the danger of accommodating ourselves to the form of this evil world, with all its materialism, its obsession with individual success, its blinding selfishness.

Jesus Christ died for our sins, to free us from the present evil world. His incarnation and his cross are the norms for the life and mission of the church. His victory is the basis of our hope in the midst of the conflict. His call is 'to equip ourselves with God's armour and to fight this battle with the spiritual weapons of truth and prayer'.

I appeal to you therefore, brethren, by the mercies of God, to present your bodies as a living sacrifice, holy and acceptable to God, which is your spiritual worship. Do not be conformed to this world but be transformed by the renewal of your mind, that you may prove what is the will of God, what is good and acceptable and perfect.

(Rom. 12: 1–2)

CHAPTER XIII

Freedom and Persecution

A. N. Observer

'It is the God-appointed duty of every government to secure conditions of peace, justice and liberty in which the church may obey God, serve the Lord Christ, and preach the gospel without interference. We therefore pray for the leaders of the nations and call upon them to guarantee freedom of thought and conscience, and freedom to practise and propagate religion in accordance with the will of God and as set forth in The Universal Declaration of Human Rights. We also express our deep concern for all who have been unjustly imprisoned, and especially for our brethren who are suffering for their testimony to the Lord Jesus. We promise to pray and work for their freedom. At the same time we refuse to be intimidated by their fate. God helping us, we too will seek to stand against injustice and to remain faithful to the gospel, whatever the cost. We do not forget the warning of Jesus that persecution is inevitable.'
(*1 Tim. 1: 1–4; Acts 4: 19; 5: 29; Col. 3: 24; Heb. 13: 1–3; Luke 4: 18; Gal. 5: 11, 6: 12; Matt. 5: 10–12; John 15: 18–21*)

(Lausanne Covenant, Clause 13)

IN THE WORLD of the mid-seventies, God's people live simultaneously in nearly all the great epochs of church history, from the days of Jesus to the present. Some suffer, as this is read, under the equivalent of Nero, Diocletian, the Inquisition, or the fierce intolerances which culminated in the massacres of the Huguenots and Waldensians.

On the one hand are grouped those nations which in their official stance leave the individual, organisations and churches completely free to practise and propagate their religious views in the context of public order; we will call these open societies. On the other hand are grouped an increasing number of nations which must be categorised as repressive regimes, hostile to active Christian faith and practice. Lip service to freedom is the official stance of a number of nations which in practice repress true Christian life and teaching.

This chapter will examine the subject pragmatically. Where necessary, the identity of those concerned has been concealed to protect individuals from recrimination. For this reason the author prefers to remain anonymous.

The Facts

The following recent cases give immediacy to the subject. In a North African nation recently, a local Christian serving the Bible Society was called before the police with his wife and intimidated with physical violence. In the background, either from tapes or nearby cells, the noise of beatings, screams and groans added an atmosphere of fear and terror. The elderly man, exhausted by several hours of interrogation, at last leaned against the table. The police superintendent whipped out his revolver and said: 'I can shoot you dead, and no one will ask a question. Don't touch my desk if you want to live.'

The real issue was the country's official stance which refused to recognise that any national could possibly admit a personal faith in Jesus Christ. The quiet but active and effective witness of this individual had somehow to be eliminated, although the Bible Society bookstore was left alone for fear of international repercussions if it were ex-appropriated. The Christian man, however, remained firm and did not deny his Lord.

In another Muslim nation a Christian young man was offered a job as a veterinarian for which he was qualified. He was told firmly, 'No Christian can hold this administrative post. If you become a Muslim you can have the job; otherwise no one will employ you in this country.' After temporising for weeks he told his sorrowing mother: 'Mama, it will hurt you, but tomorrow you will see in the newspaper a report that I have become a Muslim. I want you to know that I did this in final desperation to get a job; there was no other hope.' The irony of the matter is that this particular nation speaks out strongly on the subject of discrimination against its nationals in other countries, and pleads for western aid.

In Marxist nations of Eastern Europe and the USSR many documented facts are available. Two cases are cited. In one nation a pastor was called up by the leaders of his denomination for a first warning: 'You have had too many conversions, these must be reduced or we shall have to invalidate your preaching licence.'

'But obedience to Jesus requires that we disciple all nations. I must be obedient to him,' was the godly pastor's reply.

'Choose between survival or loss of your job,' he was told.

When I met him he was a factory worker with a shift commencing at 4 a.m., and was 'illegally' taking services for the new pastor who was absent through sickness. 'They cannot check everybody all the time. It is a calculated risk,' he commented.

Back in his radiant family circle at night — after carefully evading a hanger-on and potential informer — he told of a network of fellow workers who provided Bibles to true believers. He was a key figure in this project. 'But we always fear betrayal by informers,' he said, and this phrase lingered in my mind as I left him.

In 1970 in Camp No. 3 in Mordovia (the town of Barashevo), USSR, Father Boris Zalivako was met by Andrei Sinyavsky who was also serving a prison sentence. When Andrei Sinyavsky was freed, he reported the persecution of this man of God for his 'outstanding example of Christian service to God and his fellow man'. He added, 'In this severe regime camp, the Gospels are prohibited, and even handwritten prayers are confiscated during individual and mass searches.' The latest available information (April, 1974) indicates that the physical condition of Father Boris is extremely grave as a result of prison life, despite his being a vigorous young man in his mid-thirties.[1]

Persecution is not restricted to some Muslim nations and Marxist regimes. In an African republic recently, young Christian teenagers were subjected to intolerable pressures by the tribal elders to proceed with initiation rites. The current return to authentic African origins confronts the true follower of Jesus with decisions which few in the very tender years of puberty can handle. Parents are often too uncertain to withstand tribal pressures, and most succumb in compromise. This religious persecution is on the increase, yet few protests have been registered at international level.

In China the strictest watch is maintained over any active outbreak of vital Christian faith and worship. Yet despite all the pressures, believers are scattered among the 800 million people. More Christians may have survived the great storms of persecution over the past twenty years than are known at present. Although only two Protestant churches are known to be functioning openly, one in Peking and one in

Shanghai, heroism and a vital faith reveal themselves in the most unexpected places.

A Christian Chinese woman returning to Hong Kong from visiting relatives in China was passing the several checkpoints. At one of these, which was somewhat isolated and alone, the official looked at her and asked, 'Are you a Christian?' Panic surged, with the temptation to deny Jesus and say 'No.' But courage reasserted itself and she modestly said: 'Yes, I am.' 'Pass on,' said the official, 'so am I!'

Right-wing regimes, using police state methods and harsh repression, are also parties to persecution. It is well known that for many years in Greece the open sale of the New Testament in contemporary Greek has been an offence under law resulting in fines and prison sentences.

Truth, Lies and Prejudice

In all official contacts, perhaps with the exception of Albania, national spokesmen will tell diplomats, visitors and the public in general, that religious freedom in terms of the United Nations Charter is guaranteed to their citizens. When carefully documented facts showing a different picture are presented, the evidence is denied as fabricated or untrue.

In open societies the public has ceased to be impartial and objective in its evaluation of facts and reaction to them. For example, in October, 1974, the UN Security Council sat to discuss the expulsion of South Africa over her policy of apartheid. The unethical policy of white minority rule of a coloured majority was the major issue. Yet among those judging the issue were the USSR and China, both of whom have denied basic rights to a much greater number of individuals on the grounds that they are Christians. No voice is raised on this issue, nor on the persecution of Christians in Morocco and Algeria. Members of the World Council of Churches can wax indignant on the subject of Rhodesia and South Africa, yet remain strangely silent on the persecution and harassment of Christians. Why this partiality?

Christians in open societies have the same problem with partiality. They are easily influenced by the latest public trends in judging such issues as race (Rhodesia, South Africa), exploitation by big business and price manipulation (USA); repression (Greek and Chilean right-wing regimes). Yet, at the same time they ignore or evade even more serious matters, such as the denial of fundamental rights to fellow Christians in most nations of Eastern Europe, the USSR, China, and certain Muslim and African nations.

An important practical application of the Lausanne Covenant would be an objective and forthright prophetic voice lifted against all who crush God's people. This voice of God through his prophets should come irrespective of reprisals or the prestige and standing of the individual or nation concerned.

Survival under Persecution

An anonymous writer in *Interlit* reports:

A young American student visited Eastern Europe for the first time. As a Christian, he was interested in the situation of the church in a communist society. In addition to visiting a number of churches, he was able to meet and question a certain denominational leader. When the student returned to the United States, his experiences and observations were published in a small student magazine. As a matter of courtesy he sent a copy to the Christian leader he wrote about and quoted. He needn't have bothered. The East European had already seen the article — on the desk of the secret police officer who summoned him for questioning soon after it was published.[2]

In a Muslim nation where for thirty years a careful and discreet step by step approach had resulted in some nationals coming to faith in Jesus as the Christ, the work was halted and a number of foreign participants quietly expelled from the nation. A number of factors were responsible for government action. A candidate had unwisely announced her objective to win men and women for Christ in a public meeting. The local newspaper had headlined this; the clipping service had supplied the information to the government; and within a couple of weeks the Prime Minister of the host nation had the information on his desk. In addition, traditional western-based missionary societies and Christian aid agencies had, despite warnings to avoid publicity, succumbed to the craving of their constituencies for success news. The photographs, news items and articles had also reached the host nation. There were also other factors — such as the interest of the poor in the message of Jesus — but the point is that absolute security was required, and no western-based agency could take this.

Such cases indicate that in certain instances these agencies are actually party to the persecuting process. Few, if any, western evangelical magazines are guiltless.

Christians suffering under persecution are in the arena of conflict, and under the guidance of the Holy Spirit they themselves must determine their policies and attitudes. Would-be counsellors in the sanctuaries of open societies should be very sensitive to the repercussions inflicted on Christians in repressive regimes as a result of what is written, filmed or broadcast. The determining factor should be the consensus of godly leaders responsible for God's people in their own nation. They know when it is a time to speak and when to keep silence.

Jesus and Security

We would do well to re-examine Jesus' example and take to heart the clear warnings he gave regarding security measures. On one occasion Jesus said to a leper he had healed, 'See that you say nothing to any one' (Mark 1: 44), but his request was ignored and, as a result, freedom to work in some cities was curtailed. On other occasions Jesus also directed a security silence, but his hearers did not co-operate

(Mark 3: 12, 5: 43, 7: 36). Jesus himself withdrew from Galilee following the beheading of John, no doubt for security reasons (Luke 9: 7–10, Matt. 14: 13). On one occasion he travelled to Jerusalem 'not publicly but in private' (John 7: 10). To maintain the secrecy of the Last Supper location — because of the collusion between Judas Iscariot and the chief priests, who were awaiting an opportunity to arrest him — Jesus gave coded signals to Peter and John (Luke 22: 7–13).

Christians in western nations are influenced by contemporary pressures for uncensored media and free news coverage which do not necessarily represent a Christian stance. A much more disciplined and sensitive attitude must be developed to the situations fellow Christians face living under hostile regimes. For them these words of Jesus have special meaning: 'My kingship is not of this world' (John 18: 36); 'in the world you have tribulation' (John 16: 33); 'because you are not of the world, but I chose you out of the world, therefore the world hates you' (John 5: 19).

Degrees of compromise may lessen persecution from men, but will also reduce the privileges and honour before God accordingly (John 14: 23). Numerous cases are on record documenting the ways in which followers of Jesus have been seduced through the offer of material gain for themselves and their families. One student from Eastern Europe was offered a scholarship to study in a western seminary. He was invited to drink coffee in a café by a stranger who later identified himself as a secret police officer. 'We are prepared to let you go,' said the man, 'If you will co-operate.' Co-operation involved not only reporting the movements and contacts of other students, but membership in the espionage system. The student told the writer he had to decline the scholarship, and added that he doubted whether any student studying in the West from his nation was exempt from such conditions. He chose to obey God rather than man, and suffered accordingly.

Much discussion has ranged around the misconception that Christians are obliged at all times to 'be subject to the governing authorities . . . [for] he who resists the authorities resists what God has appointed' (Rom. 13: 1, 2). This teaching must be complemented by Peter and John's decision when the governing authorities forbade them to do what God had commanded: they chose to obey God rather than men (Acts 4: 19). In all matters where laws of the civil authority do not directly contravene the higher authority of God's expressed will, the Christian obeys. But where civil authorities pass legislation which directly contravenes God's law, that legislation is *ultra vires* or invalid. The follower of Jesus ignores it.

It is a strange irony of history that a number of Christians in western nations who reminisce on the ways and means by which Tyndale of England translated and arranged the distribution of the English Bible (contrary to the laws of local authorities) take the opposite view with reference to Bible distribution in Eastern Europe! 'Respectable' societies tend to restrict Bible sales.

The Lausanne Covenant, if properly understood, should result in those committed to it following a bolder and more definite course of obeying God rather than men in the proclamation of the Good News by every conceivable means. It must be insisted that the onus of illegality lies squarely on those who have dared to attempt to overturn God's basic commands and will, setting up their own standards instead. The *modus operandi* by which the individual or group carries out God's commands must be left to the discretion of those concerned. In the inevitable creative tension of conflicting viewpoints, weight must be given to those who live and work under oppressive regimes, rather than to those who use hit and run tactics from the safe sanctuaries of open societies.

Such conflicts are real. The summer of 1974 saw a case in an Eastern European nation where a married pastor was arrested and charged with receiving and distributing Bibles from the West. The new law under which he was charged related to material from the West which had not been officially passed by the censor. A number of local Christians protested, stating that if the pastor was not released they wished to be imprisoned also, as they were 'guilty' of the same 'offence'. When the appeal came to court, the two lawyers representing the pastor demolished the case by showing that the Bible, with its standing of over nineteen-hundred years, was not in the category of material proscribed.

The secret police intervened as the judge was about to dismiss the case and insisted the prison sentence stand. At this point one of the defendant's lawyers, a non-Christian, threw up his hands in horror and said, 'Where is justice?' Foreigners cannot effectively intervene in such cases; local Christians have to follow through the implications of faithfulness to Jesus with all the suffering that commitment involves.

Can Christians in open societies help their brothers suffering persecution for Christ's sake?

Most definitely, yes. Christians in Asia, Africa and Latin America can help more effectively than western Christians (whose opposition is constructed as pseudo-political). In the future, when Christians under pressure do request help a far more positive response should be forthcoming than has been in the past.

If subscribers to the Lausanne Covenant mean what they say in pledging themselves to 'pray and work' for the freedom of their repressed brothers and sisters, the following may provide guidelines:

The well-known case of the Christian Russian writer and historian Alexander Solzhenitsyn needs only brief comment. The widespread protests from a broad spectrum of public persons was a deciding factor in protecting Solzhenitsyn from imprisonment, perhaps even in saving his life. It is clear that repressive regimes do not wish to appear in an unfavourable light, especially before Third World nations. If Christians in open societies really meant business, they could vocalise much stronger protests than they have. In the USSR a number of Christians now imprisoned for their faith are rarely mentioned by name in any form of protest, even though their leaders have requested this, as has already been cited in the case of Father Boris Zalivako.

On March 8 and 23, 1974, only a very small group of Christians met to pray in turns, kneeling outside the Soviet embassy in London. These faithful few had responded to a request to demonstrate solidarity with a Russian Christian, Mrs Zoya Radygina of Perm, who in the summer of 1973 had been deprived of her three children because she gave them a Christian upbringing.[3] Over a million Christian believers scattered in the more than a hundred nations represented at the Lausanne Congress could have knelt in prayer outside the Soviet embassies of their respective nations had there been serious intent to help.

At the Baptist Theological Seminary in Bucharest, Rumania, matters came to a head in the early 'seventies and reached western Christians from a protesting nucleus within the Baptist Churches. They have asked western Christians to raise their voice in protest. Their spokesman is Pastor Ton, who in June, 1974, was reported to have been dismissed from his post as professor as a result of government pressure. He writes: 'Our churches have been so subjugated to the dictates of the atheist authorities and have had so much interference in their internal life from these authorities that now we can hardly speak about the freedom of the Holy Spirit in, and the lordship of the Lord Jesus Christ over the Rumanian Baptist Churches.'[4]

Ways and means of remembering 'those who are in prison, as though in prison with them; and those who are ill treated, since you also are in the body' (Heb. 13: 3) include:

— Continual prayer for specific people and situations in all meetings of the church.

— Protest letters, where recommended by national leaders, to the embassy and civic heads of repressive regimes with specific names, places and dates.

— A continual flow of carefully documented facts relating to the persecution of Christians to public media, when Christian leaders in the nation involved so approve.

— Public witness in open societies before the embassies concerned.

— Unashamed rebuke by Christian businessmen, public officials, scientists and others, especially in Third World Nations, to their counterparts in repressive regimes wherever paths cross in the course of everyday contact and at international conferences.

The noteworthy comment by Paul on the character of Onesiphorus was: 'He was not ashamed of my chains' (II Tim. 1: 16). Only time will record whether signatories and

others committed to the Lausanne Covenant are truly prepared for the public stigma of siding with the persecuted
ones of the earth.

And what of open societies? In their educational systems,
hospital and medical services, trade unions and big business
management, anti-Christian attitudes and pressures are
building up to the point of persecuting non-conformists.
Can a Christian deprive the sick of care to join a strike
based on greed and human covetousness? Can a Christian
join a strike to deprive the elderly and crippled of essential
services? Can a Christian invest his money and partake in
businesses which exploit the poor?

The comment of an experienced follower of Jesus is very
relevant to the consequences of non-conformity: 'All who
desire to live a godly life in Christ Jesus will be persecuted'
(II Tim. 3: 12).

CHAPTER XIV

The Power of the Holy Spirit

Michael Griffiths

'WE BELIEVE IN the power of the Holy Spirit. The Father sent his Spirit to bear witness to his Son; without his witness ours is futile. Conviction of sin, faith in Christ, new birth and Christian growth are all his work. Further, the Holy Spirit is a missionary spirit; thus evangelism should arise spontaneously from a spirit-filled church. A church that is not a missionary church is contradicting itself and quenching the Spirit. Worldwide evangelisation will become a realistic possibility only when the Spirit renews the church in truth and wisdom, faith, holiness, love and power. We therefore call upon all Christians to pray for such a visitation of the sovereign Spirit of God that all his fruit may appear in all his people and that all his gifts may enrich the body of Christ. Only then will the whole church become a fit instrument in his hands, that the whole earth may hear his voice.'
(*I Cor. 2:4; John 15:26, 27, 16:8–11; I Cor. 12:3; John 3:6–8; II Cor. 3:18; John 7:37–39; I Thess. 5:19; Acts 1:8; Ps. 85:4–7, 67:1–3; Gal. 5:22, 23; I Cor. 12:4–31; Rom. 12:3–8*)

(LAUSANNE COVENANT, CLAUSE 14)

THE COVENANT IS concerned primarily with the power of the Holy Spirit in relation to the church. The Christian church is not explicable purely in human or sociological terms. It is the community of God, who dwells among his people (II Cor. 6: 16), and who is often described as 'Lord of Hosts' (*kurios pantokrator*), the God of All Power.

The Holy Spirit is the executive of the godhead on earth and in the church.

The Father is in heaven. The Son is presently in heaven. When the Son was on earth, even he in his humanity depended upon the power of the Holy Spirit (Luke 4: 14). The Son ascended to sit on the right hand of power and has now poured out his Holy Spirit upon his church (Acts 1: 8). Between Ascension-Pentecost and Christ's Second Coming, the church experiences the continuing acts of the Holy Spirit (Rom. 15: 19). The Holy Spirit is referred to as the Spirit of God and the Spirit of Christ (Rom. 8: 9) so that where the indwelling Holy Spirit is, the Father and the Son have their abode also (John 14: 23).

It is through the power of the Holy Spirit revealed in preaching (I Cor. 2: 4; I Thess. 1: 5) that new congregations are brought into existence, as he bears witness to Christ (John 15: 26) and convinces the world (John 16: 8 ff.). God's method of saving us is 'by the washing of regeneration and renewal in the Holy Spirit, which he poured out upon us richly through Jesus Christ our Saviour' (Titus 3: 5, 6). These two ideas are well expressed in the Anglican

Collect for Christmas Day 'that we, being regenerated, may daily be renewed by the Holy Spirit'. Christ is the giver of the Spirit, the Living Water given to those who believe (John 7: 38, 39).

The great final objective of the Father, the goal of the work of the Son (Eph. 5: 25–27) and the chief task of the Holy Spirit is the building of the church. Christians are being built together into a Holy Temple by the Holy Spirit (Eph. 2: 22) and men are given by Christ 'for the equipment of the saints, for building up the body' (Eph. 4: 12). This is a continuing work, for the congregation (all of us) are being changed from one degree of glory to another by the Lord who is the Spirit (II Cor. 3: 18). The work of 'renewal' is not just progress in monstrous 'fits and starts' as it were, but the total continuous work of the Holy Spirit in the church. But are 'renewal' and 'revival' correctly biblical concepts at all?

How Scriptural are 'Renewal' and 'Revival'?

There are 'revivals' of true religion in the Old Testament when an apostate or backsliding people repent and are called back to obedience to the Law of God — under Samuel (1 Sam. 7: 3); Solomon (II Chron. 6, 7); Elijah (I Kings 18: 39 ff.); Hezekiah (II Kings 18: 5) and Josiah (II Kings 23: 3). Some of these were superficial and the result of legislation from above. Most remarkable was the revival under Ezra and Nehemiah (Neh. 8). There are also prayers for revival (e.g. Ps. 85: 6; Hab. 3: 2) in the Old Testament.

The concept of 'revival' is not found in the New Testament as such, although there are appeals by the prophet John to the Asian churches for congregational repentance: 'You have abandoned the love you had at first. Remember then from what you have fallen, repent and do the works you did at first' (Rev. 2: 4, 5). 'Renewal' is used in the New Testament to mean a continual ethical process rather than a spiritual crisis (e.g. Col. 3: 10, *Anakainoō*; Eph. 4: 23, *Ananeoō*), although the transformation by the renewing of your mind may, in context, possibly relate to the body life of the congregation in Rome (Rom. 12: 2, *Anakainōsis*). None of these usages seem to correspond directly to 'a visitation of the sovereign Spirit' (Acts 3: 19, *Anapsuksis*) which comes from the presence of the Lord in response to the repentance of God's people (in that context, the Jews).

The Sovereignty of God in Revival

Historically, we know that there have been such 'visitations of the sovereign Spirit of God'. Man cannot start revival: only God can do that. (John 3: 8, 'The wind blows where it wills.') Man cannot stop revival once God has started it. What man can do is to conserve its benefits: much as the disciples were commanded to collect up the fragments that remained after the five thousand were fed. What remained from miraculous multiplication had to be conserved by practical means. It was not to be thrown away in hope of another miracle tomorrow. We cannot keep a revival going — the so-called 'continuous revival' — when God in his sovereignty has determined to revert to his more usual method of operation. If the results are conserved then we may hope for 'continued revivedness', i.e., that those who have been blessed will remain on a higher plateau of spiritual experience than they were before.

Buchanan says:

The Holy Spirit is not limited to any one mode of operation in the execution of His glorious work; and His sovereignty ought ever to be remembered when we are considering a subject of this nature. It has, unfortunately, been too much overlooked, when, on the one hand, some have insisted, as we think, with undue partiality and confidence, on a general and remarkable revival, as being in itself the best manifestation of the Spirit's grace, and as being, in all cases, a matter of promise to believing prayer; and when, on the other hand, not a few have looked to the quiet and gradual success of the Gospel ministry, to the exclusion, or at least disparagement, of any more sudden and remarkable work of grace. The former have given a too exclusive preference to what is extraordinary and striking; while the latter have fallen into the opposite error, of preferring what is more usual and quiet. We think it were better to admit of both methods of conversion, and to leave the choice to the sovereign wisdom and grace of the Spirit. It is equally possible for him to convert souls successively or simultaneously; and in adopting either course doubtless he has wise ends in view. We have no sympathy with those who, overlooking the steady progress of the great work of conversion under a stated ministry, make no account of the multitudes who are added, one by one, to the Church of the living God, merely because their conversion has not been attended with the outward manifestations of a great religious revival; nor can we agree with them in thinking that the Church has any sure warrant to expect that the Spirit will be bestowed, in every instance, in that particular way. But as little have we any sympathy with those who, rejecting all revivals as unscriptural delusions, profess to look exclusively to the gradual progress of divine truth, and the slow advance of individual conversion under a stated ministry. Both methods — the simultaneous and the successive conversion of souls — are equally within the power of the Spirit; and there may exist wise reasons why, in certain cases, the first should be chosen, while, in other cases, the second is preferred.[1]

The Lausanne Covenant humbly recognises the sovereignty of God's spirit in choosing the manner of his own working. However, it is notable that even so convinced a Calvinist as Jonathan Edwards taught that Christians have a positive duty to pray for revival (see concluding section).

True and False Triumphalism

'Triumphalism' became something of a naughty word at Lausanne. Thus that thrilling document, the 'Response to

Lausanne', said: 'We confess that . . . our testimony has often been marred by triumphalism and arrogance.' This relates to the further confession of being 'unduly preoccupied with statistics' — especially with the kind of extrapolation which argues that 'if the present rate of growth continues to the end of the century, then . . .' etc. We should have learnt that this is a dangerous and presumptuous form of argument.

The great Samuel Zwemer once argued that because five sixths of the Arab world was under British rule, we could expect that eventually they would all embrace Christianity (ouch!).

A similar unfulfilled prophecy was that of Guido Verbeck who ventured:

> I am less sanguine than many others, but it is my confident belief that if the missionary societies are faithful to their charge up to the end of this century, you need not after next year send any more missionaries to Japan . . . the finishing up of the work can be safely left to the foreign force which will by that time be there, working in conjunction with the ever increasing number of native pastors and evangelists.[2]

Verbeck was writing in 1889, the year before an intensely anti-foreign militarism threw the statistical trends into devastating retreat! Eighty-five years later there are still a hundred million unconverted Japanese.

This kind of shallow triumphalism is dishonouring to God, because we are putting our trust in statistics rather than in the power of the Holy Spirit. Moreover it depends upon a dimension of church growth which is measurable (quantity) rather than one which is not (quality). The New Testament, while it does give us figures for the growth of the Jerusalem church, shows a much deeper concern for the quality of 'body life' and public testimony of the congregations. The New Testament certainly stresses human responsibility in how we build (I Cor. 3: 10). But the concept of 'church growth' is not, if we follow the biblical usage correctly, the result of human strategy and methodology at all, but of divine sovereignty: 'God gave the growth' (I Cor. 3: 6).

There is, however, a truly scriptural triumph to be anticipated: 'Thanks be to God, who in Christ always leads us in triumph' (II Cor. 2: 14). It is certain that 'he who began a good work in you [the Philippian congregation] will bring it to completion' (Phil. 1: 6). Christ promises: 'I will build my church, and the powers of death shall not prevail against it' (Matt. 16: 18). William Carey's proposal of a World Congress of Missions in 1810 fell through because there were not enough Protestant missionaries, let alone Christians, in what we now call the Third World, to attend such a conference.[3] Only two long lifetimes have passed, but it became clear at Lausanne that today the churches of the Third World are intellectually out-thinking and spiritually out-living the Laodicean churches of Europe and North America. We can see evidence of the 'fullness of the Gentiles' being brought in the remarkable growth of the church in the last 160 years. We may therefore be humbly triumphant: 'by the power of the Holy Spirit . . . [we] may abound in hope' (Rom. 15: 13).

True and False Spiritual Power

Chatting in the great lobby of the Palais de Beaulieu, Malcolm Muggeridge commented that there was a danger of seeking worldly power at Lausanne through setting up an organisation of evangelicals rather than depending upon the power of God. We are very prone to trust in human organisation.

Gottfried Osei-Mensah warned the Congress against regarding the Holy Spirit as little 'parcels of power' which we could open and use when we chose. The Covenant reminds us that it is a visitation of the 'sovereign Spirit of God', a Divine Person, that we are to pray for, and not some sensational impersonal 'power'.

Our evangelical images of power need to be calibrated afresh by the Word of God. There is a current evangelical image of the dynamic spiritual pop-star, glittering in the spotlights, revelling in the public-relations contrived personality cult. All this is a far cry from authentic apostolic experience: 'we have this treasure in earthen vessels, to show that the transcendent power belongs to God and not to us' (II Cor. 4: 7). 'The power of the Holy Spirit' did not make an apostle into a kind of superstar evangelist. Paul could say he was 'so utterly, unbearably crushed that we despaired' (II Cor. 1: 8) and were 'afflicted at every turn — fighting without and fear within. But God, who comforts the downcast . . .' (7: 5, 6). He learns that God's 'power is made perfect through weakness' (12: 9). We can scarcely argue that these men 'did not know the blessing' for biblically this is the authentic apostolic experience. We should be careful when our stereotype of the Spirit-filled leader does not measure up to his being 'in weakness and in much fear and trembling' (I Cor. 2: 3) and where his 'bodily presence is weak, and his speech of no account' (II Cor. 10: 10). God's power is not intended to make men powerful, but rather to display God's transcendent power in the scruffy earthenware of dedicated but frail human vessels.

True and False Revival

We must not be naïve and assume that all we need is revival and our problems are all solved: this is too facile a solution. Revivals bring life in places of spiritual stagnation and deadness; but they are accompanied by divisions and counterfeits, and distorted by 'excesses'. Thus Dr J. I. Packer writes:

> Revival means renewal of life, and life means energy. It is true that revival delivers the church from the problems created by apathy and deadness, but it is equally true that revival plunges the church into a welter of new problems created by the torrential overflow of disordered and undisciplined spiritual vitality. In a revival, the saints are suddenly roused from a state of torpor and lethargy by a new and overwhelming awareness of the reality of spiritual things, and of God. They are like sleepers shaken awake and now half blinded by the unaccustomed glare of

the sun. They hardly know for the moment where they are; in one sense, they now see everything, as they never saw it before, yet in another sense, because of the very brightness of the light, they can hardly see anything. They are swept off their feet; they lose their sense of proportion. They fall into pride, delusions, unbalance, censorious modes of speech, extravagant forms of action. Unconverted persons are caught up in what is going on; they feel the power of truth, though their hearts remain unrenewed; they become 'enthusiasts', harsh and bitter, fierce and vainglorious, cranky and fanatical. Then, perhaps, they fall into spectacular sin, and apostatise altogether; or else remain in the church to scandalise the rest of men by maintaining, on dogmatic perfectionist grounds, that while what they do would be sin in others, it is not sin in them. Satan (who, as Edwards somewhere observes, was 'trained in the best divinity school in the universe') keeps step with God, actively perverting and caricaturing all that the Creator is doing. A revival, accordingly, is always a disfigured work of God, and the more powerful the revival, the more scandalising disfigurements we may expect to see. Hence we cannot wonder if the revival comes to be bitterly opposed by respectable church members of limited spiritual insight, on account of the excesses linked with it; nor can we be surprised to find — as we regularly do — that many ministers stand aloof from the revival, and even preach against it and try to suppress it, on the grounds that it is not a spiritual phenomenon at all.[4]

Packer writes further on the subject when he says:

Satan is not restrained from working in times of revival. And Satan has a characteristic strategy which he employs at such times. 'When he finds that he can keep men quiet and secure no longer, then he drives them to excesses and extravagances. He holds them back as long as he can; but when he can do it no longer, then he will push them on, and, if possible, run them upon their heads.' Thus, he seeks to carry away revived believers by exploiting the strength of their feelings, tempting them to pride, censoriousness, impatience of all established order in the church, and belief that the Spirit has more freedom to work when Christians leave themselves in a state of disorganisation, and when ministers preach without bothering to prepare their sermons . . .

It is for this reason, Edwards insists, that it is so vitally important to judge spiritual movements, not by their immediate phenomena or by-products, but by their ultimate effects in the lives of those involved in them. If you concentrate on the phenomena, you can always find a great deal that is spurious, and ill-considered, and wrongheaded, and wild, and fanatical; and then you will be tempted to conclude that there is nothing of God in the movement at all. But, as we saw, the right way to assess what is happening is to see whether, amid all the tumult and disorder, the 'distinguishing marks of a work of the Spirit of God' are appearing. If they are, then we may know that it is God at work.[5]

What Edwards and Packer are saying is that revival is always a mixed work. Satan always tries to counterfeit and distort a true work of God. That is no reason, however, to be afraid of revival, for God did not give us a Spirit of timidity but of power and love and self-control (II Tim. 1: 7). There is no need to quench (I Thess. 5: 19) the fires of the Holy Spirit, or to despise prophesy, but there must be biblical discipline and we must test everything, hold fast what is good and reject what is not (I Thess. 5: 19–22). Godly men are often perplexed at first to know whether all this energy is of God or not, and the 'revived ones' may be curbed by official church sanctions or by the unofficial but undisguised disapproval of church leaders.

Recently comparing experiences in East Africa and South-east Asia, it has been an encouragement to me to discover that Scripture warns us to distinguish between genuine and counterfeit dreams and prophecies.

For example, while *dreams* may arise from bad digestion or from busyness (Ecc. 5: 3, 7) and there are false dreams (Jer. 23: 25–32), we cannot deny that in the Bible God did speak to individuals through dreams. This still seems possible especially when people cannot read Scripture in their own language. Dreams are most meaningful to the individual who dreams them. Caution is required in interpreting the dreams of others, for this approaches divination and astrology, which are forbidden (Jer. 27: 9; 29: 8–9; Deut. 18: 10–14).

Christ warned us about false *prophets* (Matt. 24: 11, 24) while Paul teaches us not to despise prophetic utterances, but to test everything carefully (I Thess. 5: 20, 21). When two or three prophets speak others are to 'weigh what is said' (I Cor. 14: 29). Merely because something claims to be prophecy, it is not to be credulously accepted without careful consideration.

It is difficult to distinguish between the counterfeit, and 'excesses' when the genuinely spiritual has been distorted by fleshy exaggeration. For example, in East Africa, 'shaking' and 'tears', originally true marks of the Holy Spirit's work, were at times regarded as mandatory. It was not true repentance unless accompanied by shaking and tears. In Sarawak, the burning of fetishes, carvings and pin-up pictures (originally a spontaneous consequence of repentance) sometimes became the central focus of preaching, instead of that whole-hearted repentance towards God which those things signified. Preachers preached to get men to burn things rather than to persuade men to repent.

I especially treasure some minutes spent with Brother Festo Kivengere by the fountains in the Palais gardens, while he expounded to me how they had dealt with 'excesses' in East Africa. It was fascinating to discover that in Sarawak, Joseph Balan Seling has written almost similar advice to those involved in the East Malaysian revival.

1. *The Centrality of Christ Crucified and Risen.* The late William Nagenda used to draw a circle and say that Jesus and him crucified must always be in the centre. If in our teaching, anything else, however excellent (whether fellowship or healing or tongues) usurped the central place, then something was wrong. Festo maintains that this is the essential test and cure for exaggerations: the centrality of Christ.

'We should have a very real sense of the overwhelming presence of the Lord in the midst of the congregation,' he said. It is not upon the gifts, so much as upon the one who is the Giver, that everything must be centred. To elevate gifts to the throne of the Giver is blasphemous. Festo went on: 'The Holy Spirit has no independence of blessing: the Spirit is grieved if you give the impression it is his own store. The Spirit simply opens your eyes to the unlimited resources in Jesus Christ.'

In Sarawak, Joseph Balan Seling wrote:

> Always look to Jesus (Heb. 12: 2), don't ever move your eyes from being fixed on Jesus. There are visions, dreams, voices, feelings, miracles, trials, difficulties, lessons to learn and many other things. But in all these, don't move your eyes from Jesus, otherwise you will be led astray by the devil's deceit.[6]

2. *Discernment and Rebuking.* Bishop Festo said that it is easy to so emphasise something genuine that it becomes an exaggeration; we need to be very sensitive. A harsh speaker in Africa was rebuked by an elderly woman who said quietly; 'When you spoke, I couldn't see the wounded hands.'

Some earnest brother was shouting in a loud voice in prayer and was politely asked: 'What has happened to your God that he is so different from the loving Lord who listens and hears like a Father?'

If hearers are uneasy and think that the content of an alleged prophecy is biblically questionable, then they should openly and courteously express their doubts about its validity, in 'weighing' what is said. If the 'prophet' replies angrily by criticising the spirituality of the person who doubts his message, then the group would judge that if it is necessary to fight for the prophecy, it may well be from man rather than from the Lord. The leaders need to express whether they are happy or unhappy about such ministry in the congregation.

3. *Firm and Responsible Leadership.* Bishop Kivengere made the point that there must be a united team of spiritual

leaders whose hearts God has touched and who can check one another, because any of us could be led astray into exaggeration at some time. When something in a meeting is not ideal it is not necessarily a question of stopping it completely, so much as correcting it with loving sensitivity. The ruling of the recognised chairman of a particular meeting must always be accepted: 'God is not a God of confusion but of peace' and 'all things should be done decently and in order' (I Cor. 14: 33, 40).

Exaggerated Fears of Spiritual Power

Fear of 'excesses' may become almost pathological, as in Germany where in some circles any religious enthusiasm is suspect as *Schwarmgeist*. For fear of being misunderstood, some even hesitate to give teaching on the Holy Spirit at all, with the danger of teaching a Two-Person Trinity. These people have swung to the opposite extreme in reacting against extreme charismatics who may concentrate on the doctrine of the Holy Spirit and neglect the Father and the Son.

Some at Lausanne were bitterly opposed to charismatics even appearing on the platform, though in the event they were not so terrifying! It seems better to insist upon being biblical and to correct overemphases from Scripture, rather than dividing God's people over this issue.

Juan Carlos Ortiz, a Pentecostal minister from Argentina, made what many found a helpful contribution, especially in his seminars on the local church. He helped us question the stereotyped poverty of Protestant hymn-sandwich worship. (Emil Brunner was equally radical in his 'Misunderstanding of the Church' and was talking 'body life' in the German-speaking world long before the present enthusiasm among Anglo-Saxons.) Many Third World churches have inherited (from British colonial and American cultural Christianity) institutional ruts much deeper than their western originals, but people are, at last, trying to climb out of them. We must not throw out the biblical baby of 'body life' because of our exaggerated fears of the enthusiastic bath-water.

'All His Fruit' and 'All His Gifts'

Howard Snyder wrote some superb things in his paper, 'The Church as God's Agent of Evangelism', to me the outstanding paper of the Congress. He is best on the nature of the church and our goals in building the church. But he rightly emphasises the place of the Spirit's gifts building the *ekklesia*. Thus 'a primary function of the Christian community is the awakening and disciplining of the gifts of the Spirit ... as the community up-builds itself in love a kaleidoscope of spiritual gifts is awakened and begins to function...'

Yet there is a serious danger that extreme dispensationalists will adopt an attitude to Scripture little different from that of destructive biblical criticism, attacking the Bible with a pair of dispensational scissors. Both 'apostles and prophets' are eliminated from Eph. 4: 11 as 'not for this age', while references to prophecy, miracles, healing and tongues must all be cavalierly cut out of I Cor. 12–14 as 'long since ceased'. If the Bible is indeed the 'only infallible rule of faith and practice' (Covenant, Clause 2) then we must be faithful to what we believe about Scripture. According to Scripture, the gifts are given by the Holy Spirit to 'edify' the body (*oikodomeō* and its cognates occurs no less than seven times in I Cor. 14).

The fruit of the Spirit is also corporate, for it is impossible to exhibit all the fruit in individualistic solitude. 'Love' demands an object; 'longsuffering', someone to suffer; another person to be 'gentle' with or 'generous' towards or with whom to display 'meekness'. Thus both gifts and fruit of the Spirit alike are given with a view to the perfecting or completion of the saints in building up the body (Eph. 4: 12–16). This great goal for the church requires that we know what is the immeasurable greatness of his power in us (Eph. 1: 19). It is defined again: 'Now to him who by the *power at work within us* is able to do far more abundantly than all that we ask or think, to him be glory *in the church* and in Christ Jesus to all generations, for ever and ever. Amen' (Eph. 3: 20, 21).

It is the power of the Spirit in the church which brings glory to God.

'We therefore call upon all Christians to pray . . .'

The Spirit is sovereign in his visitations: yet there are biblical conditions for revival. The Lord himself appeared to Solomon in the night and promised: 'If my people who are called by my name humble themselves, and pray and seek my face, and turn from their wicked ways, then I will hear from heaven, and will forgive their sin and heal their land' (II Chron. 7: 14).

Jonathan Edwards expressed it as follows: 'It is revealed that when God is about to accomplish great things from His Church, He will begin by remarkably pouring out the Spirit of Grace and Supplication (Zech. 12: 10).' He argues that Christians who desire revival not only have a strong incentive to pray for it but a positive duty to pray for it.[7] Thus Edwards writes:

> If we look through the whole Bible, and observe all the examples of prayer that we find there recorded, we shall not find so many prayers for any other mercy, as for the deliverance, restoration, and prosperity of the church, and the advancement of God's glory and kingdom of grace in the world . . . the greatest part of the book of Psalms is made up of prayers for this mercy, prophecies of it, and prophetical praises for it . . .[8]

Thus the psalmist prays, 'Wilt thou not revive us again, that thy people may rejoice in thee?' (Ps. 85: 6). The sovereign author of revival is God himself. The objects of revival are God's people. The nature of revival is to call God's people to rejoice in him. But the verse itself is a prayer that God will revive us. Thus also 'they who wait for the Lord shall renew their strength' (Isa. 40: 31). The prophet Habakkuk in his prayer prays that the Lord will 'in the midst of the years renew' his work (Hab. 3: 2).

The Lausanne Covenant is thus thoroughly biblical when it calls upon all of us to pray, but possibly less than biblical in asking for only one visitation!

We may have every confidence that through his Holy Spirit the Lord will perfect his saints, so that we may be sanctified wholly and kept sound and blameless at the coming of our Lord Jesus Christ. 'He who calls you is faithful, and he will do it' (I Thess. 5: 24). Until the great Royal Visit of the Son (*parousia*) we should certainly pray for times of refreshing when the sovereign Spirit will visit his people (Luke 1: 68; 7: 16; Heb. 2: 6 AV) and prepare us for that Day.

CHAPTER XV

The Return of Christ

Samuel Escobar

'WE BELIEVE THAT Jesus Christ will return personally and visibly, in power and glory, to consummate his salvation and his judgment. This promise of his coming is a further spur to our evangelism, for we remember his words that the gospel must first be preached to all nations. We believe that the interim period between Christ's ascension and return is to be filled with the mission of the people of God, who have no liberty to stop before the End. We also remember his warning that false Christs and false prophets will arise as precursors of the final Antichrist. We therefore reject as a proud, self-confident dream the notion that man can ever build a utopia on earth. Our Christian confidence is that God will perfect his kingdom, and we look forward with eager anticipation to that day, and to the new heaven and earth in which righteousness will dwell and God will reign for ever. Meanwhile, we rededicate ourselves to the service of Christ and of men in joyful submission to his authority over the whole of our lives.'

(Mark 14: 62; Heb. 9: 28; Mark 13: 10; Acts 1: 8–11; Matt. 28: 20; Mark 13: 21–23; John 2: 18, 4: 1–3; Luke 12: 32; Rev. 21: 1–5; II Pet. 3: 13; Matt. 28: 18)

(LAUSANNE COVENANT, CLAUSE 15)

THE FEAR THAT Lausanne '74 would opt for the imposition of a triumphalistic western Gospel through North American sales techniques was dispelled by the reality of the event. Sober voices raised among the speakers, interaction at several levels and some unexpected factors led thinking participants back to the wealth and the dynamic of biblical truth and especially to a growing awareness that the mission of God's people derives from the lordship of Jesus Christ, and not from man-made strategies. By turning to Jesus Christ as Lord in days of manifest historical importance, we also come to reflect upon the direction and end of human history, upon its culmination in our Lord's return, the subject of the final paragraph in the Lausanne Covenant.

Living in Apocalyptic Times

At the Lausanne Congress, Malcolm Muggeridge described the nature of our times with masterful literary strokes and the warmth of his personal experience. This able witness of the world scene did not limit himself to describing the gloom of a hopeless age, nor did he demonstrate the panic of the privileged when revolution and change threaten them. He ended his talk by echoing the courage and hope of the Christians in New Testament days:

So each symptom of breakdown, however immediately

painful and menacing in its future consequences, is also an occasion for hope and optimism, reminding us that truly God is not mocked ... You are surprised that the world is losing its grip and full of pressing tribulations. Do not hold onto the old man, the world; do not refuse to regain your youth in Christ who says to you: 'The world is passing away, the world is short of breath. Do not fear, thy youth shall be renewed as an eagle.'[1]

Several other voices described not only the tensions and suffering of creation and mankind in these times, but also the fact that one era of missions based upon a certain balance of world power is coming to an end, and that the church universal should prepare to continue her mission under new circumstances.

The amazing reality of a massive Third World presence at Lausanne was a confirmation that in spite of the profound changes of the past fifty years of world history, God has been calling to himself people with whom he is building his church in the remotest corners of this globe, even though it may be under persecution and through suffering. He is the Lord of history, and if he has accomplished his purpose through the past turbulent years, he will continue doing so until the culmination of his plan.

Panic and Utopianism

Is the church really driven forward in her task by the hope that comes from a biblical eschatology? Or is she more often tempted to fall into the panic of the West or the utopianism of the Third World? What is happening in what may be called the evangelical segment of the church?

A recent book by an observer of the North American ecclesiastical situation compares it to that in England at the beginning of this century and comes to this final comment:

I suggest that the proper role of the church is neither

blindly to react in a diehard support of the older establishments, which [were] often granted popularity for quite the wrong reasons, nor is it to tag on blindly to the new bandwagon, but to take its prophetic call seriously, to take another look at its Gospel and to recognise in thought and action the prophetic word it should be declaring to all societies and cultures. Indeed, nothing argues more strongly the utter irrelevance of a church and the spuriousness of its message than to see it vainly trying to hitch a ride on each popular trend as it comes along.[2]

This author is not exaggerating the temptation for the North American churches. Consider, for instance, *The Late Great Planet Earth*, one of the most popular books on eschatology in some of the evangelical groups represented at Lausanne. More than five million copies of the book have been sold; furthermore, a film has been produced about it and a whole industry built around it. The book's particular manner of handling the biblical material is clearly conditioned by an intensely conservative nationalism which is hostile to Europe, the Arab countries and communism. This hostility does *not* come from a specifically Christian stance, but rather stems from Americanism. Towards the end of the book we have this statement:

Lack of *moral principle* by citizens and leaders will so weaken law and order that a state of anarchy will finally result. The *military capability* of the United States, though it is at present the most powerful in the world, has already been neutralised because *no one has the courage to use it decisively*. When the economy collapses so will the military. The only chance of slowing up this decline in America is a widespread spiritual awakening.[3]

One is left wondering if a spiritual revival will produce the courage to use the military capability! Have we not come a long way from the New Testament?

What are the consequences of this type of literature and eschatology for missions? For example, this book has been already translated into Spanish. What vision of history and of the church's role in the modern world does it convey? Is this biblical eschatology? How should churches in countries that fear the military power of the USA react to this teaching? These questions are relevant because this approach to prophecy is probably the most popular one in the great majority of missions-minded conservative denominations in the United States.

In contrast, eschatological thought in the Third World and among some of the oppressed minorities of the developed nations is sometimes taking the shape of revolutionary utopianism. Oppression, the drive for social change and the ideological vacuum are the ideal breeding ground for Marxism. Marxism tends to be strongly eschatological when it is a revolutionary force, that is, when it is not yet in power. The revolutionary fervour is sustained by the vision of a bright future. Thus many walls of Latin American cities are painted with a sentence attributed to Che Guevara: 'What does the sacrifice of one man or one nation matter if the destiny of mankind is at stake?'

At the time of the war with Japan (around 1938), Mao Tse-tung wrote of his vision for the future:

This war ... will be greater in scale and more ruthless than the war of twenty years ago. But owing to the existence of the Soviet Union and the growing political consciousness of the world, great revolutionary words will undoubtedly emerge from this war to oppose all counter-revolutionary wars, thus giving this war the character of a *struggle for perpetual peace*. Even if later there should be another period of war, perpetual world peace will not be far off.[4]

According to this line of thought, current guerrilla warfare and terrorism, or even outright war itself, are necessary in the process of forging the future, 'liberating' the oppressed and building the classless, stateless society of the future.

Some theologians have been tempted to do for Marxist utopianism what Lindsey has done for American nationalism. Thus, they have emptied biblical terms of their biblical content and used them to speak of Marxist-style liberation. The terrestrial Marxist hope usurps the place of the eschatological hope of the Christian faith.

If the teaching about the Kingdom of God and the return of Christ is determined heavily by either of these two alternatives — panic or utopianism — we find ourselves with a very poor substitute for Christian hope.

If Jesus is Lord

Because Jesus is Lord, the church has been commissioned to be like him and to announce his name to men and nations:

> All authority in heaven and on earth has been given to me. Go therefore and make disciples of all nations, baptising them in the name of the Father and of the Son and of the Holy Spirit, teaching them to observe all that I have commanded you; and lo, I am with you always, to the close of the age (Matt. 28: 18–20).

In the early church, the lordship of Christ was the *motivation* and *drive* that moved the church forward in her mission, and at the same time the *content* of the church's message. Michael Green, René Padilla, and several others at Lausanne affirmed that according to the New Testament pattern we dare not, in our proclamation of the Gospel, separate the cross from the resurrection, or Jesus as Saviour from Jesus as Lord.

The victory of Jesus Christ and his imminent return were the source of the Christians' life-style as well as the strength for their life in a hostile world. The new life of the Christian community and its unique status as a visible sign of the Kingdom to come were made possible by the power of the resurrection, which extended to the final victory of the Lord.

In response to this truth and by the empowering of the

Holy Spirit, the church went ahead. There was an internal cohesiveness in their message: it linked the *life* of the Lord as a just man with his *death* on the cross, a death which is a victory because of the *resurrection*, and a victory that will be completed upon his *return*.

All this has to be said as a prelude to the statement, 'The promise of his coming is a further spur to our evangelism, for we remember his words that the Gospel must first be preached to all nations' (*Lausanne Covenant*). Are we to interpret Matthew 24: 14 and Mark 13: 10 to mean that by giving ourselves to the missionary task we can accelerate the return of Jesus Christ? This is a much disputed issue within evangelicalism, and we are aware of the complex debate between the different schools in relation to the millenium. There are, however, two points which can be raised without entering into the old polemic.

First, there has been an arrogant attitude (bordering on intolerance) among pre-millenialist dispensationalists who have tried to equate their particular view with orthodoxy. This position being the most popular one among active evangelical missionary societies, it is sometimes believed that missions-mindedness can only come from pre-millenialism. The many British and European evangelicals who are not pre-millenial but have tremendous missionary zeal provide ample proof of the fallacy of this position.

Second, one basic characteristic of our pragmatic, technological age, particularly in North America, is the cult of success and efficiency. This accounts in part for the strong tendency to measure the results of the missionary enterprise solely in quantitative terms. It naturally postulates a relationship between masses entering the church and a corresponding acceleration of the Lord's return. This criteria about the efficacy of human action is foreign to a biblical view of man and history, and is furthermore a superficial way of measuring the church's action in the world. Douglas Webster makes the following worthwhile observations:

'The attempt to conquer Asia for Christ has definitely failed', wrote K. M. Panikkar. 'The kingdom of the world has become the kingdom of our Lord and of his Christ and he shall reign for ever and ever' (Rev. 11: 15), says the angel in the Apocalypse. The first statement is empirical, the second prophetic. Terms like failure and success are purely relative and cannot be suitably applied to the Christian mission, because its effectiveness cannot be assessed at any given moment of time, but only at the end ... God's mission to man was completed in principle in Jesus Christ. Nothing the Church can do can add to his finished redeeming work ... Jesus achieved what he was sent to do because he was not concerned with the categories of success or failure as understood by the world. Because he was content to appear to fail in the sight of men, if this had to be the cost of witness to the truth and obedience to God, his mission gained an effectiveness which became universal.[5]

Although the New Testament church had a living hope and expectation of the Lord's return, we do not see any evidence that their missionary activity had as an aim the 'acceleration' of that return. Rather, their action grew out of their conviction of the truth, and their resultant joy and faithfulness; it was activated by the Spirit working through his Word and his ministers.

Lordship and Discipleship

For many of those at Lausanne, one of the powerful discoveries was the relationship between accepting the lordship of Christ and a radical kind of discipleship involving a definite action and life-style for the church in today's world. This was what the group that produced the document on 'Radical Discipleship' communicated eloquently:

We confess that:
We have often separated Jesus Christ the Saviour from Jesus Christ the Lord.
We have often been in bondage to a particular culture and sought to spread it in the name of Jesus.

We have not been aware of when we have debased and distorted the Gospel by acceptance of a contrary value system.
We have been partisan in our condemnation of totalitarianism and violence and have failed to condemn societal and institutionalised sin, especially that of racism.
We have sometimes so identified ourselves with particular political systems that the Gospel has been compromised and the prophetic voice muted.
We have sometimes distorted the biblical understanding of man as a total being and have courted an unbiblical dualism.[6]

Perhaps the future of the church's missionary task lies in a change of heart and mind among evangelicals. As they rediscover the real Christian hope and recapture a vision of the glorious return of our Lord, they will be able to detach themselves from their pagan environment in North America and Europe, or their wordly utopianism in the Third World, and will become radical disciples of Jesus Christ wherever they happen to be. They will then be able to understand the changes taking place in other parts of the world, and find a way to live and serve Christ wherever they are called.

If the massive nations of our world, like China and India, are going to be evangelised it will be by means of a purified church, a church that has overcome the temptations of affluence, privilege and power, and a church that does not turn her eschatology into an ideology of panic or a thinly-disguised human utopia.

For here we have no lasting city,
but we seek the city which is to come.

AUTHOR INFORMATION

Chapter I
CARL F. H. HENRY was the chairman of the 1966 World Congress on Evangelism in Berlin and is the author of some twenty books on theology and ethics. He is presently lecturer-at-large for World Vision International.

Chapter II
JOHN STOTT, Rector Emeritus of All Soul's Church, London, presided over the commission that wrote the final draft of the Lausanne Covenant. He is the author of many books and has lectured throughout the world.

Chapter III
SAPHIR ATHYAL is the principal of Union Biblical Seminary in Yeotmal, Maharashtra, India.

Chapter IV
MICHAEL CASSIDY, a South African evangelist, is the founder and director of African Enterprise, an inter-denominational evangelistic team with a ministry throughout Africa. He was the initiator of the South African Congress on Mission and Evangelism, held in 1973.

Chapter V
ATHOL GILL is the Dean of Whitley College, University of Melbourne, Australia, and has co-operated with the Australian 'Radical Discipleship' group.

Chapter VI
PETER SAVAGE, a former missionary in Peru and Bolivia, is a well-known lecturer specialising in theological education. At present he is the co-ordinator of the Latin American Theological Fraternity.

Chapter VII
HOWARD SNYDER is a Free Methodist missionary in Brazil, teaching in a seminary in Sao Paulo. He delivered a paper on 'The Church as God's Agent in Evangelism' at Lausanne.

Chapter VIII
ORLANDO COSTAS is the Secretary for Study and Publications at the Institute of In-Depth Evangelism and the Director of the Latin American Evangelical Centre for Pastoral Studies, in Costa Rica. At present he is a candidate for the doctor of theology degree at the faculty of theology, Free University of Amsterdam.

Chapter IX
JOHN GATU is the secretary general of the Presbyterian Church of East Africa, with offices in Nairobi, Kenya, and has been a key figure in the well-known 'Moratorium Debate'.

Chapter X
JACOB LOEWEN has worked for many years with the United Bible Society in anthropology and linguistics, assisting missionaries engaged in the translation of the Scriptures in South America and Africa.

Chapter XI
JONATHAN T'IEN-EN CHAO is the Dean of the newly opened China Graduate School of Theology in Hong Kong and the executive secretary of the Association for Promotion of Chinese Theological Education. He received his Ph.D. in Oriental Studies from the University of Pennsylvania (USA).

Chapter XII
C. RENÉ PADILLA has worked as a staff member of the International Fellowship of Evangelical Students in Latin America for many years and is currently Director of their literature programme in Buenos Aires, Argentina. He is the author of many articles and a lecturer with an international ministry.

Chapter XIII
A.N. OBSERVER has spent many years in areas of the world hostile to the Gospel in a ministry which includes Bible teaching, evangelism and literature work. The sensitive nature of his work prohibits the availability of the usual biographical material.

Chapter XIV
MICHAEL GRIFFITHS is the General Director of the Overseas
Missionary Fellowship, based in Singapore, and has served as a
missionary in East Asia for many years. He is the author of a
number of books.

Chapter XV
SAMUEL ESCOBAR has long been active in the work of the International Fellowship of Evangelical Students in Latin America
and recently served as General Secretary of the Canadian Inter-
Varsity movement. He is the author of several books and many
articles.

NOTES

Chapter III

1. D. Martyn Lloyd-Jones, *Authority* (London: Inter-Varsity Press, 1958) p. 10.

2. G. C. Berkouwer, 'General and Special Divine Revelation' in *Revelation and the Bible*, ed. Carl F. H. Henry (Philadelphia: Presbyterian & Reformed Publishing Co., 1958) p. 19.

3. Hendrik Kraemer, *Why Christianity of All Religions?* (Lucknow: Lucknow Publishers, 1966) p. 19. See his detailed discussion: *World Cultures and World Religions*, (London: Lutterworth, 1960) 386 pp.

4. W. A. Visser 't Hooft, *No Other Name* (London: S.C.M. Press, 1973) p. 94.

5. Paul Tillich, *Christianity and the Encounter of the World Religions* (New York: Columbia Univ., 1963) p. 97.

6. E. C. Dewick, *The Christian Attitude to Other Religions* (Cambridge: University Press, 1953) p. 20.

7. J. N. D. Anderson, *Christianity and Comparative Religions* (London: Tyndale, 1970) p. 19.

8. Marcus Braybrooke, *The Undiscovered Christ* (Madras: C.L.S., 1973) pp. 107–108. See also Raymond Panikkar, *The Trinity and World Religions* (Madras: C.L.S., 1970) 80 pp.

9. See detailed discussion on the subject for example in G. C. Berkouwer, *The Person of Christ* (Grand Rapids: Eerdmans, 1954) 368 pp. Also Carl F. H. Henry, ed. *Jesus of Nazareth, Saviour and Lord* (London: Tyndale, 1966) 277 pp.

10. J. R. W. Stott, *Basic Christianity* (London: Inter-Varsity Press, 1960) p. 32.

11. Stephen Neill, *Christian Faith and Other Faiths* (Lucknow: Lucknow Publishers, 1966, p. 16; London Oxford University Press, 1970).

12. J. R. W. Stott, *The Lausanne Covenant, An Exposition and Commentary* (Minneapolis: World Wide Publications, 1975) p. 17.

Chapter IV

1. Canon Douglas Webster, 'What is evangelism?', in *I Will Heal Their Land*, ed. Michael Cassidy (Pietermaritzburg: Africa Enterprise, 1974) pp. 87, 88.

2. Michael Cassidy, 'The Third Way', in *International Review of Mission* LXIII: 249 (January, 1974) p. 20.

3. Frances Schaeffer, 'Form and Freedom in the Church', Plenary Address, International Congress on World Evangelization (Lausanne, Switzerland, July 16–25) p. 1.

4. Dodd elaborated the *kerygma* as follows:

1. The age of fulfilment has dawned.

2. This happened in the ministry, death and resurrection of Jesus.

3. Jesus has been exalted to God's right hand as the head of the new Israel.

4. The gift of the Holy Spirit is the sign of Christ's present power.

5. There will be a consummation of the age in the return of Christ.

6. The preaching ends with an appeal for repentance and faith, the offer of forgiveness, salvation and the promised Holy Spirit.
(C. H. Dodd. *The Apostolic Teaching and Its Development* [London Hodder and Stoughton, 1963] p. 17.)

5. John R. W. Stott, 'The Nature of Evangelism', Biblical Foundation Paper for the International Congress on World Evangelization.

6. S. W. McWilliam, *Called to Preach* (Edinburgh: The Saint Andrew Press, 1969) pp. 6, 7.

7. C. René Padilla 'Evangelism and the World', Biblical Foundation Paper for the International Congress on World Evangelization, p. 5.

8. *Ibid.*, p. 6.

9. Calvin Cook, 'What is Conversion?', *I Will Heal Their Land*, *op. cit.*, p. 105.

10. 'A Response to Lausanne' pp. 1, 2 (mimeographed).

11. Cook, *op. cit.*, p. 88.

12. Helmut Thielicke, *How Modern Should Theology Be?* (London: Fontana, 1970) p. 86.

13. *Ibid.*, p. 10.

14. Alan Richardson, article on 'Preaching', in *A Theological Word Book of the Bible* (London: S.C.M. Press, 1975) p. 172.

15. Dodd, *op. cit.*, p. 7.

16. Peter Wagner, *Stop the World, I Want To Get On* (Glendale, California: Regal Books, 1974) p. 78.

17. John Stott, *Our Guilty Silence* (London: Hodder and Stoughton, 1967) p. 112.

18. Schaeffer, *op. cit.*, p. 5.

Chapter V

1. From the call of the Convening Committee to Congress participants, reprinted in A. Nichols, *Evangelicals*: Report of the

International Congress on World Evangelization (Sydney: 1975) pp. 18 f.

2. Cf. 'Evangelism', *In Unity*, XXI: (3, October, 1974) p. 6.

3. Cf. David O. Moberg, *The Great Reversal: Evangelism Versus Social Concern* (London: 1972) p. 16.

4. 'One Race, One Gospel, One Task. Closing Statement of the World Congress on Evangelism', *One Race One Gospel One Task*: World Congress on Evangelism, Berlin, vol. I, ed. Carl F. H. Henry and W. Stanley Mooneyham (Minneapolis: 1967) pp. 5 ff.

5. Paul S. Rees, 'Evangelism and Social Concern', *One Race One Gospel One Task*, vol. I, pp. 306 ff.

6. Billy Graham, 'Why Lausanne?', *Let the Earth Hear His Voice*: The International Congress on World Evangelization, Lausanne 1974, ed. J. D. Douglas (Minneapolis World Wide Publications, 1975) pp. 22 ff.

7. John Stott, 'The Nature of Biblical Evangelism', *Let the Earth Hear His Voice*, pp. 116 ff.

8. Carl F. H. Henry, 'Christian Personal and Social Ethics in Relation to Racism, Poverty, War and Other Problems', *Let the Earth Hear His Voice*, pp. 1163 ff, especially pp. 1169, 1182.

9. George Hoffman, 'The Social Responsibilities of Evangelism', *Let the Earth Hear His Voice*, pp 698 ff.

10. René Padilla, 'Evangelism and the World', *Let the Earth Hear His Voice*, pp. 116 ff. Samuel Escobar, 'Evangelism and Man's Search for Freedom, Justice and Fulfilment', *Let the Earth Hear His Voice*, pp. 303 ff.

11. The influence of this thinking is to be seen in other sections of the Covenant as well: 'The results of evangelism include obedience to Christ, incorporation into his church and responsible service in the world' (Section 4). 'A church which preaches the cross must itself be marked by the cross . . . It must not be identified with any particular culture, social or political system, or human ideology' (5). 'Those of us who live in affluent circumstances accept our duty to develop a simple life-style in order to contribute more generously to both relief and evangelism' (9).

12. 'Theology and Implications of Radical Discipleship', *Let the Earth Hear His Voice*, pp. 1294 ff. Reprinted also as 'Response to Lausanne', *The International Review of Mission*, vol. LXIII (1974) pp. 574 ff. The 'Response' is also interesting in the sections of the Covenant which it does not include on the basis of the fact that they had not been dealt with at the Congress.

13. Cf. especially Richard J. Coleman, *Issues of Theological Warfare*: Evangelicals and Liberals (Grand Rapids: 1972) pp. 167 ff.

14. Cf. Moberg, *op. cit.*, pp. 28 ff.

15. 'Wheaton Declaration subscribed by the Delegates to The Congress on the Church's Worldwide Mission convened at Wheaton, Illinois, April 9–16, 1966', *The International Review of Missions*, vol. LV (1966) pp. 458 ff.

16. Cf. especially Myron Augsburger, 'The Making of Disciples in a Secular World', *Evangelism Now*: The United States Congress on

Evangelism, edited by George M. Wilson (Minneapolis: World Wide Publications, 1970) pp. 195 ff.

17. *Evangelism Alert*: Official Reference Volume European Congress on Evangelism, edited by Gilbert W. Kirby (London: 1972) p. 11.

18. Cf. the addresses in *Christ the Liberator,* by John Stott and others (London: Hodder and Stoughton, 1972) pp. 103 ff., 113 ff., 121 ff., 189 ff.

19. 'A Declaration of Evangelical Social Concern', *The International Review of Mission,* vol. LXIII (1974) p. 274 f. Those who signed included Carl F. Henry, Bernard Ramm, William Peterson, Jim Wallis, Dale Brown, David Moberg, Samuel Escobar and Mark Hatfield.

20. Cf. Moberg, *op. cit.*, pp. 13 ff.

21. In his concluding remarks at the Symposium on Evangelism held at Louvain in September, 1973, Dr W. A. Visser 't Hooft, Honorary President of the World Council of Churches, lamented the 'really horrible problem of communication' where the small liberation programme of the World Council has been made to look 'as if it were the total World Council' and where such theological agreements as those made at Louvain are not reported at all. See 'Evangelism 1974: A Symposium', *International Review of Mission,* vol. LXIII (1974) pp. 1 ff.

22. Cf. Paul Winter (ed.), *The Evangelical Response to Bangkok* (South Pasadena: 1973).

23. *The Berlin Declaration on Ecumenism 1974*: 'Freedom and Fellowship in Christ' (Concise Version) Berlin, 1974.

24. Peter Beyerhaus, 'World Evangelization and the Kingdom of God', *Let the Earth Hear His Voice*, pp. 290, 295.

25. At the other end of the spectrum, secular theologians were celebrating the triumph of man as they prepared for the 'death of God'!

26. In some areas 'culture Christianity' concepts die hard, but the resignation of President Nixon will undoubtedly have a far-reaching affect on American evangelical theology. Perhaps, at last, corporate evil will be taken seriously.

27. Because the first drafts were prepared before Lausanne, the Covenant does not reflect in this section the emphasis on 'radical discipleship' which developed during the Congress. It was added to the preceding and following sections on 'evangelism' but omitted from the section on 'social action'. This is unfortunate for it provides the key to the relationship between evangelism and social action.

28. Joachim Jeremias, *New Testament Theology*, vol. I: The Proclamation of Jesus (London: 1971), p. 112.

29. G. Bornkamm, *Jesus of Nazareth* (London: Hodder and Stoughton, 1963) pp. 75 ff.

30. J. Behm, *'metanoeō', 'metanoia', Theological Dictionary of the New Testament*, edited by Gerhard Kittle (Grand Rapids: Wm. B. Eerdmans, 1967) vol. IV, p. 1002.

31. Cf. our forthcoming study, 'The Call to Discipleship — A Call to Mission', *Youth Outreach and Evangelism*, (Melbourne: 1975).

32. Dietrich Bonheoffer, *The Cost of Discipleship* (London: S.C.M. Press, 1959) p. 79.

33. Padilla, *op. cit.*, pp. 134 ff.

34. Had space permitted it would have been possible to show how these motifs were anticipated in the prophets and developed in Paul.

35. John Stott, *Let the Earth Hear His Voice*, pp. 116 ff.

36. Henry, *Let the Earth Hear His Voice*, p. 1181.

37. Padilla, *op. cit.*, p. 144.

38. John Stott, *The Lausanne Covenant:* An Exposition and Commentary (Melbourne: 1975) section 6.

39. This is not to say that 'the world sets the agenda', but to emphasise again that the shape of the church's ministry results from the interaction of the Word and the world.

40. Emilio Castro and Paul Little, 'Viewpoint: Proclaiming the Gospel to Every Creature', *One World*, No. 1 (November 1974) p. 16.

41. Jeremias, *op. cit.*, p. 193.

42. A number of evangelicals have recently been addressing themselves to this question. Cf. John H. Yoder, *The Politics of Jesus* (Grand Rapids: Wm. B. Eerdmans, 1972); Robert D. Linder and Richard V. Pierard, *Politics:* A Case for Christian Action (London: Inter-Varsity Press, 1973).

43. Paavo Kortekangas, 'The Social Implications of Evangelism', *Evangelism Alert*, pp. 130 f.

44. Henry, *op. cit.*, p. 1182.

Chapter VI

1. Alan Cole, *The Body of Christ: A New Testament Image of the Church* (Philadelphia: Westminster Press, 1964) p. 67.

2. The 'gathered church' is the congregation which meets in a church building for worship, fellowship and edification. The 'scattered church' would be the members of the same congregation dispersed in many secular vocations as witnesses of Jesus Christ.

3. H. Richard Niebuhr and Daniel P. Williams, *The Ministry in Historical Perspective* (New York Harper & Row, 1956) p. 114.

4. H. Richard Niebuhr and Daniel P. Williams, *op. cit.*, p. 135.

5. *Ibid.*, p. 138.

6. Lawrence O. Richards, *A New Faith for the Church* (Grand Rapids: Zondervan Publishing House, 1970) p. 14.

7. Robert H. Schuller, *Your Church has Real Possibilities!* (Glendale: Gospel Light Publications, Regal Books, 1974) p. 29.

8. *Ibid.*, p. 4.

9. P. T. Forsyth, *The Church and the Sacraments* (Independent Press Limited, 1917) p. 30.

10. Alan M. Stibbs, *God's Church* (London: Inter-Varsity Press, 1973) p. 106.

11. John Yoder, 'Radical Christianity: An Interview with John Yoder', *Right On* (February, 1975) p. 1.

12. Alan M. Stibbs, *op. cit.,* p 44.

13. H. Richard Niebuhr, *The Purpose of the Church and Its Ministry* (New York: Harper and Row, 1956) p. 22.

14. A living biblical community in a specific cultural context would, given its freedom, adopt a structure that is known and appreciated in that society. An example of this can be seen in the Garden Grove Community Church (cf. Robert H. Schuller, *op. cit.* pp. 60–71). This is merely a statement of historical and sociological fact, not a rule for faith and practice.

15. Emil Brunner, *The Misunderstanding of the Church* (Philadelphia: Westminster Press, 1951) p. 58.

16. Michael Green, *Evangelism in the Early Church* (London: Hodder and Stoughton, 1970) p. 49.

17. Paul S. Minear, *Images of the Church in the New Testament* (Philadelphia: Westminster Press, 1960) p. 163.

18. John Yoder, 'Church Growth Issues in Theological Perspective', in *The Challenge of Church Growth,* ed. Wilbert R. Shenk (Elkhart, Ind.; Institute of Mennonite Studies, 1973) p. 39.

19. Ralph D. Winter, 'The Anatomy of the Christian Mission', *Evangelical Missions Quarterly,* No. 2 (Winter, 1969) pp. 69, 88.

20. Christian Lalive d'Epinay, *Haven of the Masses* (London: Lutterworth Press, 1969) p. 224. (See also Part II, Chapter 3; 'The Life of the Congregation', pp. 45–64).

21. Douglas Webster, 'What is Evangelism?' *I Will Heal Their Land* ed. Michael Cassidy (Pietermaritzburg: Africa Enterprise, 1974) p. 96.

22. Leighton Ford, 'Evangelism in the Age of Apollo', *I Will Heal Their Land* ed. Michael Cassidy (Pietermaritzburg: Africa Enterprise, 1974) p. 118.

23. Michael Green, *op. cit.,* pp. 172, 173.

24. *Ibid.,* p. 175.

25. 'Domestication' is a process in which a member of one culture is willing to subdue and sublimate his cultural values, concerns, perceptions, in return for the material benefits that a person in another culture may offer him. He will tend to echo the desired responses and concerns that his 'master' may have expressed. Often he will dream of joining his 'master's' culture. In some cases he will become more dogmatic than his master in expressing the concerns and perceptions of his adopted culture. Unfortunately, he could become the obstacle to the full evangelisation of his people.

Chapter VII

1. See Yehezkel Kaufmann, *The Religion of Israel,* trans. Moshe Greenberg (Chicago: University of Chicago Press, 1960).

2. Second Vatican Council, *Decree on Ecumenism* (Washington, DC: National Catholic Welfare Conference, 1964) p. 1.

3. Hendrik Hart, 'Cultus and Covenant', in Robert Lee Carvill et al., *Will All the King's Men . . .* (Toronto: Wedge Publishing Foundation, 1972) p. 30.

4. Hans Küng, *Structures of the Church*, trans. Salvator Attanasio (London: Burns and Oates, 1964) p. 12.

5. Henri Blocher, 'The Nature of Biblical Unity', Biblical Foundation paper for the International Congress on World Evangelization, p. 2.

6. This affirmation is not meant to exclude the Jews, who in a special sense continue to be God's people.

7. Peter Beyerhaus, *Shaken Foundations: Theological Foundations for Mission* (Grand Rapids: Zondervan Publishing House, 1972) p. 42.

8. C. René Padilla, 'Evangelism and the World', Biblical Foundation paper for the International Congress on World Evangelization, p. 6.

9. Donald G. Bloesch, *The Reform of the Church* (Grand Rapids: William B. Eerdmans Publishing Company, 1970) p. 184.

10. *Ibid.*, p. 186.

11. It is well to remember here that the modern ecumenical movement grew out of a genuine evangelistic and missionary concern. But with time it lost its biblical theological moorings and largely went astray. Because of this, many evangelicals practically equate ecumenism with heresy.

12. C. Peter Wagner, *Frontiers in Missionary Strategy* (Chicago: Moody Press, 1971) pp. 153–60; George W. Peters, *Saturation Evangelism* (Grand Rapids: Zondervan Publishing House, 1970) pp. 76–77.

13. 'The Church as God's Agent of Evangelism' was the only plenary paper devoted to the subject of the church. Although Francis Schaeffer's paper was entitled 'Form and Freedom in the Church', Dr Schaeffer elected not to speak on that topic. The related subject of the kingdom of God likewise received little attention, as pointed out by Michael Green. The first draft of the Lausanne Covenant made no reference to the kingdom of God and inadequate reference to the church; fortunately, these symptomatic oversights were largely corrected in the final draft.

14. Billy Graham, letter to Lausanne participants, September 20, 1974.

15. Harold Lindsell, 'Lausanne '74: An Appraisal', *Christianity Today*, XVIII: 24 (September 12, 1974) p. 26.

16. Jacques Ellul, *The Meaning of the City*, trans. Dennis Pardee (Grand Rapids: William B. Eerdmans Publishing Company, 1970) p. 154.

17. Disgruntled younger evangelicals in North America, who have understandably and necessarily reacted against the theological narrowness and cultural bondage of much of American evangelicalism in their attempt to be radically biblical, need to be reminded that world-wide evangelicalism can no longer be defined

solely by its North American expression. They need to discover that there are numerous emerging evangelical leaders in the so-called Third World who share many of their concerns and perspectives and may have much to teach them.

18. Bloesch, *op cit.*, pp. 186, 187.

19. Arthur F. Glasser, 'The Evangelicals: World Outreach', in William J. Danker and Wi Jo Kang, eds., *The Future of the Christian World Mission* (Grand Rapids: William B. Eerdmans Publishing Company, 1971) p. 109.

Chapter VIII

1. Emilio Castro, 'Bangkok, The New Opportunity', in *International Review of Mission*, LXIII: 246 (April, 1974) p. 140.

2. 'The Lausanne Covenant'; Article 8.

3. Castro, *op. cit.*, p. 141.

4. See, for example, the following publications raising the question of 'the future' of the missionary enterprise: William J. Danker and Wi Jo Kang, eds., *The Future of the Christian World Mission* (Grand Rapids: Eerdmans, 1971) and the study which is being sponsored by IDOC (International Documentation on the Contemporary Church and International Documentation and Communication Centre), *The Future of the Missionary Enterprise* (New York and Rome: IDOC). Nine issues have appeared thus far.

5. By the West I mean *specifically* North America and Western Europe.

6. James Wong, Peter Larson and Edward Pentecost, *Missions from the Third World* (Singapore: Church Growth Study Centre, 1973).

7. Michael Griffith, 'Foreword', *Ibid.*, p. ii.

8. Cf. *ibid.*

9. The expressions First and Third World have more than anything else a socio-economic-political connotation. The First World (North America and Western Europe), together with the Second World (the USSR and Eastern Europe), while representing one third of the world's population benefit from more than two thirds of the wealth of the world, while the Third, which comprises two thirds of the world population, shares less than one third of the wealth.

10. For example, since the first All Asia Mission Consultation held in Seoul, Korea in September, 1973, 23 new Asian missionaries have been sent out to Africa and Latin America, 24 more 'are ready to go, and 100 are being recruited to evangelise an Asian island'. Virgil Gerber, 'When Change is Needed in Christian Mission', Keynote Address, EFMA Executives' Retreat 1974 (Winona Lake, Indiana, September 30 – October 3, 1974) p. 14 (mimeographed).

11. Al Krass, 'Lausanne '74 — Reaching the Unreached', in *Beautiful Feet*, IV: 1 (August, 1974) p. 4.

12. *Ibid.*

13. James Hopewell, 'Institute for the Study of Ministry', Unpublished paper, (Atlanta, Georgia: Chandler School of Theology) p. 1 (mimeographed).

14. For a brief but substantial account of the background of the WEF, see J. B. A. Kessler, Jr., *A Study of the Evangelical Alliance in Great Britain* (Boes, Netherlands: Oosterbaan & Le Cointre N.V., 1968) especially pp. 89 ff.

15. But note the following resolution adapted at the Sixth General Assembly of the WEF, held immediately after Lausanne '74 (July 25–29, 1974):

> That we communicate to the Continuation Committee of the International Congress on World Evangelization with a view to its considering the possibility that within the framework of the WEF the goals and wishes of the Congress which it is its objective to carry out may be achieved, and in particular we express the following opinions: (1) that channels of communication be kept open between the Continuation Committee and this Fellowship, (2) that individuals involved in both this Fellowship and the Continuation Committee should seek to keep both in concert, (3) that it is undesirable that there be any duplication of international organisations, and (4) that this Fellowship is willing to consider proposals for the alteration of its by-laws more effectively to achieve the goals of the Congress within its Fellowship and constituent members.

Quoted in 'WEF Holds Sixth General Assembly', *Theological News*, WEF, VI: 3 (July–September, 1974) p. 5.

Chapter IX

1. Walter Arnold, 'Symposium Chairman's Marginal Notes', in *International Review of Mission,* LXIII: 249, (January, 1974) p. 2.

2. Canon Burgess Carr, 'The Engagement of Lusaka', Address, All Africa Conference of Churches Assembly (Lusaka, Zambia, May, 1974).

3. Ezekiel C. Makumike, 'Evangelism in the Cultural Context of Africa', in *International Review of Mission*, LXIII: 249 (January, 1974) p. 62.

4. *Ibid.*, p. 62.

5. Leonard Broom and Philip Selznick, *Principles of Sociology* (New York: Harper and Row, p. 52.

6. Roland Oliver, *The Missionary Factor in East Africa* (London: Longmans, 1965), p. ix.

Chapter X

1. Jacob A. Loewen, 'Problems for Export I'; and 'Problems for Export II: the Paid Pastor', to be published in the *Milligan Missiogram.*

2. For a fuller account of this experience see 'Problems for Export I'.

3. For more details see Jacob A. Loewen, 'Listening with the Third Ear', to be published in the *Mennonite Brethren Herald*.

4. From Jacob A. Loewen, *Culture and Human Values in the Communication of the Gospel*, a book of essays reprinted from *Practical Anthropology*, now at William Carey Press.

5. Jacob A. Loewen, 'Socialisation and Conversion in the Ongoing Church', *Practical Anthropology*, 16: 1 (January–February, 1969) pp. 9–11.

6. Recently I received a report of the Great Slave Lake Indians in Northern Canada. It is a tribe that up to the present has resisted the Gospel but now seems to be on the verge of a breakthrough. The report stated that a leading personality had recently 'died', and when he was 'brought back to life' he reported to his people: 'For three days I was walking in heaven where Jesus is. I saw Jesus and God, but I saw no nylon, no miniskirts, no whiskey, and no adultery.' To my mind we see a new model for conversion to the process of development.

7. Jacob A. Loewen, 'Response to Dr R. Winter's paper on cross-cultural evangelism', read at the Lausanne Conference on World Evangelization.

8. Jacob A. Loewen, 'Relevant Roles for Overseas Workers', *International Review of Missions*, LVII: 226 (April, 1968) pp. 233–244.

9. Jacob A. Loewen, 'The Inspiration of Translation: A Growing Personal Conviction', to be published in a *Festschrift* for Dr E. A. Nida's sixtieth birthday. Here is an illustrative excerpt:

The second reason why translators should have direct personal contact with inspiration is even more compelling. Linguists have long recognised that languages differ in the obligatory information that must be expressed by means of their grammar, syntax and vocabulary. The Bible Societies and Bible translators in general have also been aware that some languages require the explication of information about which we have no specific indication in the source text. If the translation into these languages is to be as inspired as the original, it will require an extension of the original inspiration to give specific indication in regard to these categories.

Thus, for example, one of the languages in Paraguay requires that all nouns and proper names be preceded by a prefix which indicates whether the item or person is visible at the time of the communication. If not visible, it must be specified whether it is only currently, or permanently invisible. In the case of the former, it must be further specified whether the item is only temporarily absent, or whether it has died. In the case of the latter it must be further specified whether the item was visible only in myth age or whether it has never been seen by humans.

When the translators faced I Cor. 15: 8 where Paul says: 'I saw

Jesus Christ', the missionary translator and his Indian co-worker disagreed as to which prefix to use. The missionary explained his choice on the basis of his theology, but the Indian translator, even after listening intently to the missionary's reasoning, said, 'But I *feel* it is this one'. There is no indication in the original as to which prefix to use, because the Greek did not require the specification of this information. If the translation in this language is to be as authoritative as the original, it requires additional inspiration.

Or take those many languages in Asia and South America which recognise not only one, but several indicative modes. In fact, it is common to distinguish three degrees of factualness in the indicative: (1) by personal observation or knowledge, (2) by getting it from a reliable source, or (3) by hearsay. It takes little imagination to realise what a vast job it will be to classify all indicative statements in the Bible in one of these three required categories. As in the preceding example, ongoing inspiration is absolutely essential if the product is to be the inspired Word of God.

10. Jacob A. Loewen, Albert Buckwalter, and James Kratz, 'Shamanism, Illness and Power in Toba Church Life', *Practical Anthropology*, 12: 6 (November-December, 1965) pp. 250–280.

Chapter XII

1. *The Meaning of the City* (Grand Rapids: Wm. B. Eerdmans, 1970) p. 147.
2. At the beginning of the nineteenth century, there was no city with more than a million inhabitants, in 1945 there were already thirty, in 1955 there were sixty, and in 1970, almost ninety. It is estimated that in the year 2000, six out of every ten persons will live in urban centres.
3. To understand the applicability of the term 'consumer society' to urban centres in even the underdeveloped societies, it is helpful to consult the work of Juan Luis Segundo (*Acción Pastoral Latinoamericana: sus motivos ocultos* [Buenos Aires: Ediciones Búsqueda, 1972] p. 17). He distinguishes between the 'consumer society', which exists in any urban concentration, and the 'abundant society', which is only found in the countries where industrialisation has reached its greatest development.
4. This thesis has been elaborated in detail by R. H. Tawney in *The Acquisitive Society* (New York: Harcourt, Brace and World, Inc., 1948) pp. 8–19, 52–83.
5. *Ibid.*, pp. 37 ff.
6. *A tecnica es o desafio do século* (Rio de Janeiro: Paz e Terra, 1968) p. 418. There is an English translation: *The Technological Society* (London: Vintage Books, 1973).
The same author discusses at greater length the role of advertising

in contemporary society in *Historia de la Propaganda* (Caracas: Monte Avila, 1970).

7. 'If the overriding economic principle is that we produce more and more, the consumer must be prepared to want — that is, to consume — more and more. Industry does not rely on the consumer's spontaneous desires for more and more commodities. By building in obsolescence it often forces him to buy new things when the old ones could last much longer. By changes in styling of products, dresses, durable goods and even food, it forces him psychologically to buy more than he might need or want. But industry, in its need for increased production, does not rely on the consumer's needs and wants but to a considerable extent on advertising, which is the most important offensive against the consumer's right to know what he wants.' Erich Fromm, *The Revolution of Hope: Toward a Humanized Technology* (New York: Bantam Books, 1968) pp. 38 f.

8. It is estimated that at present sixty-five per cent of the world's population suffers from hunger. The hunger zones coincide with the underdeveloped zones which are subject to economic exploitation by the rich nations. Cf. Reginald H. Fuller and Brian K. Rice, *Christianity and the Affluent Society* (Grand Rapids Wm. B. Eerdmans Publishing Co., 1966; London, Hodder & Stoughton, 1966) especially Chapter 9, 'Starvation by 1980', pp. 150 ff.

9. The remarks of Senator Mark Hatfield at the Conservative Baptist Association of America convention in 1974 are noteworthy: 'As Americans we must no longer assume that our extra abundance can feed the hungry of the world. Our surplus supply is not enough. Rather, the world will be fed only by the sharing of resources which the rich of the world have assumed to be their unquestioned possession, and that sharing involves the changing of values and eating patterns which the affluent have barely even questioned.'

As quoted in *Eternity Magazine*, 25: 11 (November, 1974) p. 38.

10. The most recent illustration of the difficulty of enlisting the help of the rich countries in order to combat hunger was seen in the FAO meetings in Rome in November, 1974, which yielded no concrete measures to solve the problem.

11. *El libro negro del hambre* (Buenos Aires: EUDEBA, 1971) p. 88.

12. *Ibid.*, p. 69.

13. Various New Testament studies (among them H. Berkhof, G. B. Caird, M. Barth and D. E. H. Whitely) have dealt with the field of Pauline demonology and shown its relevance to social ethics. Cf. John H. Yoder, *The Politics of Jesus* (Grand Rapids: Wm. B. Eerdmans Co., 1972) pp. 135 ff.

14. 'The elemental spirits of the universe' (RSV) is a better translation of *stoicheia tou cosmou* than 'rudiments of the world' (AV). Relating to this subject, see my article 'La demonologia de Colosenses' in *Diálogo teológico*, 2 (October, 1973) pp. 37 ff.

15. Cf. George Eldon Ladd, *Jesus and the Kingdom: The Eschatology of Biblical Realism* (Waco: World Books, 1964, pp. 114 f, and 145 ff; London: SPCK., 1966).

16. *Journal of Biblical Literature*, 70 (1951) pp. 259 ff.

17. '. . . beings which in their nature are no gods' (NEB).

18. *The First Epistle to the Corinthians* (BNTC) (London: Adam and Charles Black, 1971) *in loco*.

19. *Interpreting Paul's Gospel* (London: S.C.M. Press, 1955) p. 75, note 1.

20. Juan Luis Segundo, *op. cit.* p. 83.

21. *Ibid.*

22. *Pensamiento Cristiano*, 21: 82 (September, 1974) pp. 174 ff.

23. The affirmation preceding the one cited states: 'For example, although careful studies of church growth, both numerical and spiritual, are right and valuable, we have sometimes neglected them.' It is difficult to see in what sense the neglect of church growth studies can be considered an example of the fact that 'we ourselves are not immune to worldliness of thought and action, that is, to a surrender to secularism.' Given the context — the references to the worldliness of the church, the manipulation of hearers and the exaggerated preoccupation with statistics, that defence of the use of 'studies of church growth, both numerical and spiritual', evidently corresponds more to the insistence of a pressure group upon the drafting committee than to logic.

24. Juan Luis Segundo, *op. cit.*, p. 67.

25. *Strength to Love* (London: Collins, 1974) p. 22.

26. *The Comfortable Pew* (Philadelphia: J. B. Lippincott, 1965) p. 80.

Chapter XIII

1. Andrei Sinyavsky, 'Father Boris Zalivako', in *Religion in Communist Lands*, II: 3 (May–June, 1974) p. 16. This magazine is published by the Centre for the Study of Religion and Communism, Keston College, Heatherfield Road, Keston, Kent. BR7 5JJ.

2. *Interlit* (David C. Cook Foundation, Elgin, Illinois) II: 2 (June, 1974) p. 1.

3. *Religion in Communist Lands, op. cit.*, p. 34.

4. *Interlit, op. cit.*, p. 3.

Chapter XIV

1. Professor of Free Church College, Edinburgh, writing on the Holy Spirit in 1856.

2. Quoted by Augustus Peters in *Mission Problems in Japan*, 1912.

3. Ruth Rouse, 'William Carey's "Pleasing Dream" ', *International Review of Mission*, 1949.

4. J. I. Packer, 'Jonathan Edwards and the Theology of Revival',

paper given at the Puritan Reform Studies Conference (1960) p. 20.

5. *Ibid.*, p. 26.

6. Joseph Balan Seling, letter from Kuching dated January 17, 1974..

7. Packer, *op. cit.*, pp. 27, 28.

8. Jonathan Edwards' *Works*, Vol. II, p. 291.

Chapter XV

1. *Let the Earth Hear His Voice* (Minneapolis: World Wide Publications, 1974) pp. 450, 455.

2. Robert S. Paul, *Kingdom Come!* (Grand Rapids: Eerdmans, 1973) p. 20.

3. Hal Lindsey, *The Late Great Planet Earth* (Grand Rapids: Zondervan, 1971; p. 184; London: Lakeland, 1971). Italics mine.

4. Quoted by Ninian Smart in *Mao* (London: Fontana, 1974) p. 68. Italics mine.

5. Douglas Webster, *Yes to Mission* (London: S.C.M. Press, 1966) pp. 33–35.

6. 'A Response to Lausanne', *Let the Earth Hear His Voice*, p. 1295.

J. I. PACKER
KNOWING GOD

'The author defends and restates many of the great biblical themes ... he illumines every doctrine he touches and commends it with courage, logic, lucidity and warmth ... *the truth he handles fires the heart. At least it fired mine, and compelled me to turn aside to worship and to pray.'*
John Stott, Church of England Newspaper

STUDY GUIDE:
KNOWING GOD
with a Preface by Dr Packer

Dr Packer's bestseller *Knowing God* was written to help people realise God's greatness. Here twenty-two studies, one for each chapter, bring out through pertinent questions the full content of the book. *Perfect for group Bible study, ideal for personal devotions.*

JOHN R. W. STOTT
BALANCED CHRISTIANITY

'One of the greatest weaknesses which we Christians (especially evangelical Christians) display is our tendency to extremism or imbalance,' writes the author. 'My conviction is that we should love balance as much as the devil hates it, and seek to promote it as vigorously as he seeks to destroy it.'

DONALD G. BLOESCH
THE EVANGELICAL RENAISSANCE

'I warmly welcome Dr Bloesch's critical but positive evaluation of the current resurgence of evangelicalism ... a very valuable assessment of contemporary trends.'
John R. W. Stott